The Winning Tradition

A History of Kentucky Wildcat Basketball

Bert Nelli

THE UNIVERSITY PRESS OF KENTUCKY

For my son Steve

Published by The University Press of Kentucky,
scholarly publisher for the Commonwealth,
serving Bellarmine College, Berea College, Centre
College of Kentucky, Eastern Kentucky University,
The Filson Club, Georgetown College, Kentucky
Historical Society, Kentucky State University,
Morehead State University, Murray State University,
Northern Kentucky University, Transylvania University,
University of Kentucky, University of Louisville,
and Western Kentucky University.

Editorial and Sales Offices: Lexington, Kentucky 40506-0024

Library of Congress Cataloging in Publication Data

Nelli, Humbert S., 1930-
  The winning tradition.

  Bibliography: p.
  Includes index.
  1. University of Kentucky—Basketball—History.
I. Title.
GV885.43.U53N45   1984   796.332'63'0976947   84-7306
ISBN 0-8131-1519-1

Page i, Rick Robey jumps center at the start of the UK-Tennessee game on February 15, 1978, at Rupp Arena. The Wildcats won 90-77 on their way to the SEC and NCAA championships. Other UK players shown are Jack Givens (21) and Mike Phillips (55).

Page ii, Dan Issel shoots against the Auburn Tigers. Also pictured are Mike Pratt (22) and Larry Steele, at right.

Opposite, Sam Bowie's basket helped propel the Wildcats to an 84-64 victory over a powerful Auburn Tiger team led by All-American Charles Barkley (right) on February 11, 1984. Other Wildcat players shown are Melvin Turpin (left) and Kenny Walker (34).

Page vi, Joe Hall and Leonard Hamilton confer mid-game with Truman Claytor and Dwight Anderson.

Contents

TABLES

Preface

The University of Kentucky Wildcats are one of the nation's premier college basketball programs as well as one of the major unifying forces in the state. It has not always been so. Originally basketball at UK was little more than a form of recreation to help students pass the long winter months.

In its early years, college basketball was a women's as well as a men's game. At the University of Kentucky, in fact, women played the game and enjoyed success in 1902, a year before the first men's team was organized. Women's basketball at UK merits full treatment in its own right, and in future years I hope to prepare such a study. But it is men's college basketball that has captured the loyalty of Kentuckians.

Adolph Rupp, who coached the team from 1930 to 1972, was obviously a major factor in the development of the Wildcat tradition, but he was not the only one. The tradition, in fact, was already firmly in place and developing strongly by the time the Baron arrived in Lexington. An even more significant fact is that the "Rupp system," much of which is still used by Joe B. Hall, originated not with Rupp but with his predecessor, John Mauer, and was based on the system Mauer had learned as a player for the University of Illinois Fighting Illini. Wildcat basketball owed a great deal to the "Illinois connection." Whenever the Wildcats needed a basketball coach in the late teens and the 1920's, they generally looked to the Illini for help. Even Rupp, who came to UK from a high school coaching job in Illinois, needed a strong recommendation from the Illini head coach to obtain the Wildcat coaching position.

Many myths and inaccuracies have grown through the years about University of Kentucky basketball, especially about the Rupp era. This study attempts to separate the facts from the myths. Interestingly, the truth is every bit as fascinating as the myths. The book also examines the role of Joe B. Hall in continuing the program he inherited from Rupp. Hall's accomplishments have often been obscured by his stormy relations with the press, but—as Dan Issel told me—like the Baron before him, Hall "is becoming a legend in his own right."

This volume examines important events as well as personalities in Wildcat history. These include the 1921 SIAA championship game in Atlanta, the Madison Square Garden appearance of LeRoy Edwards and his teammates in 1935, the Wildcat NIT and NCAA championships, and, on the negative side, the 1951 basketball scandal and UK's exclusively white recruitment policies prior to 1969.

University of Kentucky basketball is at a crossroads following the decision of the University Athletics Board to ask Hall to schedule regular-season games with the University of Louisville. This is the reversal of a deliberate policy of not playing regular-season games with other state schools. That policy, Hall believes, has helped make the Wildcats a national power and a unifying force within the state. Over the years, Hall has changed other integral parts of the tradition, most importantly the recruitment of blacks, with obvious benefits to the program. It may be that the Wildcat tradition will emerge even stronger than before.

Opposite, the much-awaited "Battle of the Bluegrass" saw the first regular-season meeting in over sixty years between two of college basketball's premier teams, the UK Wildcats and the U of L Cardinals. Here, forward Kenny Walker leaps over two Louisville defenders as UK drives to a 65-44 victory at Rupp Arena on November 26, 1983. Center Melvin Turpin is at right.

It is a pleasure to acknowledge the help I received during the three years of research devoted to this book. I was fortunate to have the aid of four able, intelligent, and hard-working undergraduate student assistants: Bruce Thomas, Steve Woodruff, Bill Meader, and Scott Peters. Liz Demoran of the UK Alumni Association located the addresses of former Wildcat players. Russell Rice, director of Sports Information, gave me free access to the clippings and photo files maintained in his office; from them I obtained much valuable material on current and former Wildcat players. Frank Stanger was a great help in locating material in the University Archives, while Terry Birdwhistell shared with me his extensive knowledge of oral history.

I profited greatly from discussions with University of Kentucky coaches and players from present and past squads. Jack Givens, with whom I have spent hours discussing Wildcat basketball in the years since 1978, gave me permission to use material from his unpublished autobiography. Scrapbooks and photographs were made available to me by Helen Blake Schu, widow of the 1940s star Wilbur Schu, by Louise Dorsey, sister of 1920s star Bill King, and by former players Basil Hayden, Sam Ridgeway, Aggie Sale, Paul McBrayer, James Sharpe, Red Hagan, Lee Huber, Linville Puckett, Don Mills, Lou Tsioropoulos, Dick Parsons, and Jack Givens. I want to express my sincere thanks to all of them. I am grateful to Tony Leonard for allowing us to use his excellent photograph on the dust jacket. Everyone in Photographic Services was helpful, and I thank them all.

University of Kentucky History Department secretaries Julia Bereshenyi and Dottie Leathers typed the manuscript, using the copy my wife Elizabeth deciphered and transcribed from my handwritten notes. I am grateful to them all.

This book is dedicated to my oldest son Steve, who enjoys basketball and basketball history as much as I do.

Photo Credits

All photos in this book were supplied by the Sports Information Office of the University of Kentucky Athletics Department, with the following exceptions:

Mrs. Louise Dorsey, p. 20

Joe B. Hall, p. 94

Basil Hayden, p. 18

Paul McBrayer, pp. 26, 27, 46 left, 57

Russell Rice, *The Wildcat Legacy*, p. 7 top

Mrs. Wilbur Schu, pp. 41, 62, 63

University of Kentucky Alumni Association, pp. ii, 68, 111

University of Kentucky Memorial Coliseum Sports Dedication (1950), p. 64

University of Kentucky yearbooks: 1903 *Blue and White*, p. 6; 1904 *Echoes*, p. 12; and the following issues of the *Kentuckian*: 1911, p. 11; 1912, p. 16; 1923, p. 17; 1924, p. 22; 1925, p. 25 left; 1926, p. 23; 1927, p. 25 center; 1929, p. 25 right; 1931, p. 37; 1936, p. 32; 1939, p. 40; 1941, pp. 54, 55; 1945, p. 43

Opposite, Melvin Turpin stretches his 6'11" frame to block a shot during UK's 86-67 victory over Purdue on December 28, 1983. Dicky Beal stands by for his share of the action.

1

The Tradition

Reporter Ed Ashford of the *Lexington Herald* called it "the shot that was heard around the basketball world." Ashford was describing the dramatic end of a game between the University of Kentucky Wildcats and the visiting Georgia Tech Yellow Jackets, then a member of the Southeastern Conference (SEC), on January 8, 1955. Fresh from a loss just two nights before to little Sewanee, Tech was the weakest team on the UK schedule. The Wildcats were more concerned with a game two days hence against powerful De Paul, as Coach Adolph Rupp ruefully admitted later, than with the rival at hand.

UK controlled most of the game but never held a comfortable lead and, with twelve seconds left, found itself with only a one-point lead and the ball. At that point Tech guard Joe Helms stole the ball and dribbled down court. The 5'9" Helms, the smallest man on the court, pulled up and hit a jump shot from about twelve feet out. Kentucky still had time for a set shot and a rebound but both tries bounced off the front of the rim and the game ended. Wildcat fans could not believe what their eyes were seeing. Most of the fans at Memorial Coliseum that January night remained rooted to their seats, stunned. They waited, as one fan recalled in a 1981 interview, for the public address announcer or one of the referees to inform them that the timekeeper had made a mistake and UK had one more chance. Small wonder. The Wildcats of that era seldom lost, especially at home. In fact, reporter Ashford observed, "it was the first time most of the fans in the gym ever had seen a Kentucky team beaten." The defeat was the first for the Wildcats on their own court since January 2, 1943, in a total of 129 games—an overall national record which still stands. It also was the first loss at home to a Southeastern Conference team since 1939, some sixteen years before, when Tennessee took a 30-29 decision. In addition it ended an overall thirty-two-game winning streak spread over two seasons.

Kentucky native Lake Kelly, now a Wildcat assistant coach, was a member of the Georgia Tech team. Kelly vividly and enthusiastically recalls that night. "My parents were sure we would be whipped. They were so convinced that they made sure they were off visiting my sister in Louisiana that day." Kelly and his Tech teammates shared this feeling. They would have preferred to be anywhere but Lexington. The Tech players had no illusions about their chances against the Wildcats. "All through the game we kept wondering when UK was going to break it open. They led through the whole game but never seemed to be able to move away from us. Then with about two minutes left we called time out and by then we realized we actually could win the game. I'll never forget," Kelly continues, "how the Coliseum was when the game ended. Those 12,000 fans just sat there not saying anything for about a half an hour they were so shocked."

The press and basketball fans across the nation shared the amazement of UK partisans. A "startled" *New York Times* columnist described how Tech "with a closing-second goal, ended Kentucky's dominance of Dixie opponents" and dulled the luster of UK's ranking as "the nation's number one college basketball power." The *Los Angeles Times* noted that "Tech ac-

complished what a Southeastern Conference school has been trying to do for nearly sixteen years." The *Kansas City Star* echoed Tech coach John "Whack" Hyder's sentiment at game's end: "What is there to say but 'wow.' " Cliff Hagan, a Wildcat basketball great and now UK's athletics director, recalls how he learned of the defeat. Hagan was at the time a second lieutenant stationed at Andrews Air Force Base outside Washington, D.C. During the basketball season he played on the base basketball team, leading them to two World-Wide Air Force championships and winning All-Service honors both years he was in the service. On the morning of January 9, 1955, Hagan's team was on another base preparing for a game later that day. He remembers he was on his way to breakfast when the team's sports information officer, who was traveling with the squad, came running toward him excitedly waving a newspaper. " 'You won't believe what happened last night' I remember him saying and he was right, I didn't believe it at first. It was just something that didn't happen to UK at home and especially to a team like Georgia Tech, which had such a poor record that year."

That was not the end of UK's humiliation. On January 31, 1955, the Wildcats again played Georgia Tech, this time in Atlanta. Lake Kelly recalls that before the game he had a brief talk with one of his friends on the UK team. "Rupp is furious with us," the friend confided. "He has been pushing us hard in practice all week. If we lose this one Rupp will kill us." "They were so tensed up and afraid of ol' Adolph," Kelly notes, "that they lost to us again, and by an even wider margin than they did in Lexington." Ironically, the two losses to Georgia Tech were the only regular-season defeats UK suffered that year.

Through the decades since 1903, when the first organized team played, UK basketball has evolved into a tradition of excellence and huge success. It is a tradition of which Kentuckians obviously are proud. UK is, one observer noted, "the only school anyone cares about." Coach Joe B. Hall has observed proudly that "People throughout Kentucky really care about their basketball." In fact, he continued, "businessmen tell me that business goes up or down depending on whether or not the Wildcats win."

Some people have likened what UK creates in its fans to a fever—Big Blue Fever—or a form of mass hysteria. To former governor Albert B. "Happy" Chandler, "It's a mania" and "I've been a follower of this team for 60 years. I love 'em." Whatever it is, *Lexington Leader* reporters Jack Brammer and Mike Fields wrote in 1980, "it grows larger with every UK victory." And, one might add, it is not dimmed by the team's relatively infrequent defeats.

The agony of defeat shows in the faces of the cheerleaders as UK bows to Florida State (73-54) in the NCAA Mideast Regionals on March 18, 1972—Adolph Rupp's last game.

Opposite: Top, Wildcat basketball's top fan, Albert B. "Happy" Chandler, former governor, senator, and baseball commissioner, at a 1970 game in Memorial Coliseum.

Below, UK students wildly cheer the Cats on to victory over the University of Louisville Cardinals on November 26, 1983.

Above and below, Big Blue Fever. *Left,* Jay Shidler (25) goes in for a layup against the University of Nevada Las Vegas on March 4, 1978. Mike Phillips is no. 55 and Jack Givens is no. 21.

"UK basketball is like a magnet," former Wildcat ballplayer and Assistant Coach Dick Parsons observed in a January 1983 interview, "that not only draws Kentuckians but also many individuals who didn't grow up in the state but who have developed a love for the Wildcats. There are any number of people who live out of state who loyally follow UK." One example that came to Parsons's mind was "a gentleman we called 'Tombstone Johnny.' " The man owned a tombstone business in Iowa. Apparently he developed an interest in Kentucky basketball by listening to the games on radio. Then he began to attend some of the games when UK played in the Middle West. "We would see him at Iowa and other places on the road. Eventually he made a trip or two to Lexington and just this last fall he called to tell us that he had moved to Lexington. And all this developed," Parsons concluded, "from listening to broadcasts of UK basketball. He became a Wildcat fan, he sent his son here to school, and finally he even came here to live."

Ned Jennings, a former UK starting center (1958/59-1960/61), found the appeal of Wildcat basketball to be very powerful in Eastern Kentucky. "I travel in the mountains in my work," Jennings stated in an interview, "and it is unbelievable what I run into up there. You find people who have been fans for forty years and have never seen a game but they listen to the radio and write down everything that happens." Jennings has learned from experience that the fans often remember more about the team's accomplishments than the players themselves. "You say something," he noted, "and they will pull the book out and flip through it and tell you whether you are right or wrong. You just can't believe it. It just grew over the years and got to be a way of life."

Central Kentuckians are just as ardent in their support as other citizens of the commonwealth. One local Wildcat supporter, real estate developer Dudley Webb, built a hotel in downtown Lexington in order to bolster UK's bid for the NCAA championship finals in 1985. As Webb stated in a "CBS Reports" segment on college basketball which aired on network television on January 20, 1983, "At the time the NCAA search committee was looking at Lexington they weren't sure there were enough rooms here to support the tournament, so at that time we [Dudley and his brother and partner, Donald] committed to build the hotel project. Sixty million dollars to attract the tournament."

A dream of Kentucky and many out-of-state youngsters for generations has been to wear the blue and white uniforms of UK. When the Inez Indians, from the hills of Eastern Kentucky, won the state high school basketball championship at Lexington's Memorial Coliseum in March 1954, Inez star Bill Cassady's dream came true. After the game UK Assistant Coach Harry Lancaster visited the Indians' dressing room and, amid the shouting and romping asked Cassady, "Would you like to play at the University of Kentucky?" The youngster's heart nearly stopped beating as he quietly replied, "Yes, that's what I've always wanted to do." "Would you sign a grant-in-aid?" asked Lancaster. "Yes, I'd like to," Cassady replied happily.

It would be satisfying to be able to report that Cassady went on to fame and glory at UK. Unhappily, he did not. His experience was an example of the dark side of Wildcat basketball. For Cassady, college basketball became a dream gone sour. During his varsity career (1955/56-1957/58) he was a seldom-used substitute. This experience was not, according to a former teammate, because of his lack of size or talent. Cassady was one of several players who were beaten down by Rupp's methods of motivation. As one player recalled, "Practice was all business. Games were a relief because he couldn't kill you in public." Rupp was a tough taskmaster who "seldom praised you. Some people respond to praise, others don't. You can make some guys mad and they play harder but others quit or just turn off inside." Cassady was one of several talented athletes who were unable or unwilling to deal with the psychological pressures applied by Adolph Rupp and his successor Joe Hall. UK basketball has had other negative aspects, such as the point shaving scandals of 1951. Fans and supporters generally prefer to forget or ignore the dark side, but it is just as much a part of the history of UK basketball as the brighter side, and must be examined.

Despite these negative aspects, Kentucky has become "the biggest and best [basketball dynasty] in the country," as former Marquette coach Al McGuire wrote in *Inside Sports* (December 1981). Since the first game in 1903—which, ironically, was a loss to Georgetown College—the Wildcats have won 1,358 games and lost only 423. During those 81 seasons the home record has been 756 games won and 120 games lost. Team championships include the SEC, won or shared 35 times; two National Invitational Tournament (NIT) crowns; and the National Collegiate Athletic Association (NCAA) five times, in 1948, 1949, 1951, 1958, and 1978. Individual recognition and awards have come as well. The university has produced 30 All-Americans, chosen 48 times, the first one in 1921. Adolph Rupp, who led UK to its first four NCAA championships, completed his 42-season career

in 1972 with 880 victories, 190 defeats, and a winning percentage of .822, making him perhaps the most successful coach in college basketball history.

The Wildcats' first home court, called simply "the Gymnasium," was located in the north wing of Barker Hall. The wing was two stories in height. The basement contained baths, lockers, wash stands, closets, and a swimming pool, while the gymnasium proper was on the second floor. It was equipped, noted the 1909-11 *Biennial Report* of the university, "with the best apparatus that could be procured." Unfortunately for the basketball team, the Gymnasium was also used for physical education classes until 1909. In that year, according to the 1910 *Kentuckian*, Buell Armory (which is located in the south wing of Barker Hall) "was floored and there was ample time for practice" in the gym.

The Gymnasium, later to be known as the Ladies Gym, accommodated at most 650 spectators for basketball games. But, as Sam Ridgeway, who played on the 1921 championship team, remembers, "For important games the fans would be lined up to try to get into the place. They couldn't all get in, of course, but you could hear them outside. And there was someone out there with a megaphone relaying what was going on inside. It was pretty much like it is today but on a smaller scale." For the fans who were lucky enough to get in, there was limited seating. A small bleacher section was set up at one end of the court behind the goal but most of the spectators had to stand along courtside or behind the other goal or along a track above the court. A few, Basil Hayden recalls, even hung from rafters. George Buchheit, UK basketball coach from 1919 to 1924, recalled in a June 1953 visit to Lexington that "once the spectators got in that old gym we played in there was hardly room to play the game. And I remember the poles that held up the running track that ran around the top of the gym. We always had to dodge those things."

Within twenty years of its construction in 1902 the Gymnasium was outmoded and the university, responding to a "public clamor for a better court," in the early 1920s completed plans for a new gymnasium to be built for what seemed at the time the outlandish sum of $92,000. In 1924 when Alumni Gym was built, with its then unheard-of seating capacity of 2,800, complaints were raised that too much money was being spent for a building that was simply too large for college basketball. Critics feared that the "spacious" arena might turn out to be a white elephant. While most of the spectators had had to stand in the old Barker Hall gym, in the new structure they sat on rows of benches.

Fans at the first few games played at Alumni Gym commented that the appearance was more that of a football field than of the basketball courts they were accustomed to at the time. Yet long before Alumni Gym was abandoned in favor of a newer structure, it was obvious that UK basketball had outgrown what

UK's first basketball home court, called simply "the Gymnasium." Located in Barker Hall, it was later renamed the Ladies' Gym. It lacked bleachers, and fans stood to see the games— apparently no deterrent.

The tip-off in UK's last regular-season game in Alumni Gym, the Wildcats' second home. The "biggest and best gymnasium in the South" at the time of its construction in 1924, it seated 2,800.

The Wildcats' home for a quarter century was 11,500-seat Memorial Coliseum. "The house that Rupp built" was dedicated in 1950.

once had been "the biggest and best gymnasium in the South." Its replacement, the 11,500-seat Memorial Coliseum, the "House that Rupp Built," was dedicated in 1950. The new building, which cost approximately $4 million to construct and which soon became known as the "Classic Arena in the South," was a multipurpose structure. In addition to being the Wildcats' home basketball court, the auditorium also hosted concerts, lectures, public meetings, and other programs. It boasted a large swimming pool and a complete plant for physical education as well as a host of offices for the athletics staff.

UK's home basketball games had been sold out each season since the 1930s. This tradition continued during the twenty-six seasons the Wildcats played at Memorial Coliseum and has continued at Rupp Arena, even though that structure has twice the seating capacity of the Coliseum.

When 23,000-seat Rupp Arena was opened in 1976 some skeptics expressed doubt that it would be possible to fill the building. They were wrong. The UK Athletics Department has no difficulty disposing each year of the 16,000 season tickets. Most of the rest of the tickets go to students on an individual game, first-come, first-served basis. But this policy does not begin to satisfy the demand for tickets. As *Lexington Leader*

reporter Andy Meade observed in 1980, "There simply are more people who want to watch the game in person than there is space available." The Big Blue have led the nation in attendance every season since moving to Rupp Arena. Cliff Hagan has maintained that he could fill the university's 57,750-seat football stadium for a Wildcat basketball game. As a result of the heavy demand, UK Vice President Ray Hornback notes, "It definitely is a status symbol to be seen at a UK game." It has been this way for decades.

The UK basketball program is the envy of the collegiate basketball world. When he was a member of the Atlanta Hawks, Jack Givens found that UK had "the reputation around the NBA of being the number one school in the country. Players feel it's even better than UCLA because of Rupp Arena, which . . . is sold out for every game, and because just about the whole state seems to support the team."

Many rival coaches and players consider Wildcat fans to be among the most knowledgeable in the country because they understand the nuances of the sport. They are generally more interested and informed, Givens discovered, than the typical NBA fan. "In most pro cities," he noted, "people don't go to games because they *love* basketball; they go because it's something to do, and they might just as soon go to

UK's home court since 1976 is 23,000-seat Rupp Arena. Despite its size, many fans still can't get seats. Here, UK defeats Alabama 85-70 on February 26, 1977.

For many young Kentuckians who grow up listening to games on the radio or seeing them on TV, getting tickets to a game is a dream come true. Here, Phil Grawemeyer signs autographs for young fans in 1955.

caster Denny Trease observed in an interview that "In Kentucky, where there is not much to do, basketball has become a way of life." Oscar Combs, publisher of the Lexington-based publication *The Cats' Pause*, agrees: "UK basketball is the one positive attraction all Kentuckians can identify with."

There is a certain tidiness and seeming logic to this argument, but it just doesn't hold together. Kentucky is not, for example, the only rural state in the union, but in few states if any is a college sport as important as University of Kentucky basketball is in this state. Indiana, for example, like its next-door neighbor, is essentially a rural state. The citizens of both states have long carried on a torrid love affair with basketball. But, sportswriter Mike Fields observes, "Ask a Hoosier why he thinks Indiana is No. 1 in basketball heritage. While Bobby Knight and IU will be paid their due homage, the high school game will earn the most reverential mention." By contrast, ask a Kentuckian why the Bluegrass state is "the world's basketball wonderland, and his litany of love likely will begin and end" with the University of Kentucky. Bill Harrell, who has coached both in Kentucky, at Shelby County High School and Morehead State University, and in Indiana, where his Muncie Central Bearcats won the state championship in 1978 and 1979,

a movie, or a play, or a rock concert." Kentucky is a sharp contrast. "The people who follow UK live or die basketball. If UK loses a game it's like a death in a family. Pro basketball doesn't seem to affect as many people as deeply as college basketball does in Kentucky." Linville Puckett, a star guard on the 1954/55 UK team, verified this fact when he quit the team because of a dispute with Coach Adolph Rupp over discipline. "Basketball at Kentucky isn't regarded as a game," Puckett observed, "but as a matter of life and death, with resemblance of one going to war."

Many observers believe Wildcat basketball is so special and important because of the essentially rural nature of the state which, in the words of *Lexington Herald-Leader* publisher Creed Black, makes it "the only game in town." In a large city like Philadelphia, Black's former home, sports fans "can spread their enthusiasm and attendance among professional football, baseball, basketball, hockey, and soccer teams" as well as a range of college teams and sports. "Here it's the Wildcats or else." Former Lexington television sports-

The UK Wildcat with Caywood Ledford, longtime "voice of the Wildcats"—the man who transmits the tradition to the state and to much of the nation.

confirms that in Indiana "people still turn out for high school basketball. Even if IU is playing, people are going to fill up the gym to see the Bearcats. I don't think that happens in Kentucky when UK is playing."

Emphasis on ruralness also ignores the fact that Kentucky has a major city, Louisville, which has had pro teams in a number of sports as well as a college basketball power, the University of Louisville. Even though the various pro and college teams in Louisville have won championships, they have been unable to hold the fancy of many Louisvillians, much less win the support of people in Eastern, Central, and Western Kentucky. Sportswriter Pete Axthelm's observation that basketball is a city game must be revised for Kentucky. In the commonwealth, basketball is a small-town and rural as well as a city game.

The special position UK basketball occupies in the state did not just happen. It evolved over several decades through the operation of a variety of factors. One, and not the least important by any means, has been the contribution made by radio announcers, including Claude Sullivan and Cawood Ledford, who since the late 1930s have transmitted "the tradition" from one end of the state to the other and from one generation of fans to another. Billy Reed described Ledford in a 1981 *Sports Illustrated* article as "the link between Adolph Rupp and Joe B. Hall, between Kentucky's storied past and its stirring present." Ledford and the Wildcats have built a radio network with 125 stations in Kentucky, Indiana, Ohio, Tennessee, West Virginia, and Florida. One survey found that UK games could be heard in forty states as well as Canada and the Bahamas. As a result, Al McGuire wrote in *Inside Sports*, "the kids in Kentucky start listening to the games on the radio when they are still being burped on their father's shoulder." Terry Mobley, a former UK player and now director of the university's Development Office, made this point in a December 1982 interview. A native of Harrodsburg, Mobley recalled that he was an ardent fan of the Big Blue at least by the time he was five years old. By then, he notes, he was "old enough to listen to the games on radio. The Wildcats are just a part of my heritage" he stated proudly.

Although Sullivan in his era and Ledford today are marvelous talents, the vital ingredient in the growth and maintenance of the UK dynasty, as Ledford would be the first to acknowledge, has been the athletes and their coaches. In the final analysis the role of certain individuals and certain key events has been of central importance in creating and nurturing the tradition. The first major figure was All-American Basil Hayden, and the first event was the championship game of the Southern Intercollegiate Athletic Association Tournament in Atlanta on March 1, 1921. That championship was the first of a number of milestones in UK basketball history.

Opposite, the nickname "Wildcats" was first used during the 1909 football season, and the Wildcat crest made its first appearance in the 1911 *Kentuckian.*

Part I
Origins of the Tradition

UNIVERSITAS
KENTUCKIENSIS

FELIS
CATUS

2

UK's First Championship Season

Basketball was invented in Springfield, Massachusetts, in 1891 in repsonse to a recognized need for a new sport to fill the athletic void that existed during the winter season. Football was the sport of autumn and baseball filled the needs of athletic youngsters in the spring and summer. Gymnastics, marching drills, and calisthenics were popular in Europe but did not seem well-adapted to American needs or interests.

In December 1891 James Naismith, a young gym instructor at the International Training School of the Young Men's Christian Association at Springfield (now Springfield College) solved the problem. He tacked peach baskets to the lower rails of ten-foot-high balconies at each end of the school's gym, wrote up and distributed a short list of rules, tossed out a soccer ball, and let the contest begin. One of Naismith's most important decisions was to use a soccer ball instead of a football because he wanted to avoid tackling or extremely rough play in his new game. As Naismith noted in his autobiography, if a player "can't run with the ball, we don't have to tackle!" By using a soccer ball the emphasis would be on passing rather than tackling. Although the game was eventually made less violent than football, during its early decades the sport was a far from gentle pastime. In fact, it was a very rough and tough game.

Theodore Roosevelt, while president of the United States, was concerned about the increasing violence and the growing number of injuries in college basketball as well as football. Larry Fox noted in his *Illustrated History of Basketball* that in 1909 Harvard University's president Charles Eliot "called for an end to basketball, which he said had become 'even more brutal than football.' " Others echoed these sentiments. Efforts made in the following years to bring the young sport under control met with limited success. One of the reasons for the brutality was the large number of football players who flocked to the new winter sport as a way to stay in shape and to enjoy a little violent activity during the long winter days. A measure of the savagery of the game in these early years is clearly shown in an interview conducted by University of Kentucky Sports Information Director Russell Rice with early Wildcat basketball player Thomas G. Bryant. Bryant, who played from 1905 to 1907, recalled that "we didn't play for championships but for bloody noses." Commenting on a 1907 game with Transylvania, whose players "came onto the floor wearing football pads," Bryant noted that "I've still got a tender ankle that I inherited when J. Franklin Wallace, a 6'3 1/2" 250-pound football tackle stepped on it during the game. He poked me with a left

Opposite, the earliest known photo of a UK men's basketball team, showing the 1904 starting five and their manager (there was as yet no coach). Standing, l-r: guards R.H. Arnett and J. White Guyn, center Joe Coons, and forwards C.P. St. John (captain) and H.J. Wurtele. Seated: manager Leander E. Andrews.

jab, and I came back with a haymaker to the face." In those days, Bryant concluded, "a good fight was the expected thing."

Until the 1930s, even at the University of Kentucky, games were low-scoring, slow-moving, defensive battles and on occasion brutal slugfests. Basil Hayden, UK's first All-American, noted some of the reasons that even the excellent 1921 team—which won the first championship tournament held in the South (and perhaps in the nation)—averaged only thirty-six points while holding rivals to nineteen points per game in a fourteen-game season, including four tournament games. One reason for the low scores was the way players shot. No one, Hayden recalls, shot the ball one-handed. Long set shots as well as free throws generally were taken underhanded, from the knees. Close-in shots were usually taken from the waist or chest. Even a layup was a two-handed shot although a few daring players shot a layup hook if they felt the two-hander would be blocked. Hayden tapped rebounds one-handed but he was unusual. Nearly all shots taken by all players were two-handers, and since few teams set screens, shots could be easily blocked.

Games were slow moving, with the emphasis generally on defense. There was no ten-second line so a team could hold the ball at mid-court or in the defensive half of the court if it wanted to do so. A center jump followed each basket made. Nevertheless, the clock continued to run. It also continued to run when a foul shot was taken, when violations were called, and when the ball was passed in from out of bounds. The clock was turned off only when a team called a time-out, which happened infrequently. Because the clock continued to run and teams had to move the ball around a lot to get open shots, far fewer shots were taken in a typical game than are taken now.

The most important reason for the low scores, however, was that the games were so rough. It took a lot of contact, Hayden recalls, before the single game referee would call a foul. "Generally the referees back then didn't really know the rules and you practically had to be knocked into the seats before they would call a foul." No one called a foul, he also noted, for touching a man on the arm or even the back when he was shooting which, of course, would throw the shot off. And when it came to rebounding, there was fierce action under the basket. In the battle for position to get rebounds players pushed and shoved and held. One of the techniques Hayden and other players used was to put one hand on an opponent's back, push him down while jumping, "and go up above him and push the rebound back into the basket with the other hand."

The game Naismith presented to the sports world on that winter day in 1891 was offered at the right time and the ideal place. The Springfield YMCA school was a training facility for YMCA general secretaries and physical education instructors. Sports historian Neil Isaacs has noted that the school's graduates "not only went to posts all over the country, taking their Springfield routines with them, but also returned to the school like former seminarians seeking guidance from the seat of their order. Besides, they all kept abreast of what was going on at Springfield by means of *The Triangle*, a monthly newsletter."

Collegians lagged behind YMCAs in the spread of basketball. The first known intercollegiate game took place on February 9, 1895, when the Minnesota State School of Agriculture defeated Hamline by a score of 9-3 and claimed the championship of Minnesota. The first game between eastern colleges was a March 23, 1895, match between Haverford and Temple, which Haverford won by two points, 6-4. Other contests followed between college squads in the Middle West and East but the first game involving five-man teams is believed to have been a March 20, 1897, contest between Yale and Pennsylvania. Yale won, 32-10.

Soon after the introduction of basketball in Springfield the new sport was offered in YMCAs in Kentucky. By the turn of the century collegians in the state were playing informal games as well as exhibition contests. The first recorded men's intercollegiate basketball game at the University of Kentucky (then known as Kentucky State College) took place on February 6, 1903, against nearby Georgetown College. The girls' basketball team, it should be noted, began play in 1902 and, according to the 1904 yearbook, was "successful from the start."

For what was to become the nation's most successful basketball program, it was an inauspicious beginning. On that winter afternoon the recently organized Kentucky State team, composed largely of football players, was no match for a Georgetown squad that had been playing for months. At the end of the first half the score stood at 7-1 in favor of Georgetown. "During the latter part of the game," the *Lexington Herald* reported on February 7, "State College weakened appreciably" and suffered a 15-6 defeat.

The State team, at the time called "the Cadets" because of the strong ROTC program, played two other games in 1903, both again on their home court. In that first season they defeated the Lexington YMCA team but lost to Kentucky University (now Transylvania University). State's name was changed in the following years as its status and size grew. It

Table 1. UK Basketball Team Record, 1903-1911/12

Season	Won	Lost
1903	1	2
1904	1	4
1905	1	4
1906	4	9
1907	3	6
1907/08	5	6
1908/09	5	4
1909/10	4	8
1910/11	5	6
1911/12	9	0
Total	38	49

became Kentucky State University in 1908 and the University of Kentucky in 1917. But until the 1920s the fortunes of its basketball team were mixed.

University of Kentucky basketball began "on a shoestring," as *Lexington Leader* reporter Larry Shropshire noted in 1950. The team was "a one-basketball outfit, and the ball used for all practices and games was furnished by the players, who chipped in a quarter or a half-dollar apiece to buy the heavy little balloon." It cost three dollars to buy the ball and, as Thomas Bryant, an original team member, recalled, "if something had happened to that ball, we couldn't have played."

During its first five years of competition Kentucky won only ten of thirty-five games, but the situation began to improve in the 1907/08 season when the team achieved a record of five victories and six defeats. The next season Kentucky had its first winning season and just three years later reached the pinnacle of an unbeaten season. It was, the *Kentuckian* exulted, "one glorious march from start to finish. Not only were we undefeated, but during the entire season not once was an opposing team even in the lead."

One reason for the change of fortunes was the appointment of an effective coach in 1909. In that year E.R. Sweetland, already the school's football coach, assumed the additional duties of basketball coach. The year 1909 was a landmark in UK sports history for another reason. Commenting on a 6-2 football victory over the University of Illinois on October 3, 1909, First Lieutenant Philip Corbusier, commandant and professor of Military Science and Tactics at UK, declared before a chapel audience of students that the football team had "fought like wildcats." The press soon picked up on Corbusier's term and one of the university's oldest traditions was born. Quickly replacing the previously favored "Cadets," "Wildcats" has remained ever since that day the favored nickname for University of Kentucky athletic teams.

In the wake of the successful 1911/12 basketball season the *Kentuckian* heaped lavish praise on Sweetland "for his most successful season" and outlined his methods and achievements. "He filled the boys with confidence, trained and instructed them, as only he can, and, as is his invariable custom, turned out a championship team."

Prior to the appointment of Sweetland, Kentucky had no basketball coach. Instead the team practiced on its own and all responsibilities were handled by a manager. W.B. Wendt, manager in 1906, recalled later that he was "a one-man operation. I made the schedule, printed the tickets, collected money, paid the bills, was in charge of the team on the road, and sometimes swept the floor." Although the appointment of Sweetland changed that situation, the course of UK basketball in the following years was not an unbroken string of successes. Kentucky had losing seasons in 1916/17 and 1918/19. In 1919/20, just the year before they captured the SIAA championship, they lost seven of twelve games under new coach George C. Buchheit. Despite their poor record the foundations were being carefully laid for the Wildcats' first landmark season.

Buchheit (sometimes spelled Bucheit or Buckheit) was the first of three important coaches in the short period from 1919 to 1930 who would move to Kentucky from Illinois. The others were John Mauer and Adolph Rupp. Together, the three transformed the style of play and the fortunes of basketball at the University of Kentucky. In fact, of the five men who coached at UK during the 1920s, four—Buchheit, C.O. Applegran, Ray Ecklund, and John Mauer—were University of Illinois alumni. The exception was Basil Hayden, a Kentucky basketball All-American, who coached at his alma mater in 1926/27. Adolph Rupp, who graduated from the University of Kansas in 1923, came to Kentucky in 1930 after a very successful coaching career at Freeport High School in northeastern Illinois, but even he owed his hiring in large part to a recommendation from University of Illinois basketball coach Craig Ruby. This simply emphasized the fact that during the 1920s the Illinois connection was firmly established. The connection developed primarily because of the success of the Illinois football team and its great coach, Robert "Bob" Zuppke (1913-40), as well as the close proximity of Illinois.

The starting five of UK's undefeated 1912 team. Standing, l-r: forwards Brinkley Barnett and D.W. Hart, center (and captain) W.C. Harrison, and guards R.C. Preston and J.H. Gaiser. Kneeling: team manager Giles Meadors.

Until the early 1930s Kentucky's basketball coaches, including Rupp, also served as assistant football coaches. Thus talent on the football field was often at least as important in choosing a basketball coach as ability on the hardwood. Illinois was a national football power from Zuppke's arrival in Urbana in 1913 through the 1920s, and enjoyed undefeated seasons in 1914, 1915, 1923, and 1927. Within the Big Ten the Illini won or shared the conference championship in 1914, 1915, 1918, 1919, 1923, 1927, and 1928. University of Illinois basketball teams were not nearly so successful. Ralph Jones, basketball coach from 1913 to 1920, won the conference title in 1915 and shared it with Minnesota two years later. Under Frank Winters (1921-22) and J. Craig Ruby (1923-36) the Illini shared in only two more Big Ten championships—in 1924 with Wisconsin and Chicago, and in 1935 with Purdue and Wisconsin.

Most of UK's football head coaches and assistant coaches, as well as athletic directors, during the late teens and twenties were University of Illinois graduates. Both Buchheit and Mauer had been stars in football as well as basketball at Illinois and they were to coach both sports at UK. Mauer admitted years later

that his "primary interest was football" and not his highly successful basketball teams. Even Adolph Rupp served as an assistant football coach during his first years in Lexington. Only after his success on the hardwood was a proven fact was Rupp free to concentrate on basketball and drop his other chores, which included coaching the wrestling team as well as freshman football.

Buchheit was a young man when he arrived at UK in 1919, having just graduated from Illinois, where he played football under Bob Zuppke and basketball under Ralph Jones. Buchheit brought to his new job the style of basketball play he had learned at Illinois. The *Lexington Herald* on February 24, 1921, called it "Buchheit's system," although Hayden, his star player and most famous product, referred to it as the "Illinois system." Actually this was a Big Ten style of play which all the teams of the conference used but which appears to have been developed first by Wisconsin Coach Walter E. Meanwell in the years after 1912. Under both the Buchheit and the Illinois systems one man remained under each goal while the other three players roamed the floor. Buchheit altered the system he learned from Jones in one major respect—although

both emphasized defense, Illinois played a zone defense, while UK employed an aggressive and tenacious man-to-man defense.

All teams of the era emphasized an offense that stressed passing because the ball was seldom if ever dribbled. Not until the 1928/29 season were limitations on dribbling finally removed. Buchheit used what Sam Ridgeway has called a zig-zag or figure-eight offense. Following a defensive rebound or after UK won the center tip the three men on the floor would bring the ball upcourt, one passing it to a teammate and quickly turning back toward the middle of the court and then receiving a pass from the third teammate, who was now running toward him. This, Ridgeway says, "seemed to hypnotize opponents," who apparently had never seen the offense before or had not figured out an effective defense against it. While opponents were confused by the movements of the UK players the ball was passed in to the center, who was stationed under the basket for an easy shot. Should this strategy fail, a set shot was taken from outside, and the center and the other two floor players took up rebounding positions under the basket. According to Hayden, there were no set plays. One player, a standing or back guard, remained under the defensive goal, although he might move up to midcourt or even occasionally to the offensive end of the court to take a long set shot.

Buchheit introduced his system in the 1919/20 season with limited success, winning only five of twelve decisions. But the following year he found three new players who, along with holdovers Basil Hayden and Bobby Lavin, fitted his needs and nearly brought UK a perfect season. All were native Kentuckians and all had been playing basketball for years. Hayden, for example, began playing at the YMCA in Paris, his hometown, while in sixth grade.

Each player on the 1921 team had a job to do, or to use a modern term, each was a role-player. Hayden, the team captain, Bill King, the other forward, and guard Bobby Lavin handled the ball. King was a fine goal shooter and when the team faced a zone he generally was the man who took the long outside shots. In the years prior to 1924, when a player was fouled he was not required to take the foul shots. Any player could be designated to take these shots and, for the Wildcats, King was generally that player. Lavin, who had played basketball at Paris High School with Hayden and who was the quarterback on the UK football team, was a ball handler and strong defensive player. He also helped with the offensive rebounding. The team's center, Paul Adkins, stayed under or near the offensive goal. At 6'2", Adkins was a big man for

George Buchheit, UK basketball and assistant football coach from 1919/20 through 1923/24.

the time and generally controlled the center jump which followed each goal. Adkins was an adequate rebounder but an effective goal shooter. The finest athlete was Basil Hayden, an excellent all-around player. Although an accurate shooter, he emphasized passing, rebounding, and defense. Hayden was 5'11" tall but could easily place his entire hand above the basket on a vertical leap. On defense he and other team members emphasized ball stealing as well as strong rebounding. "It's sort of devastating to a team you're playing against," Hayden chuckled in an interview, "if you get in there and get the ball when they're running in one direction and you take it away and go in the other direction." The heart of the defense and the man Hayden feels should have been named All-American was Sam Ridgeway. A strapping 6'1" sophomore, Ridgeway was a shot-blocker and an excellent defensive rebounder. "The other team didn't shoot at the basket but once," Hayden laughingly recalls, "and if they missed they didn't get it back to try again because Ridgeway was there and got it."

The accomplishments of the 1921 team were astonishing when one notes that the starting lineup was

composed of two first-year players (freshmen were not eligible), Ridgeway and King, and three juniors, Adkins (who played his first two years at Cumberland College), Lavin, and Hayden. It was not only a young team but in a very real sense a squad of "student-athletes." Buchheit recognized the talents of this group of young men and welded them into the first great basketball team in Kentucky, and Southern, history. Buchheit was ideally suited to deal with the players of the era. Ridgeway, Hayden, and the others loved basketball but they attended UK for academics rather than athletics. Ridgeway, for example, wanted to study engineering and at the time UK was the only school in the state with an engineering program. Hayden first attended Transylvania but transferred to UK at the end of his freshman year because he wanted to take an industrial chemistry course which was not offered at Transylvania.

As good as Hayden and the others were, they were not actively recruited. Neither Kentucky nor any other school offered athletic scholarships. Anyone who wanted to try out for the UK team could. In the 1920/21 season approximately thirty-five young men responded to a notice Buchheit placed on the bulletin board. Twelve made it through the cuts, and eight were on the traveling team. All were native Kentuckians. The starters were Hayden and Lavin from Paris, Ridgeway from Shepherdsville, Adkins from

Williamsburg, and King from Lexington. The three substitutes who completed the traveling team were forward William L. Poynz of Covington, center James E. Wilhelm of Paducah, and Lexington native Gilbert K. Smith, who played guard. It was, as Ridgeway has observed, not only "a group of native Kentuckians but a real team of students." And the big, quiet, sincere painfully shy Buchheit, just a few years older than his players, was perfectly suited to his team. He was as much a friend and teacher as a leader. Ridgeway recalls that Buchheit "was the kind of man you wanted to play for, to give your best for. He was the type that, without him asking, you would want to go out and play your heart out for." They probably would not have responded as well to a hard-driving, highly success-oriented coach. Adolph Rupp, whose personality and methods were ideally suited to UK's needs and interests in the 1930s, 40s, and 50s, probably would have been far less successful in 1921.

After a mediocre record of five won, seven lost in 1919/20, Buchheit's second season was a succession of victories marred only by a 29-27 loss to traditional rival Centre and capped by the SIAA tournament, which was, in Sam Ridgeway's words, "UK's first great success." The Southern Conference was composed of teams from all parts of the South, teams that now are members of the Southeastern Conference, the Southern Conference, and the Atlantic Coast Conference, as

The 1916 Paris High School basketball team with two future UK stars, Basil Hayden (front row, second from left) and Bobby Lavin (front row, second from right). Besides playing basketball, Lavin was the starting quarterback on the UK football team.

well as some that are now independents. Fifteen Conference teams were invited to participate in the 1921 tournament. In addition to Kentucky they were Auburn, Alabama, Furman, University of South Carolina, Clemson, Newberry, Birmingham-Southern, Tulane, University of Tennessee, Mercer, Millsaps, Mississippi A&M (now Mississippi State), Georgia Tech, and Georgia.

The teams converged on Atlanta in late February 1921 from all parts of the South for the first basketball tournament ever held in the region. Although Kentucky with its regular-season record of nine wins in ten games was one of the dark horses, the undefeated Georgia Bulldogs were the overwhelming favorites. This preference changed after the Wildcats' resounding 50-28 first-round mauling of a Tulane team the *Atlanta Constitution* on February 26 noted "had a record for achievement that was expected to make them a formidable factor in the final results of the tournament." Georgia also scored an impressive first-round victory over Newberry, but "the prognosticators are not talking Georgia and nothing but Georgia. They are talking Kentucky State [UK] a lot and generally they are speaking in bated breath." Kentucky's rangy and fast players, the "dazzling" passing, and the teamwork impressed all observers. King, Hayden, and Adkins were judged "three of the most scintillating goal shooters imaginable, while the defense seems almost as good as the attack." The talk of the throngs that gathered in the Atlanta hotel lobbies was Kentucky's "bewildering" and "peculiar attack," that is, its play off the center jump. On the jump, which followed each goal, Buchheit reversed the positions of his forwards and guards. When the ball was tossed up, the forwards, Hayden and King, would run past the center circle toward the offensive basket while Ridgeway and Lavin would move in the opposite direction to take up positions guarding the defensive end of the court. Because this play was new to the teams UK played and because of Adkins's height, the Wildcats generally controlled the tip and often converted it into a quick and easy basket. Basil Hayden recalls that no one was able to figure out how to defend against UK's "baffling" attack.

The Wildcats followed up the Tulane win with equally impressive victories over Mercer (49-24) and Mississippi A&M (28-13). The championship game was played on the evening of March 1 and, in what *Constitution* writer Fuzzy Woodruff termed a " 'Frank Merriwell' finish," the Kentuckians defeated the University of Georgia team. (Merriwell was a fictional hero of the day who won baseball, football, and

basketball games dramatically in the final second of action.) "More red-blooded stuff was crowded into one brief minute last night," Woodruff wrote, "than comes to most men in a span of life." With less than a minute left to play in the hard-fought game, Georgia led by only two points, 19-17. Then Georgia made a serious mistake. Throughout the game they had concentrated on containing Basil Hayden because they recognized, Woodruff wrote, that "the Kentucky captain, a blond Apollo, a Kentucky thoroughbred, if one ever stepped on the turf, has been the thorn in the side of Kentucky's opponents." Suddenly, with approximately forty-five seconds to go, Hayden was free beneath the basket for "the merest fraction of a split second." The ball was quickly passed to him. It "hardly pauses in Hayden's hands. His shot is fast, but accurate. It drops through the basket without hesitating" to tie the score.

Kentucky controlled the center jump which followed the score, quickly moved down the court and got the ball to Adkins, their center and "the surest goal shooter in the tourney." As time ran out, Georgia captain "Buck" Cheeves desperately threw himself at Adkins, who was set under the basket to shoot. The referee's whistle sounded and was followed by the timer's signal that playing time had expired. With the game on the line, Bill King, although only a first-year player, without hesitation and without consulting his coach or teammates headed to the foul line. "King is coolness personified," Woodruff noted. "He hasn't been particularly good on foul shots all night and Georgia has hopes, though it fears for the worst." And indeed their worst fears were realized. "The ball leaves his hands and King's eyes do not even follow it to the basket." After bouncing dramatically on the rim the ball fell through the net and the game was over. "Talk about your finishes," the Atlanta sportswriter concluded, "there never was such a one in reality" and all that could compare in the realm of fiction was "a Frank Merriwell finish." In interviews conducted sixty years later both Basil Hayden and Sam Ridgeway remembered the events in minute detail, as though they had just transpired. It was truly the stuff that boyhood dreams of glory are made of. Both also recalled the tumultuous reception they received on the team's return to Lexington.

Fans of the "Wildcat Five" had closely followed the fortunes of their team through each of their four SIAA tournament games. There was no radio or television coverage, of course, but fans in Lexington received up-to-the-minute reports during each game by telegraph. "A crowd of several hundred students, alumni, and rooters of the University of Kentucky jammed every

Coach George Buchheit poses with the 1921 Wildcats, "Champions of the South." Front row, l-r: Sam Ridgeway, Paul Adkins, Basil Hayden (captain), Bill King, and Bobby Lavin. Back row: Buchheit, Jim Wilhelm, Bill Poynz, Gilbert Smith, and Athletics Director S.A. "Daddy" Boles.

corner of the lobby and mezzanine floor of the Phoenix Hotel" to listen to the action in the championship game, a *Lexington Herald* reporter wrote the following day. They "whooped and 'hollered' in glee" as the telegrams recording the Wildcats' progress "were megaphoned from the mezzanine floor, and when the final wire came in and the news was shouted 'Final score, Kentucky 20, Georgia 19,' the lid flew off with a bang and bedlam ruled." As soon as the game ended plans were immediately made for a huge reception, banquet, and dance the following evening when the team arrived back in Lexington.

From the beginning, UK's participation in the tournament was occasion for a continuous round of cutting class, dances, and other forms of celebration which culminated in "a paroxysm of joy," the *Lex-*

ington Herald noted in its March 3 issue, "in the greatest homecoming reception ever accorded any athletic team in Kentucky." A huge crowd of students and fans had trooped down to the Southern Station the previous evening to meet the northbound train and welcome home the "eight modest Wildcats" and their quiet, shy coach. Despite a driving rainstorm, the crowd waited happily and patiently for the train's arrival, then it "followed the conquering heroes back to town and for two solid hours," in a scene to be repeated in future years to celebrate other championships, Wildcat supporters "kept up a continuous outpouring of praise and tribute to the team that swept everything before it in its 'march through Georgia.' "

Coach Buchheit and his "Wonder Team" were "Champions of the South."

The Illinois Connection

The year 1921 was a glorious one for University of Kentucky basketball. "The student body of the University," observed the 1922 *Kentuckian*, "became an aggregation of hero worshippers, and the Blue and White quintet became the acme of things basketball." The future seemed very bright for the "Champions of the South." The glory quickly faded and the Wildcats were unable to defend their hard-earned title in 1922 or for many years thereafter but this did not in any way decrease fan interest or support.

The magnificent "Merriwell finish" to the 1921 campaign should have provided the momentum for another highly successful season in 1922. Every member of the "Wonder Team" returned and there was every indication "that Kentucky would have a path paved with roses and leading right up to another victory in the tournament at Atlanta." Even before play began, however, the Wildcats' chances were dealt devastating blows when both Basil Hayden and Sam Ridgeway were incapacitated. Hayden, the heart of the team's offense, suffered a serious knee injury high jumping for the track team, while Ridgeway, who played a similar role on the defensive end of the court, fought a year-long bout with diphtheria and never again played basketball for UK. Although Hayden did return to the team during the season he was not fully recovered from his injury and his running and rebounding were severely limited. The leaper who the previous season had routinely touched the rim of the basket was now barely able to jump. The memory of the 1922 season still makes the proud Hayden wince.

Forward Bill King, center Paul Adkins, and Bobby Lavin, the running guard and team captain, returned, but without the vital cogs of the championship squad the 1922 team suffered through a lackluster season with only nine wins and five losses. They returned to the SIAA tournament in late February but lost to Mercer by 13 points (35-22) in the second round.

Hayden graduated in 1922 and, after a brief but far from satisfying career coaching at Kentucky Wesleyan and at his alma mater, went on to become a banker and community leader in his hometown of Paris. In his last two years of college Ridgeway, who had been a star in baseball as well as basketball, completed the requirements for his degree in engineering and participated in campus activities, especially singing with the glee club. During his senior year Ridgeway gained a fuller understanding of the importance of Wildcat basketball, even in this early period, when the glee club sang in various parts of the state. Ridgeway found himself billed as the featured attraction but not, as he recalls, because of his singing voice. "I remember that we put on a concert at Paducah, for example, and I found that I was featured in all the advertising and the newspaper writings because I had played on the championship team, even though I hadn't played in a game since, and that was at least a year and a half later."

Although basketball was important it obviously was not as crucial in the early 1920s as today. That Ridgeway, an athlete with definite All-American potential, could choose not to continue playing, and that coach and fans would not try to pressure him to use the remainder of his eligibility is, in the context of college basketball in the 1980s, all but unthinkable.

Lovell "Cowboy" Underwood, a star on UK's 1923/24 to 1926/27 teams, recalled in an interview that "professional basketball wasn't important at all in those days and we didn't think about signing big contracts when we finished school, so we played the game just for the fun we could have." As to the quality of the athletic performance, Underwood firmly believes that it has vastly improved since his playing days. "With the exception of Basil Hayden," he stated bluntly, "the players of my era did not compare in any respect with the players of today."

Even in the 1920s, of course, Wildcat basketball fans loved their team and did not forget their heroes, as Ridgeway discovered in his travels with the university glee club. Already the foundations of the UK tradition were firmly in place. Nevertheless, there were times during the decade when an observer might wonder which direction the Blue and White was going to take. While the team was moderately successful in 1921/22 their record the following season was a disaster, with only three victories and ten defeats. In 1923/24, Buchheit's last as coach, the university bounced back to win thirteen of sixteen games. After the season, Buchheit was asked to remain as coach but decided to move on to Trinity College (soon to become Duke University). His place was taken by C.O. Ap-

plegran, another former University of Illinois athlete.

Applegran's one year as coach began with an exciting 28-23 victory over the University of Cincinnati on December 13, 1924, the first game played at Alumni Gym. Reviewing the season the 1925 *Kentuckian* noted that in the wake of that season-opening victory "predictions for a championship were rife." The high hopes were not to be realized, unfortunately. "At times the Blue and White would rise to great heights and display its real skill and strength" but from the third game "to the end of the season, the Wildcat quintet played a rather mediocre brand of ball." Nevertheless, at the end of the season UK was invited to the SIAA tournament in Atlanta, where they won a narrow victory over Mississippi A&M but lost their second game, to the University of Georgia. The season ended with a respectable but not outstanding record of thirteen victories and eight defeats.

In 1925/26 under Ray Eklund, UK's third basketball coach in three seasons, the Wildcats lost only three of eighteen decisions and produced the university's second All-American in guard Burgess Carey, a tall, husky, powerful defensive specialist. James McFarland, the 1926 team captain, reminisced about Carey in a May 1983 interview: "He was just a great defensive player. He was big and tough and strong. It was

The 1923/24 Wildcats, George Buchheit's last UK team. Front row (starting five), l-r: James McFarland, Bill King, A.T. Rice (captain), Bill Milward, and Lovell "Cowboy" Underwood. Athletics director "Daddy" Boles is at left.

awful tough to get past him. He would just slam into guys and if somehow they were able to get a shot off he would just reach up and knock it off the backboard." As the team's back, or defensive, guard Carey seldom went beyond midcourt and did not shoot the ball. But he did not need to. UK had an excellent group of players including, in addition to McFarland, Will Milward, Cowboy Underwood, and sophomore star Paul Jenkins. This group, the 1926 *Kentuckian* enthused, "was the greatest team that has worn the Blue and White since the Southern Champions of 1921." This was fortunate because something, if only memories, was needed to soften the pain and frustration of the following season.

The 1927 squad compiled the worst record of any team in UK history, with only three victories and thirteen defeats. Among the opponents who whipped the Blue and White during that painful year were in-state rivals Kentucky Wesleyan and Georgetown, as well as Indiana and Vanderbilt, and Cincinnati and Tennessee, which won two games each. Although the varsity team was woefully short on experience and talent the Wildcats were blessed with an excellent group of freshmen. UK's problems in 1927 were greatly complicated when coach Eklund resigned just before the start of the season, apparently because he did not want to be saddled with a losing record. Former UK star Basil Hayden responded to the university's desperate call for help and took over the team just a week before it was to play its first game. "I wasn't able to get much coaching in," Hayden has noted. Besides that, "All the talent had graduated except for one player [Paul Jenkins, the team captain] so there wasn't much to work with and there wasn't much chance to develop anything." Although he went into coaching after graduation from college, Hayden soon decided that he was not "the coaching type" and took a job in Richmond as an insurance agent. He had been away from basketball for two years and was out of touch with the game when UK began its frantic search for a coach to replace Eklund. Hayden and his players tried hard and UK fans, for their part, hoped that tradition and enthusiasm would compensate for a lack of talent or depth, but the result was a foregone conclusion. The season began with a 48-10 loss at home to the University of Cincinnati. Although the team did not lose that badly again, the Cincinnati game, as Hayden ruefully recalls, "sort of set the tone for the whole season."

In all the annals of UK basketball Basil Hayden's experience as coach was undoubtedly the most unfortunate. A genuinely decent person, he did not deserve

Burgess Carey, a powerfully built guard, was team captain in 1925/26 and UK's second All-American.

the dubious distinction of being the most unsuccessful coach in the university's history. That this was not due to a lack of ability on his part is demonstrated by his previous record as a winning coach at Kentucky Wesleyan and at Clark County High School. Despite the unsuccessful 1927 season Hayden could have remained at UK but decided that he just "wasn't suited for coaching."

If 1927 represented the low point in Wildcat basketball history, UK's fortunes immediately improved. Moving up to the varsity in 1928 was the most talented collection of freshmen that the school had attracted up to that time, and to mold them into a unit was an able new coach, John Mauer. The starting lineup in 1928 consisted of one veteran, forward Paul Jenkins, and four sophomores. Joining Jenkins, who was for the second straight season the team captain, were Lawrence McGinnis at the other forward position and Stanley Milward at center, while the guards were Cecil "Pisgah" Combs and Paul McBrayer. Irvine Jeffries, still another sophomore, replaced McGinnis on the starting five at midseason. Jeffries was, according to the 1928 *Kentuckian*, a "clever and sensational forward," but his athletic talent was apparently not matched by an interest in academics. A starter and a star on the freshman squad, Jeffries had left school at the end of the academic year only to return in January 1928, thus missing all preseason practice sessions. He left school again, and permanently, at the end of his sophomore year after signing a professional baseball contract.

Like all of his predecessors with the exception of Basil Hayden, Mauer was hired to coach football as well as basketball. Both Mauer and his fellow University of Illinois alumnus, George Buchheit, had been collegiate stars in basketball and football. During his career with the Illini, Mauer played in the backfield with "Red" Grange, one of the greatest and most widely publicized players in college football history. In basketball Mauer was an All-Conference forward. He was also a very good student. In 1926, his senior year at Illinois, Mauer received the Conference Medal of Honor, an award bestowed each year since 1914 at each Big Ten institution on "the student demonstrating proficiency in scholarship and athletics."

A quiet, strong-willed, intelligent man, Mauer was an ideal choice to return UK to the prominence and success it had enjoyed under Buchheit. According to Paul McBrayer, whose entire varsity career was spent under Mauer, the Illinois graduate's greatest strength was as a teacher. McBrayer, an assistant coach for nine years (1934-43) under Adolph Rupp and later a suc-

cessful coach in his own right at Eastern Kentucky University, believes that "basketball coaching is teaching and selling the game and selling your knowledge to the players. It is getting across to the players that when you tell them to do something that, by God, that is the best way to do it. That if it wasn't, you wouldn't be telling them. And John Mauer did that." In addition, Mauer was a fine person who had a genuine interest in the welfare of each of his players. "He wanted us to get an education. He wanted us to play each ball game up to the hilt. He wanted us to bring out the best in ourselves in every way, and he led by example. His life was such that you could admire and respect him."

In addition to his personal qualities Mauer brought an updated Illinois system to his new job. Before he could teach that system, however, he quickly discovered that he had to work with the players on the fundamentals of the game. Twenty players came out on October 12, 1928, for Mauer's first preseason practice. (Team captain Paul Jenkins headed a group of six who were excused from practice until after Thanksgiving because they were members of the football team.) Reporter Bill Reep in the October 15, 1928, issue of the student newspaper, the *Kentucky Kernel*, related that Mauer "was somewhat surprised" by the performance of his recruits during practice "when he discovered how little the men seemed to know concerning the fundamentals of the game." The players quickly discovered that their new coach's "style of play is very much different from that [to] which they were accustomed." Mauer quickly concluded, according to Reep, that "there is a lot of work yet to be done."

Paul McBrayer still remembers that first practice session: "He started that practice as though the players had never seen a basketball or a basketball game in their lives. He gave a long speech in which he told us in detail what he wanted. As I've said, he was a fine teacher. He would correct mistakes on the spot, when they happened." Mauer turned his attention first to shooting. "We quickly found out that we didn't know how to shoot the ball right. With practice, though, we got it right." The basic shot was a two-handed set shot from the waist. No one shot the ball one-handed. To attempt such a shot at Kentucky or any other college in the country would have resulted in banishment from the squad.

By the end of the first week of preseason practice the *Kentucky Kernel* reported that Mauer was continuing to work his players hard "in order that he can have a team that can play the game and know it from 'A to Z.' " The players showed a willingness to work

Three of UK's basketball coaches during the 1920s: *left,* C.O. Applegran, 1924/25 season, the first to coach in Alumni Gym; *center,* Ray Eklund, 1926/27 season; *right,* John Mauer, 1927/28 through 1929/30. Mauer introduced much of what is now known as the "UK System." All three, along with George Buchheit, were University of Illinois graduates.

hard to correct their mistakes and to learn "the new system that Coach Mauer is teaching." Mauer continued to concentrate his attention on fundamentals "such as the bounce pass, two man offense, dribbling, pivoting, crisscross and the double pass." Players also spent time on "the art of long and short shots. Coach Mauer has one particular method of shooting these shots and the men are trying hard to follow the example that he has offered."

During the preseason the team generally practiced five days a week. Each session was three hours long and Mauer believed in using the time to the fullest. He worked the players hard and in accordance with a plan designed for each day of practice. "So much time was devoted to one thing, so much to the next, and so on," McBrayer recalls. "Then, as we got more experienced in his system, we were able to concentrate on certain things." Practice always started with a thirty-minute period devoted to shooting. Each player had his own ball and worked on the shots he would take in games. After the players were loosened up Mauer would work on the offense. "This was broken down into a series of drills. This way we would work on passing, cutting, screening, rebounding and so forth. First we would work each drill with two players,

then three, then four, and finally, the whole team. The drills were very important. Everytime there was a mistake, anywhere, it was pointed out and corrected." The same meticulous attention was devoted to the defense. Half court situations were set up to teach each man his role in the overall team defense. Like Buchheit before him and Rupp after him Mauer used a man-to-man defense. He drilled his team on how to play against various zones but never used a zone defense himself. Most of Mauer's practices ended with a full-court scrimmage under game conditions and with referees. Early in the season some of the scrimmages would be run without interruptions to point out mistakes in order to work on player conditioning. On other days every time a mistake was made play would be stopped "and it would be corrected on the spot." Later in the season, at least one day a week some time would be spent dealing with specific game situations. For example, "You've got thirteen seconds to play. You've got a one point lead. They've got the ball." Another: "You've got thirteen seconds to play. You've got a one point lead and the ball." Every day time was devoted to free-throw shooting under game conditions, defense against the full-court press and zone defenses, and other fine points, until it was second nature.

Members of John Mauer's first UK team. *Clockwise from upper left,* Paul McBrayer, Paul Jenkins (captain), Cecil "Pisgah" Combs, and Lawrence "Big" McGinnis.

To Mauer practice was of vital importance. He believed that basketball was a game of habits and that the habits developed in practice were carried over into games. The starting team was determined by performance in practice. As McBrayer recalls, Mauer's philosophy was that "you do well in the game what you do well in practice. If you don't work on something in practice you probably won't do it well under game conditions. Things don't just happen. You have to prepare, and practice is where and when you prepare."

The "Mauermen," as UK was known during Mauer's tenure as coach, were a squad of complete players. There were no specialists. Everyone was expected to be, or to practice hard to become, proficient at both ends of the court. On defense the Wildcats employed, according to the 1930 *Kentuckian*, an "unpenetrable man-to-man" which "was dependent on the speed and agility of these stars who performed like 'ten-second men.' " The emphasis was on team play but if an individual did not do his job he was out of the game. Two-time All-American Carey Spicer, who played under both Mauer and Rupp, recalled in an interview the long hours the former devoted to defense. "Mauer was a good teacher of man-to-man defense and he worked us hard on it. You didn't dare cross your feet on defense. You learned to move them fast, you know, none of that crossing over. He didn't like that," Spicer chuckled. "He wanted you to be able to move with that offensive man." Defensive assignments, it should be noted, were different in this era than today. Lawrence McGinnis, a starting player through most of his career at UK, noted in an interview that "in those days guards guarded forwards and forwards were assigned to guards. That way the good defensive players guarded the good offensive men." This was the way the game had been played from the early days of basketball but, along with many other aspects of the offense and the defense, it would be changed in the middle and late 1930s.

Team play was the hallmark of the offense as well as the defense but everyone was able to shoot, pass, and dribble. Unlike the basketball teams of the 1980s there was no playmaking guard, shooting guard, small forward, or power forward. Instead both forwards were expected to be strong rebounders as well as good

Far left, Ervine Jeffries, a star of Mauer's 1927/28 team. Jeffries quit school to pursue a career in baseball. *Left,* center Stanley Milward, who played on all three of Mauer's teams.

The 1929/30 team, John Mauer's last at UK. Front row, l-r: manager Leonard Weakley, Stanley Milward, Cecil Combs, Paul McBrayer, Lawrence "Big" McGinnis, and Carey Spicer. Middle row: Mauer, Jake Bronston, Ercel Little, Bill Trott, and George Yates. Back row: Hays Owens, Larry Crump, Milton Cavana, Bill Kleiser, and Louis "Little" McGinnis.

shooters, with a range from the corners on in to the basket. Both guards were expected to be able to run the offense. Both came down court with the ball and either could initiate the offense but they were expected to maintain a balance. That is, the ball was to be moved around the court from one guard to the other and in to the center as well as to the forwards until someone was open for a good shot. And whoever was open was expected to take the shot. Under the Mauer system of play, the *Kentucky Kernel* noted, there was little danger that one or two men would dominate the team scoring "because in his method the scoring plays are so arranged that they will give each man an equal chance to contribute to the scoring."

Mauer "startled the entire South," the 1930 *Kentuckian* observed, with "a slow-breaking offense" built around a "complicated short-pass game." A major reason for the success of this offensive was the use of

the outside screen, the first time it was seen in the South. This innovation and other aspects of the offense Mauer brought with him from Illinois demoralized opponents. "It was a joy," McBrayer reminisced, "to play when the other teams weren't familiar with what you were doing."

Another major innovation Mauer introduced to UK and southern basketball, Carey Spicer noted, was the bounce pass. This was, in the terminology of the time, the "submarine attack" and was the heart of the Wildcats' patterned offense. Contrary to general belief, UK players could fastbreak but, in Spicer's words, "we weren't encouraged to do so." Lawrence McGinnis estimated that Mauer's teams used the fastbreak about 30 percent of the time.

Mauer was blessed, from his first year with the Big Blue, with an excellent group of ballplayers. All were native Kentuckians, most from Lexington or nearby

towns. None of them was on scholarship but this was not for lack of athletic talent. College teams of the era simply did not actively recruit high school players and did not offer athletic grants. Basketball players and other athletes were still considered to be students and thus were expected to support themselves, either with money supplied by parents or by working part- or full-time. "A lot of us," McBrayer relates, "had to work our way through college. We did hard manual labor every summer."

Unlike players of the present day, athletes of McBrayer's era did not have and perhaps did not need elaborate conditioning programs to remain in shape during the off seasons. Ditch digging and other physical labor did the trick for them. Whether for this reason or some other, the Mauermen were a strapping, powerful group of young men, many over six feet in height. The starting team in both 1929 and 1930 was composed of Carey Spicer (6'1") and "Pisgah" Combs (6'4") at forward (Combs had played at guard in 1928); Stanley Milward (6'5") at center; and Lawrence McGinnis (6') and Paul McBrayer (6'4") at guard. McGinnis, who had played at forward in 1928, was team captain in 1929, an honor that went to McBrayer in 1930. All the starting players weighed between 180 and 205 pounds. It was a big team for the era but occasionally Kentucky came up against opponents who were bigger, among them Creighton with a 6'7" pivot-man. But few teams of the era exceeded the Wildcats in their combination of size, talent, technique, and discipline. The first two were there from the beginning. The technique and discipline, however, took time and hard work to develop. The team had the same nucleus through all three years Mauer coached at Kentucky and thus the improvement came from experience and maturity.

A game which probably epitomized the Mauer system, philosophy, and style of play was a January 12, 1929, meeting with Notre Dame at South Bend, Indiana. The hallmark of Mauer-led teams was a disciplined, deliberate continuity offense and a glue-like man-to-man defense resulting in a low-scoring, hard-fought game. All these variables were in evidence in the Notre Dame game. In it, the *Courier-Journal* reported on January 13, the Wildcats "played a beautiful, defensive game, time after time taking the ball after the Irish missed a toss and converting it to their own use and seldom allowing Notre Dame to take a shot within the danger zone."

McBrayer regards the Notre Dame game as "perhaps our best victory" during his playing career at UK. "Notre Dame had a fine team and in George

Table 2. Record of John Mauer-Coached Teams

Season	Won	Lost	Percentage	Points UK	Points Opponent
1927/28	12	6	.666	630	505
1928/29	12	5	.706	496	411
1929/30	16	3	.842	599	408
Total	40	14	.741	1,725	1,324

Keogan probably the best coach in the country, although he was overshadowed by football coach Knute Rockne. Probably the most interesting to a modern fan," he laughed, "was the score, which was 19-16, and we didn't freeze the ball. In those days there was no ten-second line or three-second zone and the ball was brought back and tossed up after every basket." It was, McBrayer sighed, "a completely different game, but the fans at the time found it exciting."

During Mauer's career as UK coach, the Wildcats won a total of forty games and lost only fourteen for a winning percentage of .741. Mauer's final season was more successful by one victory than that of his successor, Adolph Rupp, the following year.

The college basketball season was considerably shorter in the 1920s and into the 1930s than it has been in the decades since World War II. The Mauermen, for example, only played fifteen regular-season games in 1928 and 1929, and sixteen in 1930. In each of Mauer's three years play began in mid-December at Alumni Gym with a resounding victory. Each year the Cats were invited to the Southern Conference Tournament in Atlanta, which extended the season to the end of February or the beginning of March. In 1928 UK played three tournament games, in 1929 two, and in 1930 three. Regular-season rivals included Georgetown, Berea, and Kentucky Wesleyan. In fact, UK did not drop these schools from its schedule until the beginning of the 1940s, and even played a Berea team composed of servicemen twice during World War II. Nevertheless, by World War II UK had left its less talented and less successful former in-state rivals behind and had entered the "big time." That, however, was still in the future.

Also in the future were the spacious arenas. Most of the gyms in which UK played during the late twenties, McBrayer recalls, "were miserable places." Even the City Auditorium in Atlanta, where the SIAA (1921-24), Southern Conference (1925-32), and SEC (1933-34) tournaments were held, was less than adequate. McBrayer related an incident that "shows the

Table 3. Opening-Game Record, 1927-1929

Opening Game	Opponent	Score UK	Opponent
December 16, 1927	Clemson	33	17
December 15, 1928	Eastern (Ky.) Normal	35	10
December 14, 1929	Georgetown	46	9

conditions under which we played a lot of times. The floor in the City Auditorium was slanted. To compensate for that they put green lumber on wooden horses to make the floor level." Not only did this make running and dribbling difficult because of the many soft spots in the floor but "on one occasion while we were playing down there Lawrence McGinnis [who later was Cliff Hagan's high school coach in Owensboro] went up and got a rebound and when he came down he went right through the floor!"

Despite all the problems, "Kentucky and her stalwart stars" were, according to the 1930 *Kentuckian* "a sensation wherever they played." If the Big Blue's deliberate style of play was not exciting, that certainly did not keep people away from the games. On the contrary, the Wildcats not only performed before "S.R.O. houses" in Lexington but were "always the same drawing card on foreign floors, playing to capacity crowds on every trip."

Mauer compiled a glittering record during his career at UK, returned the basketball program to the level it had enjoyed under Buchheit, and laid a solid foundation for the even greater achievements of his successor, Adolph Rupp. The only prize to elude Mauer was the big one, the Southern Conference championship. In both 1929 and 1930 UK was universally acknowledged to have the best talent of any team in the tournament but each year they fell short. In 1929 North Carolina State defeated Duke by a 44-35 score, while the following year the Duke Blue Devils again lost the championship game, this time to Alabama by seven points, 31-24.

"Morgan Blake, Ed Danforth, and other famous Southern sportswriters," the 1929 *Kentuckian* sadly noted, agreed on a basic reason for this failure. Although "the class of the South," the Big Blue was "also a team which was incapable of rising to great heights in tournament play. The Wildcat team plays orthodox basketball, and previous tournaments have proven the fact that an unconscious flip and run [or run and gun] game fits best in the excitement and strain

of a long tournament." Another major factor, however, was also involved. Because of his personality Mauer was unable to whip up his players' emotions for the big games. Even McBrayer acknowledges that "Mauer was not a great inspirational talker." Louis McGinnis also noted in an interview that while "Mauer was a very fine person who was dedicated to his boys he did have some difficulties with the press."

When Mauer decided, after the 1930 season, to accept a coaching job at Miami University of Ohio, UK hired a man who was his opposite in personality and in ability to communicate with the press and the alumni. Louis McGinnis summed up the essential difference between the two coaches in a few well chosen words: "Mauer spent more time coaching than in public relations, which probably hurt him, in contrast to Rupp who did things the other way."

Mauer was far more than a mere footnote to Adolph Rupp, however. He became as successful a coach at Miami, Army, Tennessee, and Florida, as he had been at Kentucky. Looking back on his career at UK, the *Kentucky Kernel* in 1930 proclaimed Mauer "the Moses of Kentucky basketball." Unfortunately he took the Wildcats only part way to the promised land. It was left to Adolph Rupp to complete the journey. But it would not be a ride without cost to Rupp and the university or to some of his players.

Opposite, Adolph Rupp with four of his "runts" at the start of the 1965/66 season. Left to right: Pat Riley, Tom Kron, Rupp, Louie Dampier, and Larry Conley. The fifth starter, not shown, was Thad Jaracz.

Part II
Adolph Rupp and the Wildcat Tradition

The Baron Arrives

Adolph Rupp. The name conjures up a multitude of fond, proud, and pleasant memories in the minds of the Wildcat faithful. Adolph Rupp, the "Baron of the Bluegrass," the venerable "Man in the Brown Suit," who coached at the University of Kentucky from 1930 to 1972 and won more games than any other man in college basketball history. His 880 victories and incredible winning percentage of .822 may never be surpassed.

In the process of winning more than eight of every ten games during his forty-two years at Kentucky, Rupp-directed teams captured eighteen Southeastern Conference championships, one National Invitational Tournament Crown (when that was a very prestigious tournament), and four National Collegiate Athletic Association titles. Rupp produced some of the most memorable teams in the annals of collegiate sports, including the "Fabulous Five," the "Fiddlin' Five," and "Rupp's Runts." There were, of course, some unhappy, even bitter, memories, such as the shocking loss to Texas Western (now the University of Texas at El Paso) in the 1966 NCAA finals, and the sordid point-shaving scandals of the early 1950s. But to UK fans and probably to the sporting public in general, Rupp's achievements far outnumbered his failures and failings.

Within a decade of his arrival at UK, Adolph Rupp had become a bona fide living legend and, as usually happens in such a situation, the past was reinterpreted and rewritten to conform to the larger-than-life image he projected. The glittering success of Rupp's teams seemed, to the Wildcat faithful, to dwarf any previous achievements. Rupp came to be hailed as a miracle worker.

One of the early revisionists was Joe Creason. Later to become a sports writer and then a very popular columnist with the *Louisville Courier-Journal,* Creason in the late 1930s was a UK undergraduate and the sports editor of both the *Kernel* and the *Kentuckian.* In 1939 he wrote the basketball section of the *Kentuckian.* Reviewing the Wildcats' achievements during Rupp's tenure at the university, Creason maintained that "in the days B.R. (Before Rupp) basketball and Chinese checkers held about the same athletic rating at Kentucky. Not enough customers attended the games to furnish sides for a fast game of two-eyed cat. The teams were groping along with mediocre success, playing the slow-breaking, listless game that is so characteristic of Southern basketball. . . . Thus it came to pass," Creason concluded, "that since the eventful day in 1931 when fate sent Kentucky the soft-spoken Adolph Rupp, the Wildcats were lifted from the mire of middle class mediocrity to the peak as one of the nation's annual cage powers." The only things Creason had completely right were the use of a slow-breaking offense by the pre-Rupp Wildcats and that the Big Blue was, by the late 1930s, a major basketball power. Everything else was either a half-truth or an inaccuracy. Even the chronology was wrong. Creason believed that Rupp began coaching at the University in 1931 and had just finished his eighth season; he actually began in 1930. This lack of factual accuracy is not, however, the important point about Creason's article. What it signified was that the rewriting of UK basketball history had begun in earnest. It would continue in the following years and would gain additional embellishments. As Creason

---

Opposite, A youthful looking Adolph Rupp, during his sixth season at UK, 1935/36.

acknowledged several years later to Thomas D. Clark, the UK history department chairman and his close friend, Creason played an important early role in the formation and development of the Rupp legend.

There were other contributors. In the 1941 *Kentuckian*, sportswriter Fred Hill maintained that "before Adolph Rupp shucked his huge frame into the driver's seat of Kentucky's basketball chariot, . . . the net game in the Bluegrass made rather erratic reading. The Wildcats were a sometimes good, sometimes bad team which most of the time did well to break a little more than even." Not only was "Affable Adolph" a great basketball coach but "it would be safe to say [he] has never produced a bad team in any sport." As befitting a legendary figure, "up at Marshalltown, Illinois [actually Iowa], he built a state championship wrestling team from a book, without ever before having seen a wrestling match!"

The Baron's dynamic personality and his ability to win SEC championships obviously were vital ingredients in the near deification of the Kansan even in the years before the late forties and fifties, when he won four NCAA championships. But there was another key factor in the revision of UK basketball history that took place in the late thirties and early forties. This was the hiring by the University of Tennessee of former Wildcat Coach John Mauer in 1939. Mauer not only coached Tennessee but led the Vols to SEC championships over the Big Blue in 1941 and 1943, and to a second-place finish to UK in 1939 and 1945. These were, it should be noted, the only exceptions to UK's dominance over the Conference between 1939 and 1953. In addition, Mauer's teams administered regular-season defeats in 1940, 1942, and 1945.

Tennessee had been a major UK rival since at least the late 1920s, but with Mauer's presence the rivalry took on a new and deeper meaning. His success in bringing the conference championship to Big Orange Country radically changed the attitude of UK fans toward him. In addition, Mauer played a role in the success of Tennessee's great football squads of the late thirties and early forties through his services as chief scout for coach Robert Neyland. What this meant was that Mauer was a thorn in the side of University of Kentucky athletics not in one but in two major sports. His contributions in football notwithstanding, what made Mauer's presence at Tennessee so threatening was the success of his basketball teams and the danger this seemed to pose to the continuation of UK's control over the only conference sport it dominated. As a result, Wildcat partisans had great difficulty even mentioning John Mauer's name, much less acknowledging his current success at Tennessee or his previous

contributions to UK basketball. For example, when Mauer's basketball Vols defeated the Cats for the SEC title in 1941, the school yearbook not only attempted to downplay the three-point defeat but also ignored the Tennessee coach and his previous connection with UK. A notable exception was the gleeful reaction to a 53-29 trouncing that the Vols suffered at the hands of the UK team on February 13, 1943: "It was the worst defeat that Johnny Mauer took since handling the reins at Knoxville."

It is clear that at least part of the reason why Mauer's important contributions to Wildcat basketball have been underrated and his role in the development of the University of Kentucky (or Rupp) style of play has generally gone unrecognized was his later success as coach at arch rival Tennessee. Nevertheless, the process of downgrading Mauer and his work at UK actually began with Rupp's hiring, if not before. The Lexington and Louisville press and the campus newspaper reported the hiring of the Kansan with approval and observed that, in contrast to the deliberate style of play advocated by his predecessor, Rupp coached a relatively new but popular style called the fastbreak. The *Kentucky Kernel* on May 23, 1930, noted that with Rupp's arrival, "Kentucky will bid farewell to its well-known 'submarine' and delayed offense employed by Coach Mauer. Coach Rupp is an advocate of the fastbreak system which is the most popular system used in basketball at present." Actually, as players who were on both Mauer's last team and Rupp's first at UK have pointed out in interviews, differences between the two styles of play were not as great as the press made them out to be, although the contrast in personalities certainly was. In fact, press criticism of the Mauer system is ironic because that system was adopted in toto by Rupp.

Although Mauer was a very able and successful coach who was admired, even loved by his players, his dour, introverted personality and his inability or unwillingness to communicate with the press made him unpopular with sportswriters and, through them, with UK fans. Public and press alike were pleased with his departure and enthusiastic about the outgoing and dynamic newcomer, Adolph Rupp. The writings of contemporary sportswriters had a lasting effect. The tendency to contrast the Rupp style in his early years at Kentucky with that of his predecessor has continued to the present. In 1976 Dave Kindred, at the time a sportswriter for the *Courier-Journal*, now with the *Washington Post*, published his imaginative examination of the high school, college, and pro game in the state, *Basketball: The Dream Game in Kentucky*. In it Kindred claimed that "Rupp's teams from the begin-

ning were models of simplicity and fire. They took hold of the ball and ran. That doesn't seem much of an analysis of a system whose artful practitioners gained national fame, but then basketball is a simple game." Even Neil Isaacs in *All the Moves*, an excellent history of college basketball, states that Rupp "brought fast-breaking ideas to Lexington, where Johnny Mauer had been teaching a deliberate, ball-control game."

Actually there was a great deal more continuity than is generally realized. As Louis McGinnis, who played for both Mauer and Rupp, pointed out in an interview, "There was no reason for Rupp to make a lot of changes. Don't forget that we were very successful the previous year and that Mauer was an excellent teacher and we were strong in the fundamentals." Essentially what Rupp did was to turn the players loose but within the system Mauer had brought to Lexington in 1927 and had developed in his three years as coach of the Big Blue.

As an All-American under both Mauer and Rupp, as well as captain of Rupp's first team, and later as a personal friend of both men, Carey Spicer had a unique vantage point from which to observe the transition from Mauer to Rupp. Spicer noted in an interview that "we had the good fundamentals from Mauer, and Adolph let us use our own natural ability along with the set offense we learned under Mauer. We could use more variations which made for higher scores but we used practically the same offense we had under Mauer." Spicer had been chosen team captain by Mauer and continued in that capacity when Rupp arrived. "As captain under Mauer I had the playbook with all the plays and all the variations. So when Adolph came, and this was before the football season began, he called me to his office and sort of picked my brain about the type offense we had used," Spicer recalled. "I told him I had this playbook of John's and he said 'Would you mind if I look at it?' " Spicer soon joined the football team, on which he was one of the backfield stars. When, after the football season ended, he reported for basketball practice (which had been in progress for about three weeks) he found that "we were using all the same plays and, in fact, all the same numbers as we had under Mauer. But," he hastened to add, "Adolph encouraged us to use more variations and to use our own natural ability." Thus the plays UK uses to this day are basically the same as those used under Rupp and earlier under Mauer, but, Spicer noted, "with improved variations."

Fans and sportswriters have misunderstood two things: Mauer's UK teams did make use of the fast-break when the opportunity presented itself, but the cautious Mauer did not encourage his players to run,

while Rupp did encourage them to run, and at every opportunity. As Spicer observed about Rupp's first season at UK, "We started out with a set offense but with more fastbreaking than under Mauer. Where Mauer permitted a fastbreak but discouraged it, Rupp not only permitted it but encouraged it." But Rupp did not, also contrary to general opinion, favor a racehorse or run-and-gun style of basketball. By contrast, Ward "Piggy" Lambert, one of the originators of fastbreak basketball, and his Purdue Boilermakers (as Isaacs notes in *All the Moves*) "specialized in quick breaking whenever the ball changed hands." Rupp, instead, preferred and coached a set offense, the guard around offense, with an emphasis on short passing and as little dribbling as possible, and the use of screens, or, as they were called at the time, blocks, as Mauer had before him. Rupp made use of the outside screen and the bounce pass, two innovations Mauer had introduced to UK and southern basketball.

The contrast between the UK offense and the fastbreak was made clear by famed *New York Times* reporter Arthur Daley in his description of the Wildcats' January 5, 1935, meeting with the New York University Violets at Madison Square Garden. "The Violets displayed a brand of play that is indigenous to the East. It was one of the fast-break, the quick-cut for the basket and a short flick in. Kentucky, on the other hand, demonstrated something quite new to metropolitan court circles. The Southerners," Daley observed, "employ a slow, deliberate style of offense that is built around thirteen set plays."

By the middle and late 1930s the Kentucky system would be refined with the addition of the inside screen and the second guard around. Nevertheless, in Rupp's first year in Lexington, in McGinnis's words, "we did things pretty much the way we had the year before." There were several reasons for this. Among others, the UK players knew the style and liked it, and it was a proven success. In addition, Rupp was already familiar with it from having coached high school basketball in Illinois for five years. The system Mauer taught, it must be recalled, was essentially what he had learned as a player at the University of Illinois. This system was also used by most Illinois high school teams in the late twenties. Thus Rupp had already adjusted to much of what Mauer taught before he came to Lexington. Rupp had also adjusted to the use of more running in his offense, but this innovation was gaining popularity among high school coaches in Illinois and elsewhere.

The style Rupp used at Kentucky, it must be emphasized, was not the one he had learned as a college player at the University of Kansas. This is evident from

a February 23, 1932, *Lexington Herald* account of the Wildcats' preparations for an upcoming Southern Conference Tournament game in Atlanta against Tulane University. The Green Wave was coached by George Rody, who had been a college teammate of Rupp. "Tulane uses a style of play that greatly resembles the old Kansas style which Rupp played," sportswriter Vernon Rooks observed. By contrast, "Rupp's style falls in the 'outlaw' class, being entirely different from the Kansas system and originated by Rupp." Note that already Mauer's contributions were being ignored and the Rupp legend was forming. It is ironic that the system Rupp employed at the University of Kentucky owed more to John Mauer and to the University of Illinois than to the man for whom Rupp had played at the University of Kansas, Dr. Forest C. "Phog" Allen.

Although Rupp did not originate his system, as Lexington and Louisville sportswriters mistakenly believed, one vital ingredient of his great success was the inner fire that drove him to demand the best that he and his players could offer. Rupp's players performed to the best of their ability at all times and in every game or they did not play. Buddy Parker, who played for UK from 1945 to 1947, stated in an interview that "Coach Rupp instilled in us to be winners or we didn't last. If he taught us anything it was that there wasn't much place for second best. He did not like to lose."

Rupp maintained a constant, steady pressure on his teams all season, every season. It is not difficult for a coach to get his players up for a big game. Rupp's teams performed at their peak not only against good and great teams but also against opponents known to be inferior. And it should be noted that Rupp scheduled a lot of weak teams over the years. Nevertheless, he was able to maintain his players at a high level of intensity even for these "patsies." This is probably the most difficult task for a coach, and Rupp was a master of the art. For Rupp, as many of his former players have noted in interviews, basketball was not a game—it was a life-or-death proposition. Rupp formed this attitude toward work during his childhood years in Kansas.

Adolph Frederick Rupp was born on September 2, 1901, on a farm near Halstead, Kansas, the fourth of six children born to Austro-German immigrants Heinrich and Anna Lichti Rupp. His father died of cancer when Adolph was only nine years old, leaving a widow to tend the farm and raise the children. The result, UK Sports Information director Russell Rice has observed, was a "story of hardships, dawn-to-dusk toil

in the fields, and a close family relationship that resulted from the battle for survival on the prairie." The humble beginnings, the solid grounding in the work ethic, and the harshness of life molded young Adolph's character. Rupp the man became, as *New York Daily News* reporter Phil Pepe once observed, a "strong-willed individual who has never been afraid to voice his opinion, even if it is a minority and unpopular one."

At a very early age Rupp became interested in basketball, and the young sport became a major factor in directing the future course of his life. He became a star high school player, averaging nineteen points a game, which for that era was phenomenal. Rupp attended the University of Kansas, but his star did not shine nearly as brightly in college as it had in high school. Fated to play behind two All-Americans while a Jayhawk, Rupp recalled in an interview with Russell Rice that he usually entered games only "when things were pretty well settled, one way or another."

During Rupp's years at Kansas he played basketball for Phog Allen, one of the great college coaches and fine teachers of the sport. Interestingly, Allen was assisted at the time by Dr. James Naismith, the inventor of basketball. Thus Rupp learned basketball from two of the sport's legends. During Rupp's college career Kansas won the Missouri Conference championship in 1922 and 1923 (going undefeated the latter year) and the national championship in 1922. Following graduation in 1923 Rupp played a season for the undefeated "Ever Victorious" professional basketball team and then began his coaching career at Marshalltown, Iowa, High School, where he coached football, track, and wrestling, as well as basketball. In 1925 he moved to Freeport, Illinois, High School. During his five years there his basketball teams won more than 80 percent of their games. In 1929 Freeport won eighteen games, lost five, and took third place in the state tournament. The next season the team won twenty games and lost four, losing in the sectional meet after winning the district championship.

In addition to his activities on the basketball court Rupp was hard at work in the classroom. To advance himself in the teaching profession he spent four summers at Columbia University's Teachers College in New York and earned a Master of Arts degree in education. As it developed, Rupp had little professional need of the M.A. because his high school teaching career came to an end in 1930. But Rupp could not foresee this in the late 1920s, and it was to his credit that he devoted the time, effort, and thought to preparing himself as thoroughly as he could for his

Rupp (second from left) with other members of UK's football coaching staff for the 1930/31 season. Elmer "Baldy" Gilb (center) was Rupp's assistant basketball coach during the mid-1940s. Head football coach Harry Gamage (third from right) and Bernie Shively (second from right) both came to UK from the University of Illinois. Shively was UK athletics director from the 1940s through the late 1960s.

future. It is also significant that in pursuing a graduate degree Rupp chose the best and most prestigious school of education in the nation.

Rupp's career as high school coach and teacher came to an end when, after the 1930 basketball season, John Mauer resigned his position as coach at the University of Kentucky. When news of the opening circulated in coaching circles the university was inundated, according to the *Courier-Journal*, with seventy-one applications, among them one from Adolph Rupp. In addition to being, in the words of the *Lexington Herald*, a "graduate of the Kansas School of Basketball" and a disciple of Phog Allen, Rupp had another major point in his favor: a strong letter of recommendation for the job from University of Illinois coach Craig Ruby. Thus once again the Illinois connection was the deciding factor in filling the basketball coaching position at the University of Kentucky.

On May 21, 1930, UK Athletics Director S.A. "Daddy" Boles telephoned Rupp long distance to make a formal offer, which Rupp accepted. As formalized by a Board of Trustees meeting on May 31, 1930, Rupp

was appointed "as instructor in Physical Education, to have charge of varsity basketball and to assist in other sports." The "other sports" included football and track. Rupp received a two-year contract which paid $2,800 for 1930/31 and $3,000 for 1931/32. By contrast, instructors in academic departments received about $1,500 to $1,700 per year. By 1935 Rupp's salary had been increased to $4,250 for each of the following two seasons to serve as, according to Board of Trustee minutes, "head basketball coach and assistant in other sports."

Fans, students, and players were wildly enthusiastic about Rupp and what they thought was his new offense from the very beginning of his tenure at UK. When Rupp called his first practice, the *Kentucky Kernel* reported on October 17, 1930, he found himself "confronted with forty-six aspiring and perspiring candidates for the varsity five," and this record number did not include a number of fine athletes still playing on the varsity football team. Rupp was not only a shrewd and innovative coach and a good judge of talent; he was also blessed with excellent timing and

a large helping of good luck. His arrival in Kentucky coincided with the beginning of the decade that witnessed what sports historians Jack W. Berryman and Stephen H. Hardy termed "the first rush of national interest" in college basketball. By the end of the decade UK was a nationally recognized basketball power and Rupp had taken his place among the elite of college coaches.

Rupp's good luck was evident from the beginning of his career in Lexington. Because four of the five starters from the 1929/30 team had graduated and the Wildcats faced a tough schedule in 1930/31, sportswriters and other experts painted a gloomy picture, predicting that Rupp would be fortunate to have a winning season. These predictions removed a great deal of the outside pressure in Rupp's first season at UK. Although the fact was generally unrecognized at the time, Mauer had bequeathed to his successor the nucleus of an excellent team with talented players who were thoroughly grounded in the fundamentals of basketball. Among them were All-American Carey Spicer, Louis McGinnis, and George Yates, three excellent front-court players. In addition, Mauer's last group of recruits included Ellis Johnson and Forest "Aggie" Sale, two future All-Americans who became sophomores in 1930. Johnson had been a member of the 1928 national championship team while at Ashland High School, and at UK became one of the school's greatest all-around athletes. He was a three-year starter on the varsity basketball and football squads, and he also played baseball and competed on the university's

track team. Aggie Sale, who had played high school ball at Kavanaugh in Lawrenceburg, possessed good speed and agility for a big man, was a better than average shot, and a great rebounder. Paul McBrayer, also a Lawrenceburg native, recalls that "Aggie was a little ahead of his time as an offensive player." Harry Lancaster, who played against Rupp and UK while an undergraduate at Georgetown College and later served for many years as his assistant coach, relates in his *Adolph Rupp as I Knew Him* that "years later, Adolph was to tell me several times that Aggie might have been the best player he ever coached."

Although the success of his first season at Kentucky was based on the talented and well-coached players he inherited from Mauer, Rupp quickly demonstrated that he knew both how to adapt these athletes to his own personality and style and how to recruit other excellent players. McBrayer and other authorities agree, in fact, that the key to Rupp's success was his talent as a recruiter. Recruiting was in its infancy in the early 1930s and, at least in part because of the lack of available funds, Rupp confined his attention to players in Kentucky and Indiana. He made excellent use of the Kentucky high school basketball tournament, which was held in Lexington, and the Indiana high school tournament, to scout potential recruits. He also relied on letters from alumni and interested friends of the university to alert him to talented but unknown or overlooked players. Rupp's first foray outside the Kentuckiana area was the enrollment of New York native Bernie Opper at the Lexington cam-

Adolph Rupp with the 1930/31 basketball team, his first at UK. Front row: Ercel Little, George Yates, Carey Spicer (captain), Forest Sale, and Milton Cavana. Middle row: George Skinner, Allan Lavin, Bill Trott, Jake Bronston, Louis McGinnis, and Cecil Bell. Back row: Rupp, William Congleton, Bill Kleiser, Ellis Johnson, Charles Worthington, Darrell Darby, and manager Morris Levin.

pus in 1936. Yet, as Opper noted in a 1980 interview at his home in Los Angeles, the arrival of this future All-American guard had nothing to do with Rupp's recruiting efforts. Opper was a standout high school and amateur basketball player in New York in the early thirties and was offered a scholarship to play at Long Island University, one of the powerhouse teams of the day, but turned it down. "I saw Kentucky play in the Garden [Madison Square Garden]," Opper recalled. "Adolph came there with LeRoy Edwards [UK's star center] in January 1935 and I decided I wanted to leave New York, which was unusual in those days because everybody wanted to play there. Anyway, I wrote a letter to Adolph and told him what I had done and gave him the names of some coaches, like Nat Holman at City College, who could tell him about me. So he wrote back and said come on down and we'll see what we can do for you about a scholarship. So I went and he got me a scholarship." Such was recruiting in the 1930s.

Rupp exercised an iron discipline over his team. He made his position and expectations clear from the very beginning of his career at UK. The *Kernel* on October 17, 1930, reported Rupp's first speech to his team: "I want it understood that there will be no loafers on this team. Every man has got to play ball or get off; that's final." The Baron, as he came to be known, drove his players hard in practice in an effort to cut down on technical errors. He concentrated on basic offensive plays, a tenacious man-to-man defense and, above all, shooting. If a player could not consistently hit the basket he did not last long with the team. Rupp was not a teacher in the sense that Mauer had been. Mauer revelled in instructing his players in the fundamentals of the game—in dribbling, passing, shooting, and the finer points of defense. Rupp, on the other hand, fully expected his players to know the basics of basketball when they arrived at UK. If they were not proficient in the fundamentals or could not learn them quickly, Rupp wasted no time on them. Since many of the Wildcat recruits were deficient in at least some of the fundamentals, it fell upon Rupp's assistants to correct the shortcomings. Rupp was fortunate to find, or shrewd enough to choose, a succession of assistant coaches who were themselves thoroughly grounded in fundamentals and who were excellent teachers. In addition to helping coach the varsity, Rupp's assistant also directed the work of the freshman squad. It was during the freshman practices, which generally were held after the varsity workouts and lasted from about 7:00 to 10:00 at night, that most of the instruction in basics took place.

During a varsity practice, one former assistant recalled, the silence in Alumni Hall and later in Memorial Coliseum was almost deafening. As Rupp himself said: "Why should boys constantly chatter in a class in basketball any more than they do in a class in English? Why should they whistle and sing? If you let 'em talk and wisecrack around, they don't concentrate. I tell the boys if they want to talk, we've got a student union for visiting purposes. And if they want to whistle, well there's a music academy, too."

Rupp was extremely demanding of his players and would not tolerate mistakes. He did not play favorites, especially in his first two decades of coaching at UK, and when one of the players erred during practice Rupp would reprimand him with such sarcastic comments as: "Go back up in the stands and read your press clipping!" or "Boy, will you pass that ball to someone who knows what to do with it!" or "Some day I'm going to write a book on how not to play basketball, and I'm going to devote the first two hundred pages to you!" His thirst for perfection was demonstrated in the first varsity scrimmage against the freshman squad on December 11, 1930. The varsity won 75-21 but Rupp was annoyed because, as the *Lexington Herald* reported the next day, "thirty-one shots at the basket are too many for a freshman team to have in a scrimmage with the varsity." The Baron was somewhat happier two days later when the varsity trounced the freshmen 75-9 and allowed only six shots in the first forty-five minutes of action. He hoped that the real games would turn out the same way, and the opening contest against Georgetown College almost did.

On December 18, Rupp and "the Kentucky Wildcats introduced their new fast-break offense to the Lexington basketball fans in a convincing manner . . . by downing the Georgetown Tigers 67 to 19." Rupp used his entire squad of seventeen players in the process of running up this "overwhelming score." The press enthusiastically reported the positive response of UK partisans to the team's new style of play, which was, reporter Totsy Rose of the *Kernel* concluded, "a great deal more interesting to watch than the system used last year by Coach Mauer." Rose failed to recognize that in most respects it was the same system. The Wildcats were led in scoring by Aggie Sale (nineteen points), Louis McGinnis (sixteen), and Carey Spicer (eight), while George Yates, a substitute center, contributed ten points. Georgetown was led by sophomore guard Harry Lancaster, who scored ten of his team's nineteen points. Lancaster and Georgetown faced the Wildcats in opening-day contests in each of

Three action shots from the 1938/39 season, taken in Alumni Gym. The UK team is in white. Even then the fans turned out in droves.

the following two seasons and suffered crushing defeats in each game.

Kentucky followed the Georgetown rout with nine victories in a row. After two consecutive losses, to Georgia and Clemson, the Blue and White ended the regular season with wins over Georgia Tech and Vanderbilt and headed to Atlanta for the Southern Conference Tournament. There they defeated North Carolina State, Duke, and Florida on the way to a March 3 showdown with Maryland for the conference championship. Although the Wildcats lost by a score of 29-27, UK fans were well satisfied with the season record of fifteen wins and only three defeats. Memories of John Mauer quickly faded.

Contributing greatly to the speed and ease with which Rupp supplanted his predecessor in the hearts of Wildcat partisans was the contrasting manner in which the two men dealt with the press. While Mauer generally antagonized the press, Rupp went out of his way to maintain cordial relations by helping sportswriters meet their never-ending need for amusing and quotable statements and by displaying his unique and fascinating personality. One of the things that endeared him to sportswriters, and through them an adoring public, was his variety of widely publicized superstitions. During Rupp's very first season at UK one sportswriter described a pre-game expedition the new coach had taken with his players: "We saw, among other things, a black cat. Rupp yelled 'Boys, it's in the bag!' and proceeded to chase down to the spot where the black cat had crossed over, and follow in the footsteps of the cat. Of course, he was referring to the Washington & Lee game" which took place the next day, February 6, and which UK won 23-18.

Rupp's most famous and long-lasting superstition was his brown suit tradition. All through his forty-two seasons as UK coach he wore a brown suit, brown tie, brown shoes, and brown socks to every Kentucky game. According to Rupp, this tradition dated back to his coaching days at Freeport High School when he got a new blue suit to replace the old brown one he had been wearing. The first time he wore the new suit his team was badly beaten. Rupp took this as an omen and returned to wearing his old brown suit. Soon after his arrival at Kentucky he had his players believing in the superstition. Thus when the Wildcats faced Vanderbilt on January 21, 1931, in their first away game of the season, the team got off to a bad start and played a poor first half. At halftime Rupp asked guard Jake Bronston, according to an article in the *Kernel*, "What were you thinking of when you were going bad out there in the first half?" Bronston quickly replied, "I was thinking if you had those brown socks on."

Rupp had the brown socks on and UK went on to win the game 42-37. The press and Big Blue fans loved stories like this one, and Rupp provided a never-ending supply of them.

These were not simply stories or creations for press consumption. According to several former players, Rupp firmly believed in his superstitions. For example, Buddy Parker noted, "Coach Rupp's routine was always the same. Just like the brown suit the practices were always done exactly the same way. He always rode in the same place on the bus, just behind the driver, and before a game he always came out on the floor at a certain time and the same way. He never changed his routine." Dick Parsons, whose experience with Rupp was both as a player (1959-61) and as an assistant coach, elaborated on the superstitions in an interview. "He had a routine when he went to the locker room before the game and at halftime that must have been the same for at least thirty years. He did exactly the same thing every game. I can still see him," Parsons reminisced, "take his coat off and hang it in the first locker in Memorial Coliseum. He would go to the sink and wash his hands and come back and appear before the team. When he left the locker room he never entered the playing area until the UK Fight Song was completed." Among Rupp's other superstitions, according to Parsons, were "black cats, collecting bobby pins wherever he could find them, and he always had buckeyes in his pocket. And these were only a few of them."

Kentucky fans flocked to Alumni Gym to watch Rupp, brown suit and all, and their blue-and-white-clad heroes perform their on-court magic game after game and season after season. At a typical game "the building was jammed to overflowing and many fans had to be turned away. The student body is so large that there are only about 1,000 seats available to the other supporters." From the first season of Adolph Rupp's reign, Alumni Gym was generally filled to overflowing. The Kentucky-Washington & Lee game played on February 6, 1931, drew more than 4,000 of the faithful, while a contest with Georgia Tech three days later reportedly attracted nearly 5,000 Big Blue enthusiasts. One player from this era recalled in an interview "many games in Alumni Gym where there never was anybody ever sat down from the time they came into the building until they left."

Opponents quickly came to dread the zealous Wildcat fans, the innovative and acid-tongued Adolph Rupp, and the multitalented UK players. The Big Blue's set offense and effective use of the fastbreak and its aggressive man-to-man defense struck fear in the hearts of opposition coaches and forced many to change their

Adolph Rupp in the mid-1940s, as he stood on the threshold of his most successful seasons.

strategy. To try to run with UK was generally futile because few teams, especially those in the SEC, had the talent or depth to keep up with the Wildcats in a running game. As a result many teams used a stall in an effort to slow the tempo of the game so that, even if they were unable to win, they could at least narrow the margin of defeat. This tactic enraged Rupp, who believed it was unfair and detrimental to the future of the sport for an opposing team to be permitted to slow the game down just because their players were less talented than Kentucky's. At annual coaches' meetings and at coaching clinics he lobbied vigorously for changes in the rules. In Chicago in 1932 an effort was made to eliminate the stall. Although many coaches agreed on the need to eliminate the stall and speed up the game, they rejected a proposal to do so submitted by James Naismith, the founder of the game. It would have required the offensive team to shoot the ball within a thirty-second period after inbounding it. This suggestion was innovative. Colleges did not begin to experiment with it until the 1980s, some thirty years

after the shot clock concept was adopted by the National Basketball Association. Rupp played an important role in the passage of a compromise, the ten-second rule, at the 1932 conference. This rule, which is still in effect, allows the offense only ten seconds to move the ball from the back to the front court. If the players are not successful they lose possession of the ball. This strategy was ineffective in combatting the stall because, as Neil Isaacs has observed, "the burden of tempo remains on the defense, as Naismith continued to point out as long as he lived."

The ten-second rule, although inadequate, was a beginning. Rupp also played a prominent role in the introduction of the three-second rule at the same 1932 meeting and its permanent adoption in 1936. That rule and the elimination of the center jump after each basket, also in 1936, fell short of the intended objective of reducing the influence of the tall player, but they did help speed up the game, which was Rupp's principal intention. Rupp was also among several coaches over the years who suggested and supported an NCAA-conducted basketball tournament to choose a national champion. Thus while in New York City in January 1935 for a game at Madison Square Garden against New York University, Rupp proposed that the leading college teams from each section of the country meet in a central location, preferably Chicago, to decide the national championship. According to the *New York Times* of January 6, 1935, Rupp stated that "such a tournament would put an end to conflicting claims to so-called national championships." In addition "it would tend to further interest in this sport throughout the country" and would encourage "a more uniform code of rules interpretation." The first tournament was held in 1939 and, as Tev Laudeman has observed, it eventually did for college basketball what the World Series did for baseball. It provided a "goal and a stimulus for participants, and a focal point of interest for fans." During his career Rupp's teams won the NCAA tournament four times.

Rupp was never close to any of his players while they were team members, nor did he generally indicate a desire for their friendship. In fact, Rupp was a very private person with a small circle of close friends. Even his long-time assistant Harry Lancaster was forced to admit in his reminiscence *Adolph Rupp as I Knew Him* that he came "as close as Adolph would ever let anyone get to him. I don't think he ever had a truly close friend in his life, nor do I think he wanted one."

In his job as coach, winning was all-important to Rupp. He often told his players, "If it matters not whether you win or lose, why do they keep score?" Because he hated "quitters," Rupp constantly tested

each athlete's character by probing for physical, mental, and emotional weaknesses. He had little interest in being liked or admired by his players and insisted on maintaining a distance from them. The distance and the relationship he desired to establish with his players were emphasized by the starched khakis he and Lancaster wore at each practice. His players were treated like army recruits, while he and Lancaster, recalled former players Dan Chandler and Vernon Hatton in *Rupp from Both Ends of the Bench*, "resembled Army sergeants in all respects." The relationship changed after the players left Rupp's "army" with honorable discharges. Many, but not all, came to appreciate what Rupp had done for them. Some, like a former player who was quoted in the December 23, 1977, issue of the *Christian Science Monitor*, neither forgot nor forgave: "He made the rules and we obeyed them. There was no joking, no laughing, no singing, no whistling, no horseplay, no breaks in practice, and certainly no questioning his rules. He had us so wrapped up in basketball and winning that we didn't have time for anything else." Lou Tsioropoulos, a star forward on some of UK's greatest teams, believes Rupp behaved as he did for a definite reason—the Baron knew what he wanted in his players and was constantly testing them to see if they measured up. "Basically what he wanted were players who could concentrate, who were assertive, and who could take charge. The ones who were a little sensitive and who couldn't take his criticism didn't make it. He didn't want players who would fall apart at a crucial point in a game."

Bobby Watson, a teammate of Tsioropoulos in 1951 and 1952 and a strong admirer of Rupp, observed in an interview that "the people who got to play liked and respected him. If you didn't get to play much, though, he could make it kind of tough for you. If you weren't a starter you weren't much in his eyes." Not all of the starters admired Rupp, however, and not all of the reserves hated him. Many if not most of Rupp's pre-World War II players with whom I spoke, both starters and reserves, had negative feelings about the Baron. But members of the Rupp teams of the fifties and sixties often were reluctant to depreciate a man they all regarded as "a legend," although some spoke frankly of their feelings when I switched off my tape recorder. One who was willing to speak for the record was Ned Jennings, a 6'8" starting center on two of Rupp's teams of the early 1960s. A very honest and straightforward man, Jennings stated frankly, "I disagree with his methods. He was a very tough individual who very seldom praised you. This may work with some players but it doesn't with others." Jennings especially regretted the way Rupp beat down some

very talented players who could not or would not adjust to his personality or system. Jennings cited the example of Earl Adkins, a "Mister Kentucky" his senior year in high school who later enjoyed success in state politics but who seldom saw game action during his career at UK.

Another perspective was offered by Dan Chandler, who spent four years in the 1950s on the UK bench and never won a letter. He admitted that "many of his boys resent him for their first few years" but "after they graduate, most of them probably come to realize what a fantastic job he has done using them and others, year after year, molding them into that winning tradition." Chandler concluded that the Baron "gets immature boys, turns them into tough winners, and sends them out into life with pride and a solid accomplishment behind them."

Dan Issel, a two-time college All-American and pro star with the Denver Nuggets, who probably enjoyed the closest relationship with Rupp of any of his players, was even more laudatory. In a preface to Tev Laudeman's *The Rupp Years*, Issel expressed the appreciation and gratitude he felt for having been "fortunate enough to have played under Adolph Rupp." What he learned at UK provided the solid foundation, he maintained, for whatever success he enjoyed in professional basketball. "I will remember Adolph Rupp as a warm, compassionate man, but also as a man who would not tolerate mediocrity. He was demanding, but he recognized and appreciated a total effort."

Issel elaborated on his views during a June 30, 1983, interview. "One thing I would be willing to bet about the interviews you have had with former UK players," he began, "was that you didn't come across many who were wishy-washy about Coach Rupp. There seem to be two distinct groups: one is composed of players who hated him and couldn't stand him and the other of those who loved him. I'm certainly in that group over there because everything I have today is directly or indirectly because I came to Kentucky and played for Coach Rupp." Issel then made a very important point. "You have to keep in mind that there are two different types of players: ones that respond when you pat them on the back and others that respond when you kick them in the behind. I was one that needed the kick. Coach Rupp and Coach Lancaster had the philosophy that you kick everybody and if there was a player who needed the pat on the back why he would have to either change his ways or go down the road." For himself, Issel emphasized, Rupp was the ideal coach. "Coach Rupp made me a much better player than I would have been if I hadn't come here. I respected what he did. Then after I graduated and got

A tense moment in the 1944/45 season.

to know Coach Rupp well, I found that he was not the harsh, gruff man he portrayed in practices and on the basketball court. He wasn't like that at all." Issel emphasized that not everyone had the close and pleasant relationship with Rupp that he had enjoyed. He contrasted his own experience with that of another player from Illinois. Guard Greg Starrick, who was an excellent prospect, arrived at UK the year after Issel but never played a varsity game for the Big Blue. Starrick had compiled an excellent record while in high school, with a three-year average of 26.8 points per game and a single-game high of 70 points. Following his senior season he had been not only a unanimous All State selection in Illinois but a *Parade Magazine* first-team All American. Starrick was the type, Issel noted, "who needed a pat on the back and they just drove him off."

One fact emerges from my interviews with former players. Whether they came to admire and respect Rupp or continued to hate and resent him, he was ever in the thoughts of his "boys." For better or worse, playing for the Baron clearly was an experience that changed a person.

Rupp enjoyed great success throughout his forty-two-year career at UK. The most glittering achievements came in the late forties and early fifties. But the system which produced the "Fabulous Five" and the Spivey-Hagan-Ramsey teams was formed during the 1930s and the war years.

Rupp's Formative Era

During Adolph Rupp's first five seasons at the University of Kentucky his teams compiled a phenomenal record of eighty-five victories and only eleven defeats for a winning percentage of .885. The team won one SEC championship, in 1933, and shared the title in 1935. In the last half of the decade the winning percentage tailed off somewhat, to .745, as UK lost twenty-six of 102 contests for an average of slightly more than five defeats a year. Although the roster each season was studded with All-SEC players, the overall quality of the teams during these five seasons was not up to that of the previous squads. Despite the relative decline in athletic talent and the less impressive won-lost record, Wildcat fans did not complain but were, if anything, even more enthusiastic in their support of the Big Blue. The Cats rewarded that support with three SEC championships in the five-year period: 1937, 1939, and 1940. Rupp and UK were picking up momentum and not even a world-wide war, which the United States entered in 1941, could loosen the Big Blue's hold over its conference. By the early forties the presence of the UK team in the SEC title game was almost a foregone conclusion. Only John Mauer and his Vols prevented a clean sweep of the championship, and in the two seasons Tennessee won, 1941 and 1943, the Wildcats came in second.

Kentucky's dominance of the SEC and its status as one of college basketball's major powers was an established fact. To many it seemed preordained. It was not. It was based on a number of factors and although Adolph Rupp was one of them, if not the most important, he was not the only one. Rupp's achievements were built on a solid base—the work of

his predecessors, especially John Mauer. Rupp added his own unique personality and a new and popular style of play. Ralph Carlisle, who was an All-Southeastern Conference forward on UK's 1936 and 1937 teams, observed in a December 1982 interview that Rupp "had a leadership aura about him. Even before he became known as a great coach and an important man he had a quality about him you just can't describe. He was amazing," Carlisle continued. "He could walk into a room filled with people he didn't know and who didn't know him and in no time at all he was the center of everything. He always seemed to have something to say that was appropriate for the moment," noted Carlisle (who is himself regarded by many people as an excellent speaker and a dynamic personality), "and he always seemed to be able to draw the attention that he wanted to draw. He just knew how to do it. Now, that's not a bad quality, is it?"

Two Rupp assistant coaches of the era merit special mention for their contributions to the program. Both Paul McBrayer, 1934-43, and Harry Lancaster, who assumed the position in 1946, played important roles in training players in the fundamentals of the game, helping with recruiting and scouting, and serving as buffer between the players and an increasingly autocratic and irascible Rupp. According to several players from the thirties and early forties, McBrayer along with Blanton Collier was responsible for many of the patterns, plays, and variations that UK teams use down to this day and contributed the minute details of the tenacious man-to-man defense he learned from John Mauer in the late twenties. When he became assistant coach, Lancaster, who had played for Col-

lier while at Paris High School, helped perfect the superbly synchronized and coordinated offense (he fully developed the fastbreak's potential) and the sticky defense that distinguished the UK teams of the late forties and fifties. It was to Rupp's credit that he permitted assistants the latitude to develop their role fully and to contribute to the program. Rupp was a highly intelligent man. In addition, he had a genius for picking other people's brains and for absorbing new ideas and adapting them to his own use so they became his ideas. Like their coach, Wildcat teams adapted to changing situations. Although Rupp and his players loved the fastbreak, UK basically employed a guard-oriented patterned offense. Even the fastbreak was carefully planned and coordinated. The first pass, for example, was to go upcourt. It was never to go to the side because that slowed the break.

Rupp's use of the fastbreak was an important element not only in the success of his teams but also in their public appeal. Most of the Southern teams of the era employed one variation or another of a slow-down offense. Many did so because they could not compete with UK at its own game. They did not have enough quality players and either did not or could not recruit them.

Although basketball scholarships, according to Aggie Sale, were being awarded, by 1932 (not 1935, as some books have reported), most SEC teams in the thirties and early forties carried as few as two or three scholarship players. Most team members were on football scholarships.

There was also a dearth of first-rate coaches. Quite simply, basketball was not considered as important at other conference schools as it was at UK. Many of the coaches were assistants on football teams who were pressed into duty to direct the basketball squads. Even in the late forties, noted Wallace "Wah Wah" Jones in an interview, "at some schools one assistant football coach would take the job this year and another assistant would take it the next year. Rupp's success eventually forced them to take basketball more seriously." Even Mauer, at both Kentucky and Tennessee, divided his attention between basketball and football. No other basketball coach in the SEC, as several former Wildcats noted in interviews, took the sport as seriously or concentrated as completely on his job as Rupp. Rupp also was fortunate in that, when the SEC was formed in 1933, Maryland, North Carolina, Duke, and North Carolina State did not join the new league. All had been members of the Southern Conference and would have been formidable rivals. Instead, other than UK, the teams that helped form

the SEC were oriented toward football more than basketball.

The final ingredient in UK's success was the players themselves. The Big Blue was blessed throughout the thirties and early forties with a steady stream of talented athletes, more than any other SEC rival of the era was able to assemble. Although some of the UK players during this formative era were outstanding, there was not the profusion of "blue-chip" athletes that would distinguish Wildcat teams during the decade commencing in 1943/44. Nearly all of the early UK players were Kentucky natives, many of them from the Bluegrass area. With few exceptions the out-of-staters were from nearby sections of Indiana and Ohio.

Strangely enough, considering the success he would soon enjoy in the SEC, during his first two seasons in Lexington Rupp was unable to improve on the record of his predecessor, John Mauer, in the Southern Conference tournament. In 1931, following a 12-2 regular season, the Cats were invited to the Southern Conference Tournament in Atlanta, where they swept to easy victories over North Carolina State, Duke, and Florida, only to fall in the finals to Maryland in the final seconds of play. In that March 3, 1931, contest UK made only two field goals and three foul shots in the entire first half. Incredibly, the Cats took twenty-one shots before they sank their first goal. Holding the Big Blue "to two field goals in one half of a game," Ralph McGill (at the time a sportswriter) marvelled in the March 4 issue of the *Atlanta Constitution*, "is perhaps the greatest guarding feat in the eleven years of tournament history." Kentucky rallied in the second half and held a 27-25 lead with only forty second to go in the game. That was when Maryland's star guard, Lewis Berger, "broke out in a tremendous one-man attack that won the game 29-27. . . . The uprising of Lewis Berger," wrote Ed Danforth in the same issue of the *Constitution*, "was the greatest single exploit the eleven years of the Southern conference basketball tournament has produced." Louis McGinnis, who played forward on the 1931 UK team and was the leading scorer in the conference tournament, recalled in an interview that a little known factor in the defeat was Maryland's use of a zone defense. "I think that was the first time that Rupp ran into the zone defense. We weren't prepared for it and we couldn't work our offense against it and our guards weren't hitting over it. The zone was a deciding factor in the game." Although they did not win the tournament the Wildcats placed three men on the All-Southern team, the first time they had accomplished that feat. The three were McGinnis, referred to in the press as "the

diminutive forward," center George Yates, who played "masterful basketball" despite an illness, and team captain and forward Carey Spicer, who also made All-American for the second time. Guard Jake Bronston made second team All-Southern. Guard Ellis Johnson, a starter during most of the regular season, suffered an ankle sprain in midseason and did not play in the tournament, while Aggie Sale was hampered by a painful hip injury which limited his playing time through most of the season.

Kentucky's style of play that year, both offense and defense, was similar to what it had been the previous season under John Mauer. The players were used to the Mauer system and Rupp, as a new coach fresh from the high school ranks, was smart enough not to try to introduce a new system. Instead, with Carey Spicer's copy of the Mauer playbook as guide, Rupp retained the same plays and even the same play numbers. Thus the Number Six play in 1929/30 was still Number Six in 1930/31 and, in fact, today. Rupp even held three-hour daily practices, as his predecessor

had. By the fifties the Baron's highly organized and intense practices were generally concentrated into a period of no more than an hour and a half. Rupp, it must be emphasized, was a quieter, more modest person that first year than he would be later in his career. Or so his early players maintain.

Louis McGinnis noted that "we just sort of carried on with what we had been doing and worked the fastbreak in as we always did when we got the chance." Mauer's slowbreak, McGinnis observed, was what is now referred to as a deliberate offense. During Rupp's first season, "there was still a lot of screening and passing to open things up for a close in or a layup shot. That is, we just took our time to get a good shot and then we took it. If a fastbreak was available we took it." A difference, however, was that Mauer did not encourage his players to take advantage of a fastbreak opportunity and Rupp did. The players could be more innovative under Rupp. He permitted them much more freedom within a structured system than Mauer had.

Three All-Southern members of Rupp's first team at UK, in 1930/31: l-r, Louis "Little" McGinnis, who played forward; Carey Spicer, team captain and All-American selection; and George Yates, who played center and was voted All-Southern for his performance in the 1931 Southern Conference tournament. All three were also on Mauer's last team.

Rupp's second UK team (1931/32) boasted three future All-Americans: Forest "Aggie" Sale, John DeMoisey, and Ellis Johnson. Front row, l-r: Cecil Bell, Ercel Little, Gordon George, Harvey Mattingly, Evan Settle, Bill Kleiser. Middle row: Bill Davis, C.D. Blair, Darrell Darby, Johnson, Howard Kreuter, Charles Worthington. Back row: assistant coach Leonard Miller, James Hughes, DeMoisey, Sale, George Skinner, Rupp.

The season following Rupp's arrival (1931/32) was the first in which the conference permitted the awarding of athletic scholarships to members of the basketball team. Before then the only assistance the university provided was in helping players find jobs in Lexington. With the money they earned the boys paid for room and board which, Aggie Sale noted in an interview, could be found for as little as four dollars a week. "You could get a meal at a rooming house on Upper Street for twenty-five cents and it was just as good as what you can find now for seven or eight dollars."

UK again had a very successful regular season in 1931/32 but also once again fell short in the tournament. After an injury-plagued sophomore season, Sale and guard Ellis Johnson came into their own. They, along with fellow juniors Darrell Darby and Howard "Dutch" Kreuter at forward, senior Charles Worthington at guard, and sophomore John "Frenchy" De Moisey, a starter at forward until he was sidelined for

five games by academic problems, rolled to a fourteen-victory regular season record that was marred only by a final game loss by one point to Vanderbilt. UK entered the conference tournament as co-favorites with Maryland. Led by Sale with twenty-one points, Darby with seventeen, and reserve forward De Moisey with six points, the Wildcats crushed Tulane on February 26 by twenty points (50-30) in their first tournament game, only to fall short by one point the next afternoon to North Carolina. The Maryland "Old Liners," as the team was called, fared even worse than UK. In their first-round game the overconfident Maryland squad, one reporter observed, "stood around like craven images, no doubt thinking Florida would be paralyzed by the Old Liners' mighty presence."

With the formation of the Southeastern Conference, UK's luck in tournament play soon changed. As *Atlanta Constitution* sportswriter Ralph McGill observed in the aftermath of the 1933 SEC championship game, "What Kentucky needed, it seems, was to get out of

Among the stars of the powerful 1932/33 team were *(l-r)* Bill "Racehorse" Davis, Ellis Johnson, Forest "Aggie" Sale, and John "Frenchy" DeMoisey. Davis and Johnson were all-around athletes, starring in football as well as basketball; Johnson, an All-American guard in 1933, was also outstanding in baseball and track. Rupp later said that Sale, who was college player of the year in 1933, may have been the best player he ever coached.

the Southern conference." The Wildcats fielded a veteran team with Sale and De Moisey alternating at center and one forward and with Darrell Darby at the other forward. George Yates, an All-Conference performer in 1930/31, did not play the following season and was a little-used substitute at center in 1932/33. The guards were Ellis Johnson and Bill "Racehorse" Davis, the latter the only sophomore on the starting team. Johnson and Davis were excellent ball handlers and passers who could sink the outside set shot when necessary, but most of the scoring was handled by the forwards and center. Sale and De Moisey, both of whom measured around 6'5" in height, complemented each other beautifully. Sale was much the better leaper; he generally jumped center (remember that a center jump followed each basket) and handled most of the rebounding but also could shoot a two-handed set shot. De Moisey, who was not as mobile as Sale, usually stationed himself on or near the foul line (there was no three-second area at the time) and took his favorite shot, a turn-around half hook or, as Sale described it, a "flip" shot.

The Wildcats lost three regular-season games—to Ohio State, Creighton, and South Carolina—but reached their peak in the SEC tournament. On four successive days, February 25 through 28, the "Ruppmen" roared to overwhelming victories over Mississippi, Florida, LSU, and Mississippi State. The closest game of the four was that against LSU, which UK won by only thirteen points, 51-38. In the championship game the Big Blue led at half-time by a score of 29-7 but substituted freely in the second half and finished

the game with a 46-27 victory and the title.

De Moisey, Sale, and Johnson were chosen to the All-Conference team. Ralph McGill thought this was ridiculous. His choices were De Moisey, Darby, Sale, Johnson, and Davis, all of Kentucky. "There were other great players," McGill admitted, "but the all-conference *team* is Kentucky's." The captain of the UK squad, Aggie Sale, was, McGill bubbled, "redoubtable, versatile, clever, skilled, capable, brilliant, scintillating, dazzling and otherwise dominating." McGill obviously was not alone in this opinion. In addition to All-American honors, Sale was chosen by the Helms Athletic Foundation as the college basketball player of the year. UK was chosen the team of the year.

In 1933-34 the Ruppmen won all fifteen regular season games and outscored their opponents by an almost two-to-one margin, 656 points to 340. De Moisey and Davis were joined on the starting team by junior forwards Dave Lawrence and Jack Tucker and Milerd "Andy" Anderson, a sophomore guard. The squad travelled to Atlanta with high hopes of repeating as SEC champions, but their hopes were quickly dashed. Although De Moisey and Davis were named to the tournament first team, UK was eliminated in the first round by Florida (38-32).

Going into the game the lightly regarded Florida Gators were given little chance of beating the undefeated Wildcats, who were the top-seeded team in the tournament. Instead, the Gators accomplished what reporter Bert Prather, writing in the February 25, 1934, issue of the *Courier-Journal*, termed "one of the biggest upsets in the history of Southern basketball."

Unfortunately for UK, "the Gators were charged up to the sky for the encounter," were as fast as the Wildcats, and "proved superior" in playing defense. If all this was not bad enough, UK's offensive star, De Moisey, had a poor game and got in foul trouble early in the second half. The Wildcats were probably lucky to lose by only six points.

The tournament format was dropped in 1935 (though it was reinstated the following year) and UK shared the championship with LSU. The departure of 1934 All-American Frenchy De Moisey and the decision of Bill Davis not to return for the 1934/35 season were hardly felt. The three returning starters—Lawrence, Tucker, and Anderson—were joined by two members of the undefeated 1933/34 freshman team, Warfield Donahue and LeRoy "Cowboy" Edwards. Another member of that group, Ralph Carlisle, who would be an All-Conference forward in 1936 and 1937, was a substitute in 1934/35.

The Rupp system began to take definite shape in the 1934/35 season with the arrival of Edwards, Donahue, and Carlisle and the hiring of former Wildcat All-American Paul McBrayer as assistant coach. McBrayer would bring an attention to detail,

a passion for hard work, and a number of innovative ideas to the program, among them the inside screen and the second guard around, the latter originally used by Blanton Collier at Paris High School. (Years later, Collier would become a head football coach, first at Kentucky and then with the Cleveland Browns of the NFL.)

The Edwards-led team of 1934/35 set a trend and a standard for future UK teams that would not be matched until the late forties. Although only a sophomore and just 6'5" in height, Edwards was the prototype of the modern center. As McBrayer recalled, "He had a lot better moves around the basket than most centers did at that time, he was much stronger in the upper body and he had a good touch for the basket in close." Teammate David Lawrence also marvelled at Edwards's strength and shooting ability. In an interview, Lawrence noted that the big center had "a good close-in jump shot, an excellent hook shot with either hand, and could rebound above the basket."

The 1934/35 season was the only one Edwards played at UK, but because of him it was memorable. He was named All-SEC and All-American and the

Outstanding members of the 1934/35 team included LeRoy Edwards (25), voted All-American and college player of the year in his only varsity season; and Ralph Carlisle (14), an All-SEC selection at forward in both 1936 and 1937.

LeRoy "Cowboy" Edwards, a scoring and rebounding sensation whose single varsity season (1934/35) was memorable. Edwards was All-SEC, All-American, and college player of the year.

Helms Foundation Player of the Year—and he was only a sophomore. Unfortunately for the Wildcats and their faithful fans, his was a spirit more akin to that of the "do-your-own-thing" sixties than the Depression thirties. Edwards returned to his hometown, Indianapolis, at the end of the school year, never to return to the University of Kentucky. The following season he played basketball on a semi-pro team and in 1937 became a professional when he joined the Oshkosh (Wisconsin) All-Stars, one of the premier teams of that era. Edwards was a great player, and one can only guess what he would have accomplished if he had remained at UK and completed his eligibility.

During 1934/35 the Wildcats won nineteen games,

lost only two, and finished the season as co-champions of the SEC. One of the losses, to New York University, was in a sense a triumph rather than a defeat. As Tev Laudeman has noted, "It broke Kentucky out of the mold of being just a good southern team." It had a number of other important results as well, including the favorable attention it brought Rupp and the team in the *Times* and other New York papers, and the important part it played in helping to promote intersectional play as well as highlight the differences in officiating between the East, the South, and the Middle West. When, after the game, Rupp complained bitterly that what had transpired in the contest bordered on a steal, many sportswriters agreed with him.

The NYU game was part of a double header, the second one ever played at Madison Square Garden. According to one newspaper account it "was so exciting that the capacity crowd of 16,539 fans nearly went wild." The two teams offered contrasting styles. While the Violent Violets employed a fastbreak offense, the Wildcats used set plays, quick short passes, and the setting of screens. The screens, or blocks, were an integral part of the UK offense. Unfortunately referees in the East considered them illegal because most were moving picks. Every time the Cats set a screen the referee called a foul. (There was, Lawrence explained, only one referee and NYU chose him.) Edwards had three fouls within a few minutes after the start of the game. At the time four personal fouls brought expulsion from a game. Edwards lasted until the last minute of the game but played much more cautiously than normal and scored only one field goal. His game and that of his teammates were thrown off during most of the first half by the rough play of the NYU players, especially their center, Irving Turjesen. One reporter described it as verging on "warfare."

Although Turjesen scored only one point in the contest his pushing, shoving, and jabbing effectively neutralized Edwards. The referee was much more indulgent of the NYU tactics than of UK's use of the moving screen. The Wildcats seemed bewildered during the early going by the NYU fastbreak, the rough play, and the referee's interpretation of the rules. Nevertheless, they fought back from an early 4-0 deficit to take the lead for the first time after more than twelve minutes of the first half had elapsed. It remained a close and rough game thereafter but the Big Blue held the lead through nearly all of the second half. Then, with a minute left to play, the Violent Violets' captain Sidney Gross sank a field goal to tie the score at 22 all. The Wildcats controlled the following center tap and set up their offense for a game-winning basket but at this critical juncture Edwards was called for set-

ting an illegal block. Gross stepped to the foul line for the Violets. Arthur Daley, in the January 6, 1935, *New York Times*, described the dramatic moment: "The ball teetered on the front edge of the rim with agonizing uncertainty and then toppled through the net to give the New York University quintet its twenty-second successive victory over a two-year span in Madison Square Garden." Although nearly a minute still remained in the game after the successful free throw, the Wildcats were faced with an impossible task. Without Edwards, who had fouled out, the Cats were unable to control the center tap. The Violets took possession of the ball, the *Lexington Leader* reported ruefully, "and iced the game by freezing it during the remaining seconds."

Although Edwards was held to only six points in the NYU game, he scored the phenomenal total, for that era, of 343 points for the entire season. By contrast, Carey Spicer's team-leading total for the 1930/31 season had been 190 points, and Aggie Sale had managed to tally 194 points in 1931/32. Edwards scored more than twenty points each in six of UK's twenty-one games during the 1934/35 campaign, with a season high thirty-six-point performance against a very good Creighton University team on February 22. This is impressive when one notes that UK rivals were able to score twenty or more points only eleven times during the season.

Big Blue fans looked forward to 1935/36 with high expectations. They were to be disappointed, of course, because Edwards did not return. The big center was ahead of his time in many respects, including the belief that college basketball should bear immediate financial rewards for players as well as coaches and sponsoring institutions. According to former UK players, Edwards made monetary and other demands of Rupp and the university that they could not or would not meet.

Although guards Anderson and Donahue were back, the entire starting front line was lost because forwards Lawrence and Tucker had departed through graduation. Junior Ralph Carlisle and sophomore Joe "Red" Hagan quickly moved into the starting forward positions and proved to be at least the equal of their predecessors, with Carlisle winning All-SEC honors in both 1936 and 1937. But filling Edwards's shoes proved an impossible task, not only in 1936 but for several years to come. Compounding the problem in 1936 was the fact that Rupp had arranged a very demanding schedule. In addition to tough SEC rivals Tennessee, Alabama, and Vanderbilt, the Wildcats faced intersectional powers Notre Dame, New York University, Michigan State, Butler, and Creighton.

Top: Warfield Donahue, who played guard from 1934/35 through 1936/37. *Above:* Louisville native David Lawrence, an All-SEC forward in 1934/35.

And, recalls Ralph Carlisle, UK just did not have the talent that season.

Carlisle, who blossomed as a star in 1936, contrasted the games in Madison Square Garden with and without Edwards. In 1935 "we could have beaten NYU if they hadn't held Edwards all night long. Oh, it was terrible. The things Rupp said after the game didn't really go far enough because it was just highway robbery." The next year was a different matter entirely. "We went up there to New York and we just got beat and that's all there was to that. They won 41 to 28. That year they were just a better team than we were. We just plain didn't have much." In the opinion of Tev Laudeman that situation lasted into the early 1940s. During those years (1936-43), wrote Laudeman in *The Rupp Years*, "hard times came to Adolph Rupp." To a certain extent, it must be emphasized, this was relative. It was in comparison to the achievements of the pre-1936 period and what the Wildcats were to accomplish after 1943. And these eight so-called lean seasons at any other SEC school would have been glory years. The Big Blue not only won the league championship four of the eight years but placed nine players on the all-SEC team (three of them made the first team in two different seasons) and two were All-American selections. The All-SEC performers were Ralph Carlisle, forward, 1936 and 1937; Warfield Donahue, guard, 1937; Bernie Opper, guard, 1938 and 1939; Mickey Rouse, guard, 1940; Marvin Akers, forward, 1941, and guard, 1943; Lee Huber, guard, 1941; Ermal Allen, forward 1942; and Melvin Brewer, center 1943. The All-Americans were Opper and Huber. Some of the others, especially Carlisle, might have made the honor teams if UK's won-lost record had been better. Although UK had some good centers, among them Melvin Brewer, what was lacking during this era was an outstanding player in the pivot who, like Edwards, and after 1945, Alex Groza, could dominate a game.

Several players of that era give a great deal of credit for what UK achieved to assistant coach Paul McBrayer. Bernie Opper recalled in an interview that McBrayer "was very, very influential. He was an excellent teacher of defensive and offensive basketball and rebounding. Mac was a strong believer in defense and he put us through the paces. He just loved to see somebody shut somebody out." In those years, Opper noted, "if you scored in double figures it was

Like other Rupp teams of the period, the 1938/39 SEC champion Wildcats were stronger at guard positions than in the front court. Front row, l-r: Rupp, Lee Huber, Waller White, Harry Denham, Keith Farnsley, Bernie Opper, Elmo Head, Layton Rouse, Donald Orme, and assistant coach McBrayer. Back row: trainer Frank Mann, James Goodman, Fred Curtis, Homer Thompson, Marion Cluggish, Stanley Cluggish, Carl Staker, Rogers Nelson, manager J.B. Faulconer.

Three outstanding players of the late 1930s. *Above left*, Bernie Opper, star guard and Rupp's first recruit from the New York area, All-SEC in 1938 and 1939 and All-American in 1939. *Above*, Lee Huber, two-time All-American guard (1940 and 1941), who came to UK on a tennis scholarship. *Left*, Ermal Allen, a small but fierce and rugged competitor who was an All-SEC forward in 1941, as well as a star halfback on the football team.

phenomenal. In the year I made All-American I think I averaged four or five points a game. If a team scored forty points that was good. Just a few years before LIU was being advertised as a point a minute team. That is, they scored forty points a game!"

Ken Rollins, who was team captain and starting guard in 1946/47 and 1947/48, was a sophomore starter on the 1942/43 team. In an interview Rollins recalled that McBrayer was "a very vital participant in coaching tactics and had complete charge of the freshmen." He worked with the freshmen "on all of the basic fundamentals of basketball. You would have thought that we had never been taught anything before, but that's good. Don't take anything for granted." Freshmen were also run through all of the drills and plays that the varsity used in preparation for their moving up. "When it came to the varsity," Rollins continued, "Coach McBrayer was at one end of the floor and Coach Rupp at the other and during practice we caught it at both ends. Coach McBrayer had what appeared to me to be a lot of authority. Coach Rupp listened an awful lot to what Coach McBrayer was saying and suggesting." In sum, McBrayer "contributed to everything that was done."

Former star forward Red Hagan recalled in an interview that during his varsity career (1936-38) "at least two-thirds of the team looked to Mac for everything they did. I know I did and I think the others did too. Mac didn't want it that way but it just was because just about everyone on the team felt Adolph was not very knowledgeable about basketball." It was only later, "when Adolph became more successful, that his word almost became law on the team, and I guess even the campus."

Ed Lander, who played at UK during the early forties and served as a scout later in the decade, also reminisced about Rupp and McBrayer in a January 1983 interview. Lander knew Rupp from around the age of thirteen when the Rupps moved into a house across the street from where the Lander family lived. While still in high school, 1937 or 1938, Lander started watching UK practices. In 1940 he entered the university as a freshman. Over a period of several years he developed an admiration for Paul McBrayer. In the Kentucky system "Mac did all the teaching and he was superb at teaching the mechanics of the game. He really made us better players than our talents warranted." (Several other players made this same point.) But McBrayer's contributions went far beyond that in both the late thirties and the early forties. "Mac coached all phases of the game. Any time something needed to be explained or corrected or something new was put in, he did it. Before and during the games Rupp said the inspirational things and Mac explained what we were supposed to do. After the war Harry Lancaster took over what Mac had done, which was pretty much the actual preparation for the game and the coaching during the game." Rupp's approach, Lander noted, was specific and direct. "It was to go out and do it. For him the important thing was the end result, to win. He knew how to win. He wasn't that interested, though, in the basics, in teaching. But he was smart enough to get Mac and then Lancaster who were."

Tom Parker, who was a co-captain and forward on Rupp's last team, in 1972, made essentially the same point in an interview. "Coach Rupp had a unique ability to attract good people. Not only athletes but assis-

tant coaches." While Parker was at UK Rupp's assistants were Lancaster, who became athletics director in 1968, Joe Hall, and Dick Parsons. In Parker's view Lancaster was a major contributor to UK's success. "Not to take anything away from Coach Rupp, those four NCAA championships he won, you can give Coach Lancaster half the credit." Parker considers Rupp to have been "a master tactician, a General Patton-type" and a master psychologist and motivator. But "when it came down to a specific play, or to needing a basket or something specific done Coach Lancaster was the one that did the job. And then after he left the coaching ranks and took the AD job Coach Hall filled that need."

Ed Lander offered specific examples of McBrayer's contributions. "He put in a back block system and I remember a play he put in after a defensive free throw. Actually, in basketball you can only block [or set picks] two ways, inside or outside, but he was constantly refining variations on those two types of blocks. He also taught us how to handle things in ball control situations like at the end of the game when we had a small lead. He taught that more than forty years ago and it is identical to the way [Indiana University head coach] Bobby Knight teaches it now." Lander remembers observing McBrayer develop his techniques at the practices he attended while still a high school student. The system McBrayer taught "was really, as I understand it, a refinement of the basic offense Mac learned from Johnny Mauer when he coached at Kentucky. And it, in turn, was the system Rupp continued to use during the rest of his career."

McBrayer entered the service in 1943 expecting to return to his position as assistant coach after the end of the war. In this hope he was to be bitterly disappointed because Rupp hired Harry Lancaster. Lancaster, who had played for Georgetown in Rupp's first game as UK coach, had worked as an instructor in the UK Physical Education Department before being called into the Navy in 1944. In his book *Adolph Rupp as I Knew Him* Lancaster recalled that "Rupp had told me after McBrayer went into the service that he did not want Mac back after the war. I got the idea that Adolph thought Mac was after his job." Although it cannot be proved, another possibility is that Rupp felt he no longer needed McBrayer. A successful program was under way with a style of play that was pleasing fans and winning games and league titles. Effective drills, plays, plans, and procedures were now in place. Obviously McBrayer had played a major role in standardizing and rationalizing the system but, looked at in a cold-blooded way, he was no longer essential to its continued functioning. Another former Mauer player, Elmer "Baldy" Gilb, filled Rupp's needs from 1944 to 1946 and helped guide the Cats to an NIT championship in 1946. A UK assistant football coach at the time, Gilb was not, he explained in an interview, interested in a full-time basketball assistant coaching position, so Harry Lancaster was awarded the job in the spring of 1946.

Lancaster resembled McBrayer in many respects and filled much the same function as his predecessor, but he also differed in several important ways. Unlike McBrayer he did not have a connection with the University of Kentucky prior to Rupp's arrival nor did he have a power base of his own either in the univer-

The 1940/41 season inaugurated Rupp's second decade. *Far left*, Milt Ticco shoots against West Virginia in the season opener, which UK won 46-34. *Center*, Marvin Akers helps boost UK to victory over Tennessee, 37-28, on February 15. *Near left*, Mel Brewer (15) tips off against perennial power Notre Dame. UK lost 48-37. Rupp's Wildcats didn't beat Notre Dame until 1943.

sity or in Lexington. While Lancaster had been a star in both basketball and football at Georgetown College he had not been an All-American as McBrayer had. As a player, it might be noted, McBrayer's record overshadowed Rupp's own accomplishments. Contrary to some later reports, Rupp had been a substitute and not a starter on the 1923 University of Kansas national championship team. Neither did Lancaster have a direct connection with John Mauer, as McBrayer did. With McBrayer's departure, a key link with Mauer, the source of much if not most of the Kentucky style of play was severed and the system became fully the "Rupp system."

Nearly everyone who was connected with Rupp acknowledges that he had a giant ego, and having to share credit for the success of the Big Blue could not have been pleasant for him. What was worse, in the words of Red Hagan, a star forward from 1936 to 1938 and later a successful coach, "Knowledgeable fans and all the players knew Mac was really running the team. During a time-out at least three-quarters of the players turned to McBrayer to find out what to do." In the post-World War II period all ideas had to emanate from Rupp. One did not sell him an idea either, relates one player who after graduation served for several years as a scout and recruiter. "You had to implant the idea in his mind so it was his idea and not yours. You had to turn it around so it came from him. Coach Lancaster was a master of that."

Ironically, it is extremely doubtful that any of Rupp's apparent worries about his status were justified. Except in the aftermath of the basketball scandals of

1951, Rupp's position was never in jeopardy nor his high standing in the coaching profession in doubt. Even during the relatively lean years of the late thirties and early forties Rupp's reputation was constantly on the rise nationally. As for the local situation, it is doubtful that the majority of students or other fans were greatly concerned about who the assistant coach was so long as the head coach was Adolph Rupp. The question of who contributed what to the program was also of far less significance to them than whether or not the Cats won. In this they reflected the attitude of the Baron. As more than one player has observed, Rupp knew how to win and how to produce a pleasing product. The 1941 *Kentuckian* quoted what it claimed to be Rupp's motto: "Always a good show." Whether or not Rupp had a formal motto, it did epitomize the Baron's wide appeal.

The passion of the Kentucky basketball faithful for their Big Blue team and especially for its head coach did not cool in the early forties despite the war. If anything it became even more ardent.

The first phase of Rupp's career came to an end in 1943. During this era the Wildcats became the dominant basketball power in the Southeast. However, as one former player has noted, "Our record when we went across the river [that is, to the Middle West and the East] was just so-so because in terms of scholarships and emphasis on basketball they were probably ahead of Kentucky. We really didn't fare too well." UK gained some important intersectional victories and savored some memorable moments but there were also many bitter defeats.

The 1942/43 Wildcats, Paul McBrayer's last team as assistant coach. Front row, l-r: Carl Althaus, Bill Turley, Bob Atherton, Ed Fish, and Tom Moseley. Middle row: Rupp, trainer Frank Mann, Wilbur Schu, Clyde Parker, Mulford Davis, Kenny Rollins, Bill Barlow, William Hamm, and McBrayer. Back row: Milt Ticco, manager Bob Landrum, Marvin Akers, Melvin Brewer, Jim Weber, Hoyt Moore, Ed Lander, E.S. Penick, and Paul Noel.

56

Paul McBrayer, an All-American guard while a player, served as UK's assistant basketball coach from 1934 through 1943, when he went off to war. Rupp did not rehire him at war's end and McBrayer became the highly successful head coach of the Eastern Kentucky Colonels, a position he held until his retirement.

An event that provided Adolph Rupp's greatest thrill in all the years his teams played at Alumni Gym took place on February 14, 1938. UK was playing a fine Marquette squad that had beaten Notre Dame and several other powerful teams. It was a game the Wildcats were not expected to win but they were holding their own. With only twelve seconds to play the score was tied at 33 and UK had the ball out of bounds. The ball was put in play and after a couple of passes it was in the hands of forward Red Hagan. With only six seconds remaining, Hagan sank a two-hand shot from beyond midcourt and UK won 35-33. The crowd went wild and A.B. "Happy" Chandler, then governor, immediately sent for a hammer and nail. Rushing from the stands Chandler went to the spot where Hagan had taken his shot. There, forty-eight feet, two and a quarter inches from the basket, Chandler drove a nail to immortalize the occasion.

During that same 1937/38 season the Big Blue gained one of its most important intersectional victories of the era—a decisive 40-29 win over the Pittsburgh Panthers in the Sugar Bowl Tournament. Actu-ally it was not a tournament because only two teams were invited to New Orleans for the contest, which took place on December 29, 1937. The game was intended to bring together a team regarded by the Sugar Bowl Committee as the strongest in the North and the most powerful squad in Dixie. In 1937 Pitt, with an unbeaten record, appeared to be a worthy representative for the North. Pitt Coach Doc Carlson was one of the famous coaches of the time, but he still used the old figure-eight offense, and that proved easy for UK to handle. The figure eight involved continual movement of the ball and was intended to free a man for an easy layup. Carlson did not permit his players, Bernie Opper remembers, to shoot the ball from beyond the free throw line. "If they tried Carlson would pull them right out." Opper described what Pitt tried to do. "Every time they ran the figure eight the man I was guarding moved out so they would set up a play. So I saw in the first quarter that he kept moving out and moving out. One time," Opper chuckled, "when he moved out instead of going with him I stopped in the middle and broke up the criss cross. They didn't know what to do. There I was picking off passes and they were still running that same pattern."

The Wildcats followed up their important victory over Pitt with a disastrous "trip across the river" on which they lost three games in a row to Michigan State (43-38), Detroit (34-26), and Notre Dame (47-37). For several years playing Notre Dame was a painful experience for Rupp. Before his arrival, UK under the direction of John Mauer had played the Fighting Irish only once, winning a 19-16 decision at South Bend in 1929. Rupp scheduled Notre Dame, a nationally recognized power, for the first time during the 1935/36 season. When the Baron made the arrangements he thought LeRoy Edwards would be on his team. The two schools met on February 10, 1936, and the Wildcats were badly outclassed, losing by the score of 41-20. Even with Edwards in the lineup the Big Blue would have had problems because Notre Dame was a perennial national power with excellent players and one of the truly great coaches of the era, George Keogan. As Wildcat All-American Lee Huber recalled in an interview, "Notre Dame was the biggest rival we had. The three years I played at UK, they beat us every year." The Big Blue, in fact, lost seven straight regular-season games to the Irish until 1943, when Rupp gained his first decision over a Keogan-coached team.

By the end of the 1942/43 season Rupp's team had won a total of 214 games and lost only 57. The Baron reigned supreme in the Southeast. The following decade would witness UK's emergence as one of the major basketball powers in the nation.

Wildcat Basketball's Golden Decade

The "glory years" of Kentucky basketball spanned the period from 1943/44 to 1953/54. Although this covered eleven seasons, UK played only ten of them. The Wildcats were under an NCAA suspension in 1952/53 and did not compete on the intercollegiate level, play being limited to four intrasquad games. During this era the Big Blue scaled the heights of glory with championships in both the NIT (1946) and the NCAA tournaments (1948, 1949, and 1951), as well as capturing the SEC championship in each of the ten seasons the Cats competed in the conference. Unfortunately, in the aftermath of the point-shaving scandal of 1951, the program also plumbed the depths of humiliation.

When the UK squad assembled for practice in preparation for the 1943/44 season not even the most loyal of Big Blue fans would have dreamed that the Wildcats were embarking on the most successful decade in the university's basketball history. This was the height of World War II when able bodied young men were needed for military service. Some universities were fortunate enough to have the use of army or navy trainees. UK was not. Rupp had to make do with military rejects and youngsters who had not yet reached the draft age of eighteen. As a result, the team he assembled may have been one of Adolph Rupp's most important. In the belief that the shortage of experienced players rendered the building of a competitive squad impossible, Rupp and Athletics Direc-

tor Bernie Shiveley seriously considered dropping basketball for the 1943/44 season, if not until the end of hostilities. Rupp admitted to a reporter in January 1944 that the youngsters "surprised me as much as anyone. They're just a bunch of kids who showed up for basketball practice last fall when we decided for sure to have a team."

The team's veterans were two sophomores, forward Wilbur Schu and guard Tom Mosely. The other fifteen players were freshmen. It appeared that the most that could be expected was to suit up a team. No one anticipated a representative team, much less a squad that would lose only one regular-season contest, win the SEC championship, and place third in the NIT Tournament in New York. Variously referred to as "the beardless wonders," "the freshmen," and "the Wildkittens," the 1944 aggregation was one of the top teams in the nation and lent great luster to the coaching reputation of Adolph Rupp.

Although the "Wildkittens" of 1944 boasted some excellent individual talents, the secret of the squad's success was that it functioned so effectively as a unit. The "beardless wonders" hustled and scrapped all season long and achieved some things no previous UK team had, including the first victory over Indiana University, the first win over Big Ten champion Ohio State in Columbus, and the first victory in New York's Madison Square Garden, a 44-38 win over St. John's,

---

Cliff Hagan goes in for a layup during his record-setting performance against Temple on December 5, 1953. His 51-point single-game score was unbroken until 1970. He has been UK's athletics director since 1975.

which had been NIT champion in both 1943 and 1944. They also defeated Notre Dame for only the second time in Rupp's tenure at UK and whipped an excellent University of Illinois team 51-40 in Lexington on February 7, thus avenging the only loss of the regular campaign. At season's end three freshmen won spots on the SEC first team, center Bob "Tank" Brannum and guards Jack Parkinson and Jack Tingle. Wilbur Schu placed on the second team while fellow sophomore Tom Mosely and freshman Rudy Yessen won honorable mention. Brannum later was named an All-American.

The "Wildkittens" capped the season with their first appearance in the NIT, the premier tournament of the era. Only eight teams were invited to the tournament and UK only had to win three games to capture the championship. They got off to an auspicious start with a 46-38 trouncing of a fine Utah squad but were upset two days later by St. John's, a team they had beaten during the regular season. The "beardless wonders" met Oklahoma A&M (now Oklahoma State University) and seven-footer Bob Kurland in the consolation game, while St. John's played De Paul and its giant center George Mikan for the championship. UK and St. John's neutralized the play of the big men with excellent team play and won their March 26 contests. In fact, although Kurland stood under the basket and batted away shot after UK shot (goaltending was legal then) the kittens soundly thrashed the Aggies, 45-29.

Above, Bob Brannum, All-SEC and All-American during his freshman year in 1944, was unable to break into the starting lineup when he returned from the service in 1946, and transferred to Michigan State.

Right, members of the 1943/44 "Wildkittens," all freshmen except for Wilbur Schu and Tom Moseley. Their 19-2 season brought UK its sixth SEC championship and first appearance in the NIT. Front row, l-r: Nathaniel Buis, Rudy Yessin, Jack Parkinson, Buddy Parker, and Moseley. Back row: manager Allan Abramson, Schu, Truitt DeMoisey, Bob Brannum, George Vulich, Jack Tingle, and Rupp.

Ironically the Idaho "Blitz Kids," because of their early elimination in the NIT, were free to accept an NCAA bid when Southwest Conference co-champion Arkansas withdrew from the tournament following the injury of two starters in an auto accident. An all-civilian squad which averaged just 18.5 years in age, Utah became the Cinderella team of the tournament and emerged as the NCAA champions of 1944.

The following season, 1944/45, UK performed brilliantly again for a group of fuzzy-faced seventeen-year olds and military rejects. Back from the 1944 team were Jack Tingle and Wilbur Schu at forward and Jack Parkinson at guard. Each was an All-SEC performer during the previous campaign. Gone was All-SEC and All-American center Bob Brannum, who had left for the service, but his departure was hardly felt, at least during the first part of the season. Taking Brannum's place was Martin's Ferry, Ohio, native Alex Groza. Although only an eighteen-year-old freshman, Groza already displayed "the perfect basketball hands," the "great team spirit," and the "uncanny ability at hitting the basket" that would later mark his play as a member of the "Fabulous Five." Although the 6'7" pivotman played only in UK's first eleven games of the campaign, he scored enough points to lead the team in scoring for the entire season.

When Groza left for military service the Wildcats had a perfect record. This included victories over such strong teams as Indiana, Wyoming, Temple, Long Island, Michigan State, and Ohio State. The most satisfying triumph for Groza was that over Ohio State on December 23, 1944, at Alumni Gym. Groza noted in a May 1983 interview that he had wanted to attend his home state university but the interest was all one-sided. To defeat Ohio State would thus be sweet revenge, especially since the Buckeyes also boasted a great center, Arnie Risen, who would later star as a professional player. Ironically the 6'8" Risen was a Kentucky native from Williamstown. The two teams entered the game undefeated and the Buckeyes were defending Big Ten champions. It was, in other words, a *big* game. The two teams and their marvelous centers exchanged baskets throughout the contest. The score was tied at the end of regulation time but UK pulled ahead in the five-minute overtime to prevail by five points, 53-48. Groza finished with sixteen points, followed by Tingle and Parkinson with fifteen each. The only Ohio State players in double figures were Risen and forward Don Grate, each with fourteen points.

Following Groza's departure Kentucky suffered its only regular-season losses to Tennessee, Notre Dame, and Michigan State. The Wildcats recovered by the end of the regular season, swept to the championship of the SEC tournament, but lost in the first round of the NCAA to Ohio State, a team they had defeated during the regular season while Groza was still in the lineup. It is not beyond the realm of possibility that the Big Blue, with Groza in the lineup for the entire season, would have gone undefeated and perhaps even won the NCAA. This is not meant to denegrate his replacement, Kenton "Dutch" Campbell. The 6'4" freshman was talented enough to be voted first-team All-SEC center in 1945. Nevertheless, Campbell simply was not in the same class as Groza, who after the war was a three-time All-American, Helms Foundation Player of the Year, and one of the greatest pivotmen in the history of college basketball.

The foundations of the great post-World War II University of Kentucky teams were laid in the 1943/44 and 1944/45 seasons. The latter campaign was the first in which the Big Blue won twenty or more games, now (in the 1980s) the yardstick of a successful season. Rupp, whose position as one of the nation's foremost coaches was already securely established, emerged from the triumphs of these two seasons as a veritable miracle worker because of the great performances of his all-civilian teams in victories over such intersectional powers as Notre Dame, Indiana, Illinois, Ohio State, St. John's, Long Island University, Utah, and Oklahoma A&M. All this, however, was but a prelude to what was soon to come.

In the 1945/46 season Rupp had back the nucleus of the fine 1944 and 1945 teams—senior Wilbur Schu and juniors Jack Tingle and Jack Parkinson, as well as Kenton Campbell, who had won All-SEC honors in 1945 as a freshman. Despite their earlier accomplishments Campbell lost his center position to a freshman, Wallace "Wah Wah" Jones, while Schu was forced to share his forward position with yet another freshman, Joe Holland. Still another freshman, Ralph Beard, walked (or rather ran) into a starting guard position. Jones arrived at the Lexington campus as the greatest high school player in the nation but Beard was not far behind in either publicity or talent. At UK both Beard and Jones quickly proved that they fully deserved all the superlatives showered upon them. The powerful rebounding of Jones and the speed of Beard made the Wildcat fastbreak sizzle. The Big Blue completely dominated the SEC and finished the season with twenty-eight victories and only two defeats. The Wildcats overpowered their opponents in the conference tournament in Louisville and placed four players on the All-SEC first team (Tingle, Jones, Beard, and Parkinson) and their fifth starter, Schu, on the second team. Parkinson, an excellent shooter both from

outside and on drives to the basket, also won a spot on post-season All-American teams.

The Big Blue capped the 1945/46 season by winning the NIT championship, an achievement that previously eluded Rupp and his Wildcats. UK entered the tournament as heavy favorites and swept to an easy 77-53 triumph over Arizona in its first-round test. That proved to be the Wildcats' only breather. The West Virginia Mountaineers fought the Big Blue on even terms in the semifinals. The score was tied fourteen times before UK broke the game open with about two and a half minutes left and scored eight straight points to take a 59-51 decision.

The championship game against the Rhode Island Rams and their magnificent star Ernie Calverley was an even tougher game. The score was tied twelve times in this contest, the last time with only forty seconds to play. At that point, with the score knotted at 45, Calverley fouled Ralph Beard. Beard recalled in an interview that he was scared to death as he stepped to the free-throw line with Madison Square Garden's 18,000 fans screaming for him to miss. The Rams, who had entered the tourney as 20-1 underdogs, had quick-

ly become the Cinderella team and the darlings of the Garden crowd and the New York press. The Rhode Island dream ended as Beard sank his free throw (at the time one free throw was awarded for a non-shooting foul) and UK took the lead, 46-45. The Rams tried desperately, but unsuccessfully to score in the final few seconds. This was one of Rupp's biggest victories. The NIT was not only the first national tournament, dating from 1938, it also had the most prestige—at least until the basketball scandals tarnished it, along with Madison Square Garden and New York City basketball in general. Until then the Garden was the "Mecca of Basketball" and it was especially sweet for the Wildcats to gain a major victory there.

Rupp lost only three lettermen from the NIT championship team, and such was the quality of the 1946/47 team that their departure was hardly felt. Departing through graduation were part-time starting forward Wilbur Schu and reserve guard William Sturgill, while junior guard Jack Parkinson was called up for military service. It was unfortunate for Parkinson—who had been team captain, leading scorer, and an All-

Tension and exhaustion are evident on the faces of Rupp and his 1945/46 starting five, a team that bagged the SEC trophy and UK's first NIT championship. Left to right, Wilbur Schu, Wallace "Wah Wah" Jones, Ralph Beard, Jack Parkinson (captain), Jack Tingle, and Rupp.

American in 1946—that he had to depart for a year of duty in the army because when he returned for the 1947/48 season he could not even crack the starting lineup much less become a star on the "Fabulous Five" team.

Amazingly, Parkinson was one of three All-Americans who languished on the Wildcat bench during the 1947 and 1948 campaigns. The others were Kansas native Tank Brannum, who had won All-American honors at center for UK as a freshman in 1944, and West Virginian Jim Jordan, who was named All-American in both 1945 and 1946 while a naval trainee at North Carolina. Jordan, who played at guard, arrived in Lexington as a freshman with four full years of varsity eligibility still available, while Brannum still had three more years. Brannum, Jordan, and Parkinson obviously were not lacking in talent. Their misfortune was simply that in 1946/47 and 1947/48 Rupp had players who were even more richly blessed with playing ability than these former All-Americans.

If UK and Adolph Rupp had a problem in those seasons it was an overabundance of talented athletes. Rupp had nineteen players on his team roster in 1946/47 and eighteen the following season. By 1948/49 the squad was down to a more manageable twelve players. The prospect of playing for the great Rupp attracted these and many more quality athletes to Lexington. Some of the players had started at the university before or during the war only to have their careers interrupted by military service. Among these were Cliff Barker, Ken Rollins, Mulford "Muff" Davis, John Stough, and Jack Parkinson. The others were either recruited by Rupp or were attracted by his reputation. Once again Rupp's luck came to the fore. Before the 1945/46 season the United States Army asked him for a favor—to develop a sports and recreation program for soldiers in Europe. While he was overseas, noted Buddy Parker in an interview, Rupp sold the UK program to some of the fine athletes he came across. Among these were Dale Barnstable and Jim Line, both of whom were All-ETO (European Theater of Operations) players. Both later contributed greatly to the UK program. So many out-of-state players arrived, in fact, that in the 1947/48 season, for the first time in the history of UK basketball, native-born Kentuckians comprised a minority, six of eighteen players on the Wildcat roster. This continued in 1948/49 when only four of twelve varsity players were from Kentucky. Among the four were seldom used sophomore guards Joe Hall of Cynthiana and Garland "Spec" Townes of Hazard.

In the years from 1945 to 1948 the university came

Wilbur Schu rebounds a missed shot in a 1946 game against LSU. "Wah Wah" Jones is no. 41.

to resemble a revolving door for basketball talent. Wave after wave of talented ballplayers arrived only to learn that for one reason or another they did not quite measure up to Rupp's standards, and sooner or later they departed. Players transferred from UK who possessed the ability not only to start but to star on other college teams. Thus Frenchy De Moisey's younger brother Truett and Deward Compton, both of whom played either center or forward, transferred to the University of Louisville, while former All-American center Bob Brannum and richly talented guard Albert Cummins (who languished on the UK third team) moved to Michigan State. After graduation Tank Brannum went on to star in the NBA for six years, four of them with the Boston Celtics.

One of Adolph Rupp's basic rules throughout his career was to decide on a starting lineup and stay with it. He generally substituted as little as possible. During the immediate post-war years, Buddy Parker observed, Rupp did bend this rule, but only in games

where the Wildcats badly outclassed their opponents. In those contests Rupp "would suit up part of the team at halftime. The boys who played the first part of the game would shower and change into street clothes and be up in the stands with their girlfriends. I don't reckon," Parker laughed, "that's ever been done at any other college in the country." Parker noted that UK had three teams with enough ability "to have probably beaten ninety-five percent of the teams in the SEC." In fact, "some of the scrimmages between the first and second teams were better played and more competitive than most of the conference games we played." It was indeed an embarrassment of riches but UK fans did not complain.

To help him mold the magnificent groups of athletes who flocked to UK in the postwar years into championship teams Rupp had the services of Elmer "Baldy" Gilb through the 1945/46 season. Gilb, however, preferred football to basketball coaching and decided not to continue as Rupp's assistant. The Baron's prewar assistant coach, Paul McBrayer, had gone off to military duty in 1943 but with his discharge from the service was once again available. Unfortunately for McBrayer, who loved the university, Rupp had ap-

Harry Lancaster, who played against UK in Rupp's first game as coach, became the Wildcats' assistant coach following World War II. In 1968 he was named athletics director, making him Rupp's boss.

parently long before determined not to ask him to return to the staff. Several interviewers maintained that although he was approaching the pinnacle of his success Rupp was apparently in constant fear that his job and his reputation were in jeopardy. This was perhaps a carryover from the insecure years of his youth in Kansas. Whatever the reasons, several former players have observed that Rupp found it extremely difficult to bear other people receiving publicity he felt should be his. And the Baron was well aware that many people, including some sportswriters, held McBrayer's coaching ability in high regard. Obviously Rupp could not accept the idea of having McBrayer back as assistant coach and thus as rival for control of the team and of publicity.

With McBrayer out it was necessary to find someone else to serve as assistant. According to Lee Huber, a pre-World War II UK All-American, he was tapped for the job. In an interview Huber related the process by which Rupp had Andy Anderson sound him out before the 1946/47 season. Rupp did not conduct the negotiations personally or directly, Huber noted, "because he wouldn't risk being turned down." Huber was not interested in the job and Rupp turned to physical education instructor Harry Lancaster, a personal friend who had proved his worth to the basketball program on a number of scouting trips for the team. This was a fortunate choice because Lancaster complemented Rupp's talents and personality so perfectly. Lancaster served as assistant coach until 1968, when he accepted the position of athletics director at the university.

The UK record in the post-World War II era was truly spectacular. During the four seasons from 1945/46 through 1948/49, the Cats won 130 of 140 games played, for an average of 32.5 victories a season. The record was only slightly less impressive over the next four seasons the Big Blue played, as the Wildcats won 111 games and lost only ten, for an average of nearly 28 victories a season. The Blue and White captured the SEC championship every one of those eight seasons. UK also won the NIT championship in 1946 and the NCAA in 1948, 1949, and 1951.

In the opinion of Harry Lancaster, UK could have won at least five straight NCAA championships. In an interview he pointed out that "we won the conference in 1950 but the representative from our district, the Athletic Director at Virginia, didn't invite us to participate in the NCAA and at the time you had to be invited. Instead of us, he invited a team from his own conference." Lancaster noted how ridiculous the situation was. "Here we were defending champions two years running and we weren't invited. So we

skipped that year but we came back in 1951 and won it and we might have even won it in 1952 but Spivey was lost to us because of the scandal." The Cats did not play a schedule in 1952/53 but returned the following season with a vengeance. They posted a perfect 25-0 season record and the conference championship in 1953/54 but did not participate in the NCAA tournament because the team's three best players—Hagan, Ramsey, and Tsioropoulos—were ineligible, as they were graduate students. (The rule has since been changed.)

Of all the achievement-filled seasons during this period probably the greatest was 1947/48, the season of UK's most famous team, the "Fabulous Five." The Wildcats not only posted a 36-3 record and held the conference title and their first NCAA championship, but also provided half of the U.S. Olympic basketball team which went on to win a gold medal at the Olympic Games in London.

The starting five were Wah Wah Jones and Cliff Barker at the forwards, Alex Groza at center, and Ralph Beard and Ken Rollins at guards. Rollins, a senior, was team captain for the second straight season. In an interview Rollins noted that although this group did not come together as a starting team until the 1947/48 season, World War II was responsible for the "Fabulous Five." The twenty-six-year-old Barker, Rollins, age twenty-four, and Groza, who was twenty-one, were ex-servicemen as were the majority of the team's substitutes. The result, was, as Rollins noted, an excellent mixture of maturity and youth. Thus Barker started at UK "in 1939, played just part of his freshman year, fell in love, went home, got married, and joined the air force. I started in 1941, played my freshman and sophomore years, and got drafted into the Navy. Groza," he continued, "arrived in '44, played part of a year and was drafted. Then in 1945 along came some great talent straight out of high school in the persons of Beard and Jones. Then you have us all coming together after the end of the war" when Groza, Barker, and Rollins returned to UK in time for the 1946/47 season. "It took us a full year to get everything together," Rollins stated, "for us to be comfortable together and get that chemistry."

The great success achieved by the 1947/48 team, Rollins believes, was a combination of a number of factors, including speed, size (for the era), unselfishness, good shooters, and a certain chemistry. It must also be rememberd that all the players were hard workers. "None of us was ever lazy or ever slacked off" either in practice or in games. "Another thing we had," Rollins continued, "was the killer instinct. I get so disturbed with teams that get fifteen or so point

Kenny Rollins started at guard in 1942/43 but his career was interrupted by military service. He returned to star on the 1946/47 and 1947/48 teams.

leads at half-time and fritter it away in the second half. Brother, if we got twenty on a ball club that was just the beginning," he maintained, slapping the desk to emphasize his point. "We weren't satisfied. We wanted twenty more and more often than not we got them. No mercy! None whatsoever. We never had compassion for anyone," he laughed.

Rollins, Jones, Groza, Beard, and Harry Lancaster in interviews discussed the contributions of each member of the starting five to the team's success in the 1947/48 season. They noted that every successful team needs at least one player who is willing to sacrifice his personal glory for the success of the squad and who is also willing to take a leadership role. The 1948 team was especially fortunate because it had not one but two such players. Both Barker at forward and Rollins at guard got as much pleasure from making a good

pass as from scoring a basket. Rollins was, in Lancaster's words, "our coach on the floor." Groza, Beard, and Jones did most of the scoring but Rollins also was a good if not great shooter. He had an excellent long set shot and a jump shot from around the foul line. Rollins also scored points on the fastbreak. Barker, on the other hand, was not a scorer. Ironically he had been an excellent shooter before the war but somehow had lost his touch during the fifteen months he spent in a Nazi prisoner-of-war camp during World War II. Most of the points he made were on rebounds or fastbreaks, although he did occasionally hit a jumper from eight or ten feet out. Amazingly, considering his poor shooting touch, Barker hit the longest field goal in Wildcat history, a 63' 7 1/2" missile unleashed against Vanderbilt on February 26, 1949 at Alumni Gym. Barker characteristically downplayed the shot when we talked in November 1983, claiming that it was just luck and not very important anyway. Barker's major contributions to the team were excellent defense, strong rebounding, and great ballhandling. He was often the trigger on the fastbreak because of his strong defensive rebounding and his ability to get the ball out quickly on the break once he had the rebound. His passing was legendary. As one of his teammates observed, "He could do just about anything with a basketball except shoot it."

The team's chief offensive weapon was the center, Alex Groza. He was very quick and fast for a big man and often got downcourt on the fastbreak. He had good hands and an excellent scoring touch. All he needed, a teammate recalled, was "a little operating room." Therefore the team constantly worked on ways to get him open because "once you got him the ball, that was it. He was an excellent faker and he had a variety of shots and was a great rebounder." His chief attribute, though, was a combination of floor balance and court sense.

The 6'4" Jones, also a football and baseball star, was a powerful rebounder who was especially effective on the offensive boards. He had an excellent two-hand shot from above his head which he took from the corner and from around the foul line. Beard had a variety of shots including a long two-hand set shot and a one-hand jump shot from medium range. If guarded too closely, the 5'10" Beard, who was extremely fast

Ralph Beard's jump shot against Georgia Tech in the 1948 SEC championship helped UK to a 54-43 victory. "Wah Wah" Jones is no. 27, Alex Groza is no. 15.

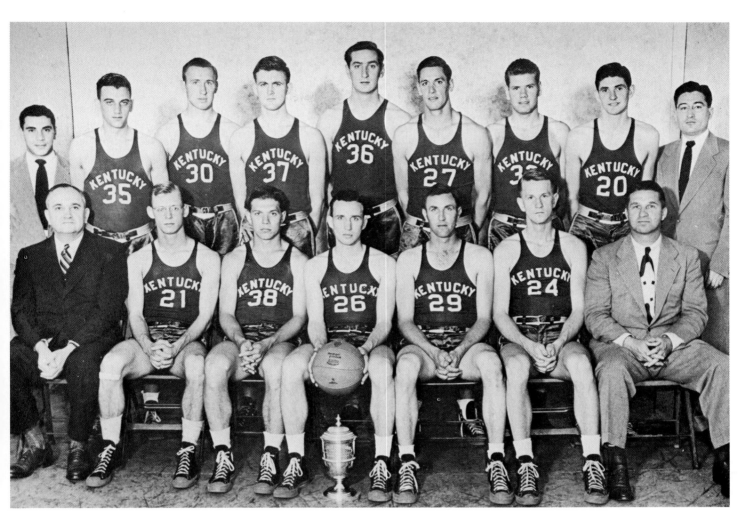

The 1948 NCAA champions, probably UK's greatest team. Front row, l-r: Rupp, Johnny Stough, Ralph Beard, Kenny Rollins (captain), Cliff Barker, Dale Barnstable, and assistant coach Harry Lancaster. Back row: manager Humzey Yessin, Garland Townes, Jim Jordan, Joe Holland, Alex Groza, Wallace Jones, Jim Line, Roger Day, and trainer Wilbert "Bud" Berger.

and had great quickness, could get by his man for a layup. Like the other guard, Ken Rollins, Beard scored many of his points on the fastbreak.

Harry Lancaster reminisced about the "Fabulous Five" and their fastbreak. "They were a beautiful team," he observed. "They had the finest fastbreak I have ever seen, before or since. It was just magnificent the way Groza got the ball off the board." When Groza or Barker got the rebound "he would hit Jones around the head of the circle. He would hit Rollins at about midcourt and Rollins would hit Beard going under the basket. Beard and Rollins were just so quick." Lancaster also noted that when the "Fabulous Five" ran the fastbreak "the ball might touch the court once or twice but never more. None of this dribble, dribble, dribble. It was bing, bing and in it went." Lancaster closed his discussion of the "Fabulous Five" with the observation that while "Rupp would never admit

it but that was the best team we had man for man."

Only Rollins was lost from the great 1948 team. Dale Barnstable, a 6'3" junior from Antioch, Illinois, took Rollins's place in the starting lineup. At the beginning of the 1948/49 season Barnstable played at guard but it did not take long to see that a better passer was needed. The happy solution was to move Barnstable to forward and shift the team's best passer, Cliff Barker, to guard. The result was another glitteringly successful season. The Cats won thirty-two games and lost only two en route to a second straight NCAA championship. Beard and Groza won All-American honors for the third season in a row and were joined on the honor teams in their senior season by forward Wah Wah Jones. In 1949 Alex Groza became the third UK star to be named the Helms Foundation Basketball Player of the Year. Two years later another Wildcat center, Bill Spivey, became Player of the Year.

Spivey, UK's first seven-footer, joined the varsity in the 1949/50 season and led an inexperienced team composed largely of sophomores to a very respectable 25-5 record and yet another conference championship. After being snubbed by the NCAA the two-time defending national champions accepted an invitation to play in the NIT. It quickly became evident that this was a mistake because they met a City College of New York team that administered the worst drubbing Rupp had ever suffered. What made the defeat even more humiliating at the time was that the CCNY team entered the tournament with a deceptively lackluster 17-5 regular-season record. In the wake of the basketball scandal which began to break in the summer of 1951 evidence was uncovered that the squad had shaved points in games throughout the 1949/50 season. CCNY did not begin to play up to its potential until tournament time, when it won not only the NIT but the NCAA championship. No other team in college basketball history has ever matched this accomplishment, although UK and other teams of the era tried.

Three-time All-American Alex Groza scores against Georgia on his way to a record-setting 38-point game total on February 21, 1949. UK downed the Bulldogs 95-40.

The Wildcats achieved another thirty-win season (32-2) and an NCAA Championship in 1950/51. Along with Spivey, who was named All-American and College Player of the Year while still a junior, UK had a talented squad that included senior Walt Hirsch and junior Shelby Linville at forward and junior Bobby Watson and sophomore Frank Ramsey at guard. Reserves included future college coaches Guy Strong and C.M. Newton as well as Lucian "Skippy" Whitaker, Lou Tsioropoulos, and Cliff Hagan, who became a sophomore and joined the varsity at mid-season.

The 1950/51 season shines brightly in Bill Spivey's memory, especially a December 16 game at Memorial Coliseum with Kansas in which he outduelled another great center, Clyde Lovellette. In an interview Spivey recalled it as "my best game at UK. The press from coast to coast was playing it up and Rupp was really anxious to win because he had played for the Kansas coach, Phog Allen." By the time the game started "I was really psyched up because of the press and because of clippings Rupp had been pasting on my locker saying how good Lovellette was." UK crushed Kansas 68-39 and Spivey assured himself the Player of the Year award by completely outclassing one of his major rivals for the honor. Spivey was so emotionally charged up that at one point in the game he treated Wildcat fans to their first view of a dunk during a game. Dunking was legal at the time but Rupp did not permit it during games although he did in practice. But, Spivey remembers, one time in the game he got carried away. "I stole the ball from Lovellette under the basket and it took me only about three bounces of the ball to get to the other end and I went up and slammed it through the basket. I just couldn't help it." Spivey laughed. "I was so fired up I even beat the guards downcourt. The fans went crazy. They went absolutely wild."

The 1950/51 team was one of the most successful in Wildcat history but fans were expecting even more the following season. And their expectations were justified. With Bill Spivey in the lineup the 1951/52 team had the potential to be one of the greatest college basketball squads in history. Even without him it was excellent. With the 7' Spivey at center the team would have boasted 6'4" junior Cliff Hagan and 6'5" senior Shelby Linville at forward, and 6'3" junior Frank Ramsey and 5'10 1/2" senior (and team captain) Bobby Watson at the guard positions. Among the sixteen available reserves were 6'5" junior Lou Tsioropoulos at forward and center, and 6' senior Skippy Whitaker and 6'1" sophomore Bill Evans, who played at both forward and guard. This aggregation possessed talent,

size, and depth. It could have become, as Spivey noted, an even better team than the "Fabulous Five."

Unfortunately, injury to Spivey and the basketball scandal intervened. Spivey injured his knee prior to the start of the season, and before he was ready to return to action he was implicated in the fast-spreading scandal. Although Spivey was never convicted of wrongdoing he never played in another game for the Wildcats. His place in the lineup was taken by Cliff Hagan who, although only 6'4" tall, had good jumping ability and an awesome hook shot. UK lost only three of thirty-two games but one of the defeats was to St. John's in the Eastern Regional of the NCAA by a 64-57 score. The loss was especially painful because the Cats had smashed the same St. John's team by forty-one points (81-40) in a regular season meeting. Spivey might have made a difference in the tournament game but he was under investigation by law enforcement authorities in New York City.

The existence of corruption in college basketball was first publicized in 1945 when five Brooklyn College players were expelled from school after admitting they had accepted bribes to lose a game. The extent of the point shaving and game fixing did not become evident, however, until 1951 when Manhattan College star Junius Kellogg reported to the District Attorney's office that he had received an offer of $1,000 to control the point spread in a game. Although the scandal centered on New York area teams and Madison Square Garden games, investigations disclosed the fact that between 1947 and 1950 fixers had tampered with at least eighty-six games in twenty-three cities and seventeen states. Authorities named thirty-three players as having participated in the fixes and there were rumors that many more were involved.

As the revelations began to appear in the press Adolph Rupp made what soon proved to be an unfortunate statement. In an interview in Lincoln, Nebraska, on August 15 he maintained that "the gamblers couldn't get to our boys with a ten-foot pole." The team, he continued, was under "constant and absolutely complete supervision while on the road." Furthermore, the Baron bragged, "nowhere was that supervision more complete than in New York." New York authorities soon demonstrated that gamblers had indeed been able to "get to" some of UK's players, and with money rather than poles. The press and New York sportswriters in particular gleefully turned Rupp's words against him. Larry Fox pointed out in his *Illustrated History of Basketball* that when "the scandal 'hit in the family,' Rupp no longer urged leniency for players who 'only' shaved points." In this unfolding drama Rupp did not perform with distinction.

Bill Spivey, UK's 7' center, dominates Kansas star center Clyde Lovellette in the Wildcats' resounding 68-39 defeat of Rupp's alma mater on December 16, 1950.

In the fall of 1951 Ralph Beard, Alex Groza, and Dale Barnstable were taken into custody and admitted sharing $2,000 in bribe money to shave points in a 1949 NIT game against Loyola. The Wildcats were ten-point favorites going into the game but suffered a stunning 67-56 defeat and elimination in the opening round of the tournament. Soon Jim Line, a star of the 1950 team, Walt Hirsch, team captain and star forward in 1951, and Bill Spivey were implicated. All but Spivey admitted accepting money and when they came to trial received suspended sentences. Spivey, who adamantly proclaimed his innocence, was indicted for perjury but was found innocent.

Beard, Groza, and Barnstable appeared before Judge Saul S. Streit of the Court of General Session in New York on April 29, 1952, to hear their sentences. As with the athletes of other universities who appeared before him and admitted their guilt, Judge Streit was relatively lenient. But the judge was not as under-

Wildcat captain and forward Walt Hirsch fights for a loose ball in a January 8, 1951 game against DePaul during UK's first season in Memorial Coliseum. The Cats won 63-55.

standing in his dealings with gamblers, universities, coaches, and alumni. In an earlier trial when passing sentence on the game fixers Judge Streit maintained that "the responsibility for the sports scandal must be shared not only by the crooked fixers and corrupt players, but also by the college administrations, coaches and alumni groups who participate in this evil system of commercialism and overemphasis."

As the school with the most successful basketball program in the nation the University of Kentucky came under particularly close scrutiny and, in Judge Streit's opinion, was found wanting. The judge, in a sixty-seven-page opinion delivered on April 29, 1952, found the university to be "the acme of commercialization and overemphasis." The magistrate complained that "intercollegiate basketball and football at the University of Kentucky have become highly systematized, professionalized and commercialized." He also found "covert subsidization of players, ruthless exploitation of athletes, cribbing at examinations, 'illegal' recruiting, a reckless disregard of their physical welfare, matriculation of unqualified athletes by the coach, alumni, and townspeople, and the most flagrant abuse of the 'athletic scholarship.' "

Judge Streit was particularly critical of Adolph Rupp who, in his view, "failed in his duty to observe the amateur rules, to build character and protect the morals and health of his charges." After their experience with Rupp, Beard and the other players were "ripe for plucking by the Fixers."

Judge Streit also decried Rupp's relationship with Lexington bookmaker Ed Curd. As Russell Rice noted in *Big Blue Machine*, Curd was "the undisputed 'king' of Lexington bookmakers at the time" as well as "a nationally known gambling figure who operated in comparative security above the Mayfair Bar on Lexington's Main Street. He was friendly with the 'right' persons, made his contributions to charity—Rupp had gone to Curd's home to solicit for the local children's hospital—and operated a 340-acre farm near Lexington. His name was mentioned at least twice in the Senate Crime Committee investigation as Lexington's betting commissioner."

In testimony before the court Rupp admitted knowing Curd (misspelled "Kurd" in the court records) and agreed that it was "general knowledge" that Curd was a bookie who operated a bookmaking establishment in Lexington. Rupp further acknowledged that Curd

had on at least two occasions joined the Baron and others of the Kentucky traveling contingent at meals at New York's Copacabana night club and had traveled on the train to at least one game with the team. The Baron denied the allegation of some of his players that he frequently telephoned Curd to learn the point spread on UK games.

The university and its president, Herman L. Donovan, defended Rupp and refused to dismiss him even when it became evident that such action would spare the team punishment by the SEC and the NCAA. On August 11, 1952, the Executive Committee of the SEC announced its findings and decision. The punishment meted out was harsher than the university had feared. The Wildcats were barred for one season from conference play and participation in postseason tournaments. Three months after the league ruling, the

NCAA asked all member schools not to schedule UK during the 1952/53 season.

A few days after the NCAA announcement President Donovan informed UK alumni that he had ordered an internal investigation of Rupp, which had produced a report that exonerated the basketball coach of any wrongdoing. "From all we could learn," Donovan maintained, "Coach Rupp is an honorable man who did not knowingly violate the athletic rules." The announcement pleased Big Blue fans but not, apparently, the university's football coach, Paul "Bear" Bryant.

The Bear, who had arrived in Lexington in 1946, brought UK its first success and national prominence in football, but felt that he and his program were not fully appreciated on campus or in the state. (Bryant's immediate predecessors as head coach were A.D. Kir-

The 1950/51 SEC and NCAA champion Wildcats. Front row, l-r: Lindle Castle, Lucian Whitaker, Bobby Watson, Guy Strong, and Charles Riddle. Middle row: Rupp, Cliff Hagan, C.M. Newton, Walt Hirsch (captain), Paul Lansaw, Dwight Price, and assistant coach Lancaster. Back row: Frank Ramsey, Shelby Linville, Bill Spivey, Roger Layne, Lou Tsioropoulos, and Read Morgan.

wan, later a UK history professor and university president, and Athletics Director Bernie Shively, who also assumed the duties of football coach in 1945.) Both Rupp and Bryant were coaching geniuses, both had enormous egoes, and both needed a large stage on which to perform. It proved impossible for them to coexist on the same campus. Supposedly Bryant was under the impression that Donovan would dismiss Rupp and was angry to learn instead that the Baron had received a vote of confidence. Thus instead of forcing Rupp's departure from the university, the basketball scandal precipitated Bryant's departure.

For Rupp, who always feared failure, the entire affair must have been a humiliating and debilitating experience. Gerry Calvert, who played on UK's varsity from 1953/54 through 1956/57 and who later became Rupp's attorney and good friend, maintained in an interview that the Baron's problems with his eyes and with diabetes began much earlier than most people realized and that the pressure on Rupp during the various investigations had a great and adverse effect on his health.

If the scandal was a traumatic experience for Rupp, it was devastating for the players involved. The very promising professional basketball careers of Alex Groza and Ralph Beard were cut short by the scandal, while Bill Spivey, who had the potential to be one of the greatest of all pro players, never got an opportunity to play in the NBA. In the 1949/50 season Groza and Beard, together with former "Fabulous Five" teammates Cliff Barker and Wah Wah Jones, began their careers as players and part owners of the Indianapolis Olympians, a new franchise in the newly formed NBA. The Olympians finished their first season as Western Division Leaders (the league was made up of three divisions). Although the Olympians were defeated in the second round of the playoffs, the season was a success both on the court and at the ticket office. Groza and Beard quickly emerged as two of the league's brightest stars. At the end of the 1949/50 season both were among the league's top ten scorers and Groza, with a 23.4 points per game average, finished second to the Minneapolis Lakers' great center George Mikan and his 27.4 average. Beard and Groza played just one

Five stars of the 1953/54 Wildcat squad, UK's first undefeated team since 1911/12, pose with a beauty queen. Left to right: Phil Grawemeyer, Bill Evans, Lou Tsioropoulos, and co-captains Cliff Hagan and Frank Ramsey.

more season before the scandal broke. Claiming it was necessary to protect the reputation of the young league, Commissioner Maurice Podoloff declared the two players "ineligible for life" and forced them to sell their shares in the Olympians for a fraction of the real worth. Spivey's fate was equally tragic. Even though he was never found guilty of wrongdoing, Spivey was banned for life from playing in the NBA even before he had a chance to play his first pro game.

Rupp and the university were penalized for one year; Groza, Beard, and the other players paid for their mistakes with their careers. Each was successful in picking up the pieces of his life, but the full potential of every one for an athletic career went unfulfilled.

During the 1952/53 season the Wildcats were prohibited from intercollegiate play but not from practice or intrasquad scrimmages. Rupp and Lancaster used the season, as Laudeman noted in *The Rupp Years*, "to polish up the team's offense and defense without the pressure of preparing for a particular game." The team also held four public scrimmages which attracted a total of nearly 35,000 spectators. The smallest turnout was on the worst night of the entire winter when 6,500 fans braved the cold and the icy streets to attend a scrimmage between a squad composed of varsity players and the freshmen. The spectators learned at these scrimmages that UK would be loaded with talent when the 1953/54 season rolled around.

Led by the "Big Three"—Cliff Hagan, Frank Ramsey, and Lou Tsioropoulos—the Wildcats returned to the basketball wars with a convincing 86-59 drubbing of Temple University before more than 13,000 screaming fans at the Coliseum on December 5, 1953. Hagan, in particular, had a sensational game as he broke the SEC single-game scoring record with fifty-one points. Although he was only 6'4" the hook-shooting Hagan performed brilliantly at center throughout the season. He had one of the smoothest and most effective hook shots in the history of the game and was an excellent rebounder. While Hagan was small for a college center, Ramsey at 6'3" was taller than most guards in the 1950s. In addition to size Ramsey was fast, aggressive under the boards, and a good but not great outside shooter. His points usually came from driving layups, rebounds, or the fastbreak. Few opponents were able to stop him when he moved to the basket. He was also an excellent defensive player. Both Hagan and Ramsey were named All-Americans for the second time. According to teammate Phil Grawemeyer, the 6'5" Tsioropoulos, who made the All-SEC second team in 1954, was the team workhorse. "A lot of people didn't realize it," Grawemeyer observed, "but he was a good shooter. He didn't get much of a chance to show what he could do because we needed other things he could do more." Among other things Tsioropoulos "was an excellent rebounder and a terrific defensive man. If we needed it he could even guard a guard. He was fast, he was strong, and he was tough."

The Wildcats swept through the regular season undefeated and whipped LSU in a playoff to determine the league champion and representative to the NCAA tournament. The Cats declined an invitation, however, when the NCAA declared Hagan, Ramsey, and Tsioropoulos ineligible to participate in the tournament because they were no longer undergraduates. It is indeed ironic, as Hagan noted in an interview, that "we were penalized for the year we were forced to sit out and that was for something we had not been involved in. If we had taken five years to graduate we wouldn't have had a problem. So we were penalized for trying to do the right thing. Isn't that something?"

Thus UK's "Golden Decade" ended on a bittersweet note. The Big Blue crowned an era of brilliant basketball performance with a perfect regular-season record, a rare achievement indeed. What happened off the court proved once again to be the Wildcats' undoing. For the second season in a row the lingering effects of the scandal denied UK's three best players the opportunity to compete for the national championship even though there was no suspicion of personal involvement on their part.

In the four years from 1948 through 1951 Adolph Rupp made college basketball history when his teams won the NCAA tournament an unprecedented three times. The Baron would win only one more national championship in the remainder of his long career and that triumph would appear, even to Rupp, to be something of a fluke.

7

The Afterglow

During Adolph Rupp's last eighteen seasons as head coach (1954/55-1971/72) the Wildcats compiled a record of 384-107 for a winning percentage of .782. Although no longer perennial SEC champions, the Big Blue won the conference title outright nine of the eighteen seasons and shared it in another two. Interestingly, UK not only participated in NCAA postseason play each of the eleven seasons it won or shared the conference title but also represented the SEC three other times: in 1956 when Alabama refused an invitation because it might have to play against teams containing black players, and in 1959 and 1961 when Mississippi State declined for the same reason. Thus UK appeared in fourteen of the eighteen NCAA tournaments played between 1955 and 1972 but did not approach the glittering record of success achieved by Big Blue squads of the late forties and early fifties. Only twice during these years were the Wildcats able to get beyond the regionals. In 1958 the "Fiddlin' Five" won the national championship and in 1966 "Rupp's Runts" were runners-up.

Lack of greater success in postseason play as well as with regular-season conference and intersectional foes was a source of frustration for the aging Rupp. All through his career, but particularly during his last two decades of coaching at UK, Rupp exhibited great concern about records and reputation. In an interview, Ned Jennings noted that when he played at UK (1957-61), the Baron made the team very conscious of the fact that "he had never been beaten on TV, never been below .500, never lost an opening game, anything that was a first." Jennings recalled a December 28,

1959, game against Ohio State and its sophomore stars Jerry Lucas, John Havlicek, and Mel Nowell. "They had us down pretty good at the half. Nobody had ever scored 100 points on us on UK's floor and that was his main concern at halftime. 'Just slow the game down,' he said. Well, we wound up beating them [96-93] but his big worry was that someone would set a record against him."

Despite his many records and achievements, Rupp was in some ways a tragic figure during the last part of his career. These years were filled with physical pain and an increasing sense of professional frustration, in large part because of the spectacular success of John Wooden and the UCLA Bruins.

Prior to Wooden's amazing achievements in the sixties and seventies only Rupp and UK had won as many as four NCAA titles and only UK, Oklahoma A&M, San Francisco, and Cincinnati had won two in a row. The Baron wanted very badly to be the first coach to capture five titles. Instead, this honor went to Wooden, the "Wizard of Westwood." Wooden's Bruins did not stop with five NCAA championships, however. In the twelve years between 1964 and 1975 the Bruins won ten NCAA titles. In addition, UCLA set a collegiate record of eighty-seven straight victories, and three of Wooden's squads completed undefeated seasons—two during the career of Lew Alcindor (later Kareem Abdul-Jabbar) and one during that of Bill Walton. To Larry Fox this was "a dynasty unmatched and unapproached in college basketball" history. In fact, Fox maintained, Wooden's achievement far exceeded that of pro basketball's best—Red Auerbach's

---

eight straight and eleven of thirteen NBA championships with the Boston Celtics. "Wooden had to keep his streak going with a continuously changing cast: no player could remain more than three seasons. With small teams, big teams, shooting teams, defensive teams, Wooden kept on winning."

To a man as jealous of his achievements and reputation as was Adolph Rupp, John Wooden's outstanding success during the twilight years of the Baron's career was undoubtedly a source of frustration and bitterness. In addition, Rupp during this period suffered greatly from physical ailments. "In fact," Harry Lancaster observed in an interview, Rupp "didn't coach the last fifteen years he was here. He was out of it as soon as the game started." Responsibility for directing the team during the game, as several knowledgeable people have noted, fell to Lancaster, who apparently was always able to maintain a level head, even during the most tension-packed moments of a contest. Rupp "was a sick man," Lancaster continued. "He had back problems. He had had his spinal column fused and that bothered him. . . . Then he wound up as a diabetic and had a hole in one foot that wouldn't heal. Rupp suffered a lot of pain." During Rupp's later years, according to Lancaster, "there was drinking and it was noticeable on his Sunday night [television] program."

In addition to various health problems, Rupp had another major concern: the increasing importance during the late fifties and the sixties of the black athlete. During the fifties Wilt Chamberlain, with his intimidating dunk shot, and the defensive genius Bill Russell helped revolutionize the college game. On offense the use of the jump shot and the dunk permitted play to move closer to the basket than in the era of the two-hand shot from the chest. This change, in turn, placed increased emphasis on defense especially on the use of a variety of zones. It was difficult for Rupp to adjust to the new style of play. As one former player theorized, the Baron "didn't really understand zones because he had seldom been forced to play against a zone." Rupp and Harry Lancaster did finally make use of the zone in the mid-sixties, but with great reluctance.

With his devastating zone press, John Wooden demonstrated that he recognized and accepted the growing importance of the defensive game. Wooden also made excellent use of black players to develop the UCLA dynasty, among them Walt Hazzard, Lucius Allen, Curtis Rowe, Sidney Wicks, Henry Bibby, and perhaps the greatest player in basketball history, Kareem Abdul-Jabbar.

There is some disagreement about Rupp's real attitude toward blacks. Black students at UK during the mid-sixties charged that Rupp was a racist who had no intention of recruiting or coaching black players. Bill Russell, a star player and later a playing coach with the Boston Celtics of the NBA, agreed. In his autobiography *Second Wind: The Memoirs of an Opinionated Man*, Russell wrote of Rupp: "I know many players who had been coached by him at the University of Kentucky, I'd met him myself, and nothing I ever saw or heard of him contradicted my impression that he was one of the more devout racists in sports. He was known for the delight he took in making nasty remarks about niggers and Jews, and for his determination never to have black players at the University of Kentucky." Rupp apologists, on the other hand, maintained that the Baron was indifferent to race. His only interest was an athlete's playing ability and he would have recruited blacks if the conference had permitted him to do so. On Rupp's behalf it should be said that he did schedule games with intersectional rivals that had black players. UK played away games against blacks as early as the 1940s. The first black to play on UK's home court, according to Bobby Watson, was St. John's University's Sollie Walker. The Wildcats had played the St. John's Redmen several times at Madison Square Garden but the December 17, 1951, game at Memorial Coliseum was the Redmen's first visit to Kentucky. It was not a pleasant experience for the visitors—St. John's was thoroughly whipped, 81-40.

Competing against an occasional black in intersectional play was not the same, though, as actually recruiting blacks. The excuse that Rupp did not recruit blacks because the SEC would not permit it is spurious. On the contrary, Harry Lancaster recalled in a 1983 interview, "There was no regulation within the SEC or even here at UK against recruiting blacks. In fact, when John Oswald was president here [1963-68] he drove Adolph crazy telling him to recruit blacks." Lancaster noted that "Adolph always used the excuse that he didn't want to recruit one and have him sitting on the bench. Oswald would answer, 'You've got whites sitting on the bench and you don't seem to object to that. What's the difference if a black sits on the bench?' Adolph would come back from talking with Oswald and say, 'That son of a bitch is going to drive me crazy. He's unreasonable. He's unreasonable.' "

By the 1960s the Baron was a dominant figure not only in the League but nationally. Throughout his career he had been an innovator who was not afraid to take chances. Yet instead of pioneering within his conference, Rupp waited until Vanderbilt, a private university, integrated the SEC before he signed his first black, Tom Payne of Louisville, to a scholarship. With great reluctance one is led to the conclusion that Rupp

did not recruit blacks earlier because he did not want to.

In a sense Rupp was a captive of the great success he had enjoyed during his "Golden Decade" from 1943/44 to 1953/54. During that period the Baron was freed from the need to recruit star players actively. Although he did often engage in personal recruitment, he seldom needed to because excellent ballplayers were eager to come to him. In addition, the method of recruitment was different in the forties than later. Instead of having to go to the players, coaches were permitted to bring high school seniors to the college campus for tryouts. As Ken Rollins, Cliff Hagan, and other stars of the era noted in interviews, Rupp brought droves of players to Lexington for tryouts. Rollins, for example, was brought in with forty-nine other athletes for a week of workouts. Only three of this group were offered scholarships. Other groups worked out in the weeks before and after the Rollins contingent. By all accounts Rupp and his assistants, McBrayer and Lancaster, were masters of this type of recruitment. In the aftermath of the basketball scandals of 1951, campus workouts were prohibited. By the late fifties droves of outstandingly talented players were no longer knocking at Rupp's door begging to be permitted to play at UK. In addition, quality athletes tended increasingly to be blacks.

The changing environment was evident as early as the 1954/55 season when Rupp searched for a replacement at center for All-American Cliff Hagan. Dissatisfied with the players coming up to the varsity from the freshman team and with the reserve centers returning from the undefeated 1953/54 squad, Rupp turned to the junior college ranks for help. At Lon Morris Junior College in Jacksonville, Texas, the Baron found and recruited Bob Burrow, the nation's leading junior college scorer and the JC "Player of the Year" for 1954. The 6'7" Burrow possessed a variety of shots, was a powerful rebounder, and more than held his own on defense. The Texan was named to the All-SEC team in both 1955 and 1956 and was an All-American in the latter year. Rupp was so pleased with Burrow that he turned often to junior colleges in the following years with results that were sometimes, but not always, worthwhile. For example, while Adrian Smith became a starting guard on the 1958 NCAA championship team and guards Bennie Coffman and Sid Cohen made important contributions in the 1958/59 and 1959/60 seasons, the highly talented and eagerly awaited Vince Del Negro, a center and forward, and Doug Pendygraft, a guard, proved to be bitter disappointments in 1960/61. In large part because of their experience with Del Negro and Pendygraft, and although UK during the early sixties was in desperate need of quality players, Rupp and Lancaster discontinued recruiting in the junior colleges.

Cotton Nash, a three-time All-American (1962-64), ruefully recalled UK's recruiting problem during the early sixties. In an interview Nash noted that for lack of taller players he had to play at center, although he believed he would have been more effective at a forward position. "I'm just sorry Rupp didn't [actively recruit] because I spent four years there at 6'5" and he couldn't find anyone bigger than me to bring in to play center and let me get out there at forward. I didn't want to play center," Nash emphasized. "I'd have preferred not to play there. The only thing I've regretted was that he didn't go out and recruit some bigger guys to go with us little guys." During his senior season, 1963/64, the Wildcats' front line consisted of sophomore Larry Conley and senior Ted Deekin, both 6'3", at forward and the 6'5" Nash at center. The backcourt consisted of Terry Mobley and Randy Embry. "We had to emphasize the fastbreak because we were always outmanned physically. Then toward the end of my last year we even put in a zone defense. UK teams had always been strictly man-to-man on defense before that."

The early 1960s was a traumatic period for ardent fans of the Big Blue. In fact, during the six seasons from 1959/60 through 1964/65 their team won only one SEC championship (1963/64), shared another (1961/62), and lost an average of eight and a half games a year, a previously unimaginable figure. By ordinary standards UK's record during this six-year period was a good one, a total of 112 victories and a winning percentage of .717. But Wildcat fans had come to expect something more than "good." Little did they realize that the worst was yet to come. After a rebound in 1965/66 which boasted a 32-2 season record, an SEC championship, and second place in the NCAA tournament, the 1966/67 season brought disaster—a 13-13 season. This was the nadir of Adolph Rupp's long and illustrious career. For the first time fans and sportswriters seriously suggested that the game had passed by the Man in the Brown Suit, and that he should consider retirement. Instead, the Baron coached five more seasons and proved that he could return UK to a position of dominance within the SEC, winning or sharing the championship each of the five seasons. Success in the NCAA tournament, however, still proved to be an elusive goal.

Although it was not recognized at the time, the downward slide had begun in the 1954/55 season. On the eve of the season everyone connected with UK basketball, from coaches to fans, expected the seem-

ingly endless successes of the preceding decade to continue. The Wildcats compiled an excellent 22-2 record, but the two losses, both to Georgia Tech, may have been harbingers of future problems within the SEC. That, at any rate, is the opinion of Phil Grawemeyer, who was a starting forward on the 1954/55 team. "I believe that was the beginning of a change in the SEC," Grawemeyer stated in an interview. Other schools began to feel that it was possible to beat UK and they devoted greater attention and more resources to basketball. "Not all of them, mind you, but different ones at different times developed strong teams. Through that period after I was in school Mississippi State, Vanderbilt, LSU, Tennessee, Alabama, and Auburn had some good years. The SEC developed to the point where no team had a guarantee it would win the title."

Fans seemed to have ample reason to be confident of UK's chances in 1954/55 because Rupp had another strong team, at least during the early part of the season. The starting five consisted of 6'6" Jerry Bird and 6'8" Phil Grawemeyer at the forwards, 6'7" Bob Burrow at center, and 6'1" Bill Evans and 6' Linville Puckett at guards. It was a well-balanced team with one of the tallest front lines in the country, and with shooting ability and strong rebounders. The Wildcats seemed to have all the ingredients for a second con-

secutive undefeated season. The first loss to Georgia Tech dashed that dream. The second defeat, also at the hands of the Yellow Jackets, was the prelude to an attempted Wildcat rebellion. Following the Tech game in Atlanta the UK team returned to Lexington. Since Rupp had not scheduled a practice the next day, a Sunday, most of the players decided among themselves to take a break and go home. Unfortunately for them, Rupp got wind of their plans, sent someone to check the players' rooms, and called a practice for Sunday. Somehow the players found out about the change and got back to campus in time.

In a 1983 interview, Linville Puckett described the succeeding events. He had not left town because "the girl I was dating, who is now my wife" lived in Lexington. Puckett recalls that on Sunday afternoon he was at the Jack Cook Service Station just down the street from the Coliseum and Stoll Field. Cook's was a meeting place for members of the basketball and football teams. "Well," Puckett reminisced, "I was sitting there at the service station and the players came in and told me that Adolph had found out they had left town, and would I say I had left town, too. So I agreed to say I had gone home." The players had heard that Rupp planned to take some of their privileges away and they agreed that if he did so they would quit the team as a group. They went to the Col-

The 1954/55 starting five plus one. Left to right: Gayle Rose (first reserve guard), Jerry Bird, Bob Burrow, Rupp, Phil Grawemeyer, Bill Evans (captain), and Linville Puckett. The photo was taken before Rupp and Puckett had their run-in.

iseum for the meeting called by Rupp. After asking each player if he had gone home, Rupp announced that he was going to take away their movie passes and $15-a-month laundry allowance for a specified length of time.

Puckett had been asked to serve as the players' spokesman because he had never been afraid to express his views. After Rupp's announcement, Puckett immediately responded, " 'If you need mine for that long you can keep them for the rest of the year.' That kind of shocked him," Puckett noted, "and he went on down the row and every one of them said the same thing. They all agreed that if Rupp was going to do what he said, we would quit. So we did quit. We went outside the Coliseum. Everybody but Bill Evans." Evans, the team captain, was married and had not been involved in any of the plans.

Outside the coliseum the players discussed what had happened and agreed that "if Rupp would let us keep our movie passes and our $15 a month for laundry, we would stay on the team. They [Rupp and Lancaster] sent Evans out to tell us all to come back in. So we went in." Rupp did not, as most accounts of the events claim, attend this second meeting with the team. "Adolph went to his office," recalled Puckett, "and had Harry and Bill Evans speak to us. Harry told us what a mistake we were making if we quit the team, so all of them agreed to go in and practice except me. Old hardheaded me went the other way." Puckett is convinced that everything would have blown over and Rupp would have welcomed him back to the team if the incident had not received widespread publicity. He understood that "the team manager worked for the *Courier-Journal* and quick as he saw what went on he went and called the paper and told them what had happened. When that hit the paper there wasn't anything more that could be done. Happy Chandler got Harry to speak to Adolph, but Adolph said it was all there in the papers and he would look bad if he took me back." Even though the rest of the players returned to the team, they "didn't get to keep their passes and laundry money." According to Puckett, Rupp followed through on his threat to withhold these from players who had quit the team, even temporarily.

Puckett and teammate Billy Bibb transferred to Kentucky Wesleyan, where they joined two other former Wildcats, Logan Gipe and Pete Grigsby. With this nucleus the Owensboro team nearly pulled an upset over Louisville and did defeat Coach Ed Diddle's Western Kentucky Hilltoppers. "It was the first time that Wesleyan beat them in Bowling Green in thirty-nine years," Puckett related.

At UK, reserve Gayle Rose moved into the starting

Wildcat captain Phil Grawemeyer, plagued by injuries during the 1955/56 season, wears a protective headpiece in a December 10 game against Temple.

lineup, but Puckett's departure had an impact felt especially during postseason play. According to Phil Grawemeyer, "The team really missed Puckett because he was a terrific passer. No one else we had was as good." Combined with the loss of two other starters, Puckett's departure was to prove disastrous when UK got into the NCAA regionals.

Grawemeyer was the second player lost to the team. During a close contest with De Paul in Chicago (which UK eventually won 76-72), he fell and broke a leg while driving toward the basket. This was Grawemeyer's second serious injury of the season. Before the season started he had suffered a fractured skull in practice and wore a special headgear through much of the season. At the time he broke his leg, he was averaging thirteen points and thirteen rebounds per game. Despite a slim build he was a strong rebounder, had excellent speed, an accurate jump shot from long range, and a hook shot from around the foul circle. His place in the starting lineup was taken by 6'4"

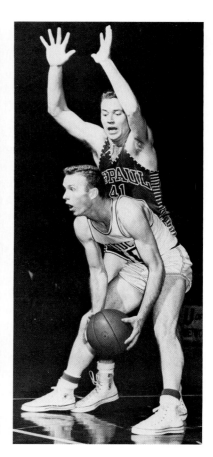

The Wildcat way to victory. *Left,* Bob Burrow guards a Vanderbilt player on February 20, 1956. Vernon Hatton *(center)* and Gerry Calvert *(right)* battle DePaul for a Kentucky victory on December 12, 1955.

sophomore John Brewer, who showed great promise but could not match Grawemeyer's contributions on defense or under the basket. Nevertheless, the Wildcats with Brewer in the starting lineup closed out the regular season with four straight victories over conference foes. For the NCAA regionals UK was to lose yet another regular. Bill Evans, the team leader and an All-SEC performer, was ineligible for postseason play because he was a graduate student. Sophomore Gerry Calvert became a starter at guard and performed well. With only two of the original starting five, UK went down to defeat in the opening round of the Eastern Regionals at Evanston, Illinois.

The 1954/55 team worked so hard and overcame so much adversity that it was dubbed the "Desire Kids." The following season Rupp had regulars Grawemeyer, Burrow, and Bird back for their senior seasons. They were joined in the starting lineup by junior Gerry Calvert and sophomore Vernon Hatton at the guards. Burrow won All-SEC and All-American honors, while Hatton performed so effectively he was selected SEC "Sophomore of the Year." With this blend of experience and youth the Wildcats should have had an excellent year. Instead, they experienced their worst

season since 1942. Team captain Phil Grawemeyer recalled that "nothing seemed to go as it had the year before. We had the players but we just couldn't get it all together and clicking right. I guess coaches see it all the time but can't do anything about it." UK lost its opening game at home, an almost unheard of event. As if this disaster was not enough, the Wildcats also lost the UK Invitational Tournament for the first time since it was inaugurated in the 1951/52 season. Another first UK did not find pleasant was its loss of the SEC championship to Alabama—for the first time since 1942/43. Because Alabama declined an invitation to the NCAA tournament, the Big Blue made its annual appearance in the postseason event but with less than satisfying results. The Wildcats had the misfortune to meet the Iowa Hawkeyes in the finals of the Eastern Regionals on the Hawkeyes' home court. "I guess I learned then how other teams felt when they came into the Coliseum," Grawemeyer laughed, "because I knew there had to be some Kentucky fans there but you couldn't hear them. It was all Iowa and those fans just roared." It was, Grawemeyer summed up, "just one of those years."

With the graduation of the excellent front line of

Grawemeyer, Burrow, and Bird, little was expected of the 1956/57 squad. With Vernon Hatton and team captain Gerry Calvert returning, there was strength at guard but the front line was a question mark. The freshman team had produced only one player of note—but what a player! Stoop-shouldered, slow-moving, and frail-looking off the basketball court, 6'4" Johnny Cox was a whirlwind on it. A native of the Eastern Kentucky mountain community of Hazard, Cox was a star from the beginning of his varsity career. He had an accurate one-handed jump shot from medium range and a devastating hook shot with either hand from closer in, and was an effective rebounder. Cox had an excellent sophomore year which he capped by being named to the All-SEC team.

Even with Johnny Cox in the lineup, the Wildcat front line lacked the overall height, scoring punch, and rebounding skill of the previous season. Rupp found it necessary to use at least six different starting lineups during the 1956/57 season in order to squeeze the most out of the available material. Hatton was injured for a month in midseason and was never, during the remainder of the season, up to the level of performance he had shown in the previous campaign. This put even more pressure on Cox to score. The Wildcats confounded the experts who freely predicted that "this could be the weakest Kentucky team in the past fifteen years." They finished the season with a 23-5 record, won their eighteenth SEC title, and appeared once again in the NCAA tournament. The Big Blue actually was favored to sweep the Midwest Regionals because they were to be played at Memorial Coliseum, but the anticipated easy time did not materialize and UK was blitzed by Michigan State, 80-68.

Undoubtedly the high point of Adolph Rupp's last eighteen years as a college coach was UK's victory over Seattle University and its great star Elgin Baylor in the finals of the NCAA tournament on March 22, 1958. This victory, which fulfilled the Baron's vow in the aftermath of the gambling scandal to win another national title and return himself and UK to the top of the college basketball world, also was one of the great, albeit pleasant, surprises of Rupp's long career.

Entering the 1957/58 season, UK boasted a veteran team composed largely of seniors. Rupp quickly became disillusioned about the team's chances as it lost three early-season games, including a UK Invitational

Few held out much hope for the 1957/58 team at the beginning of the season. They emerged as NCAA champs. Front row, l-r: Rupp, Adrian Smith, John Crigler, Ed Beck, Don Mills, Johnny Cox, Vernon Hatton, and assistant coach Lancaster. Back row: student manager Jay Atkerson, Earl Adkins, Bill Smith, Phil Johnson, Bill Cassady, Lincoln Collinsworth, and Harold Ross.

Tournament contest with West Virginia. "We've got fiddlers, that's all," Rupp confided to the press. "They're pretty good fiddlers; be right entertaining at a barn dance. But I'll tell you, you need violinists to play in Carnegie Hall. We don't have any violinists." By that, said Phil Johnson in an interview, Rupp meant that UK no longer had the type of player that had characterized the team during the golden era.

The success of the 1958 team, noted Harry Lancaster, was entirely unexpected. Compared to UK's previous NCAA championship squads, "we had no real ability at all but we had everybody doing the thing he could do best." Despite, or perhaps because of, the lack of individual talents this was a well-balanced team on which each player had a role he understood and accepted. Ed Beck was a fine rebounder and a very effective defensive center. "He couldn't score," Lancaster stated, "but if he could cut that high-scoring center on the other team down from twenty-five or thirty points to eight or nine, which was about Ed's average, why it leveled things down beautifully." The other starters were John Cox and John Crigler at the forwards and Vernon Hatton and Adrian Smith at the guards. Together they comprised the "Fiddlin' Five." Cox was an excellent shot, especially from the outside, and Hatton thrived on pressure, as he proved several times during his career as a Wildcat. Smith was an underrated player while at UK but he proved his ability during a long and successful career in the NBA with the Cincinnati Royals.

To Lancaster, "the unknown and unsung player on the team" was John Crigler. "He had no particular abilities but he was the only true driver we had. Cox had a fine jump shot but he wasn't fast and didn't drive well to the basket." Thus it is surprising that in the title game of the NCAA tournament the Seattle coach, John Castellani, assigned his All-American forward Elgin Baylor to guard Crigler. "We couldn't believe our good luck," Lancaster recalled with a chuckle. "We had Crigler drive on Baylor and almost immediately we had three fouls on him. He was in foul trouble the rest of the game." UK won by the surprisingly wide margin of twelve points, 84-72.

Rupp's fourth NCAA championship was certainly not a fluke. As Tev Laudeman noted in *The Rupp Years*, three of UK's six defeats in the 1958 season were by only one point, and the Cats played "the toughest schedule in the school's history up to that time. Almost every non-conference opponent was a veteran team, on the way to winning a conference championship or finishing high in the race." The "Fiddlin' Five" squad was helped by a factor Laudeman does not mention— geography. The NCAA tournament field at the time

contained only twenty four teams, so that UK had to play only four games to win the championship, and all four were played in the state of Kentucky before highly vocal and supportive Wildcat fans. The first two games, against Miami of Ohio and Notre Dame, were played at Memorial Coliseum in Lexington, while the tournament finals were played only eighty miles away in Louisville, where the Big Blue always enjoyed ardent support.

Full and effective use of the home court and home fan advantage also underlines the fact that the "Fiddlin' Five" were a team of opportunists. Most certainly it was not a great team, but it was a successful one. Several other teams during Rupp's last years had better individual talents and more successful regular-season records, but for one reason or another each fell short in the NCAA tournament. The very next year, in fact, with All-American Johnny Cox and All-SEC Bill Lickert leading the way, UK compiled an excellent 23-2 regular-season record. Amazingly, this was only good enough for second place in the final conference standings behind Coach James "Babe" McCarthy and his Mississippi State Bulldogs. Fortunately for the Big

Rupp with Johnny Cox, the lone returning starter from the "Fiddlin' Five" championship team, show off a warm-up jacket listing UK's four NCAA titles, at the time an unprecedented accomplishment.

Table 4. Record of Adolph Rupp-Coached Teams, Selected Years, 1961/62–1970/71

Season	Regular Season		NCAA	
	Won	Lost	Won	Lost
1961/62	22	2	1	1
1963/64	21	4	0	2
1965/66	24	1	3	1
1967/68	21	4	1	1
1968/69	22	4	1	1
1969/70	25	1	1	1
1970/71	22	4	0	2

Three-time All-American Cotton Nash (1962, 1963, 1964) goes in for a layup despite close guarding by two St. Louis defenders. UK emerged the victors (86-77) in this December 11, 1961, contest.

Blue, the Bulldogs refused to participate in the NCAA tournament because they would have had to play teams with blacks on them. UK eagerly departed for Evanston, Illinois, were it met the University of Louisville in the opening round of the Mideast Regionals. Although the Cardinals had a lackluster 17-10 record, in their contest with the Wildcats they played a half-court pressing defense that UK could not solve, and crushed the Cats 76-61. "We had them down by seventeen points in the first half," recalled Don Mills, "but they started using that press. It was the first time we faced the press in a game all season. For some reason we didn't work on defensing the press in practice, either. Then our shooting turned cold and when they started coming back the Evanston crowd got behind them and that was a big help for them, too. But the press was probably the big factor."

It was difficult to live down the defeat, Dick Parsons related in an interview. Although only a sophomore, Parsons was a starting guard on the 1958/59 team. "I'll never forget what Coach Rupp said after the game: 'By God,' he said, 'I'll tell you one thing, you'll never forget this game.' And we haven't," noted Parsons ruefully. "No one will let us forget." Perhaps Louisville's victory over the Wildcats in the 1983 NCAA regionals will soften the memory of the 1959 contest.

The UK Wildcats compiled good regular-season records and won or shared conference titles in 1961/62, 1963/64, 1965/66, and 1967/68 through 1970/71. With one exception, the Big Blue ended each season in the NCAA regionals.

The exception was the 1965/66 season, when "Rupp's Runts," with no starter taller than 6'5", nearly won a fifth NCAA championship for the Baron. In an interview published in the June 27, 1982, *Courier-Journal*, Pat Riley recalled that the Runts "started out

as a team that people didn't have a whole lot of faith in. . . . We were very small and we had lost a lot of our top players. So we started out in the preseason as a team that wouldn't be one of the contenders." During the previous season the Wildcats had struggled to a miserable 15-10 record. The 1964/65 team had contained three effective seniors—Randy Embry, Terry Mobley, and John Adams—and four of the stars of the following season—juniors Larry Conley and Tom Kron and sophomores, Pat Riley and Louie Dampier. Little wonder UK fans were caught unaware by the stunning achievements of the team. "But once we started to play," Riley observed, "it was like a snowball going downhill, we began to believe that we were a great team."

"Rupp's Runts" may not have been a great team overall, but they were, in the opinion of Harry Lancaster, "one of the finest that we ever had for moving the basketball." Lancaster also noted, in a 1980 interview, that "they were so intelligent and even though small they were very quick." Riley freely acknowl-

The Afterglow 83

edged the vital contributions of Larry Conley and Tom Kron. He believed the contributions "were never chronicled the way they should have been. They literally sacrificed themselves for the team. Louie Dampier and I were parasites off what they did." Although scoring stars in high school, Conley and Kron decided that with so many good shooters on the team they could contribute more to the success of the Wildcats as playmakers and passers than as scorers. "They were the reasons," Riley continued, that he and Dampier were named All-Americans, "though I didn't fully appreciate it until I was in the pros. It's easy to shoot the ball and not have a whole lot of other responsibilities." Conley and Kron, he emphasized, "did what it took to win." The fifth member of the starting team, and the only sophomore, was Thad Jaracz. Although only 6'5" Jaracz played center and contributed a good shooting touch from close to the basket as well as speed and quickness. Spelling Jaracz when UK needed more size in the pivot was another sophomore, 6'8" Cliff Berger.

With Jaracz in the starting lineup, "Rupp's Runts" averaged 6'3" in height, with Riley and Conley (both 6'3") at the forwards, and Dampier (6') and Kron (6'5") at the guards. Jim LeMaster, now Majority Floor Leader in the Kentucky House of Representatives, was a sophomore guard on the Runts' team. In an interview, LeMaster maintained that the principal ingredients in the team's success "were quickness and teamwork. There was just an excellent chemistry on that team. Everybody, the whole team, just worked so well together. And all the players were just so unselfish." LeMaster also noted that all the starters and most of the reserves were good shooters but for the good of the team each was a role-player. Kron was the playmaker as well as the defensive star of the team; when UK played the one-three-one zone, he played the point. Conley had a fine touch but concentrated on passing, at which he was excellent. The best shooters on the squad, according to LeMaster, were Dampier and Riley, while Riley and Jaracz were the best rebounders. The only player with leaping ability was Riley. "We got our rebounds with team defense and blocking out. That is, with good fundamentals."

Like Riley, LeMaster emphasized that before the season not much was expected of the 1965/66 team, but "once we started playing everything seemed to jell." Because of their lack of size the Runts emphasized the fastbreak and were so effective that they had a perfect record until the final week of the regular season. The only loss came in the next-to-last game of the season against Tennessee in Knoxville. Ironi-

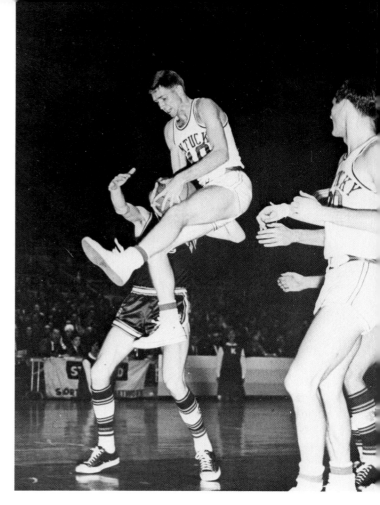

Larry Conley, one of the unsung heroes of "Rupp's Runts" in 1965/66. He and guard Tom Kron sacrificed their own records for the good of the team.

cally, UK at home had trimmed the Vols just the week before by fourteen points.

In the NCAA regionals played in Iowa City the Cats faced two tall and talented teams and defeated both. In the first game, on March 11, 1966, UK played Dayton with its 6'11" center, Henry Finkel, who later would play with the perennial NBA champion Boston Celtics. The next day the Wildcats outplayed All-American Cazzie Russell and the Michigan Wolverines. The following weekend the Big Blue traveled to College Park, Maryland, for the NCAA finals. UK faced the Duke Blue Devils, the second-ranked team in the nation, in a March 18 contest that many rate one of the best played and most exciting college games ever played. Although Kron and Conley were weakened by flu, the Cats outplayed the Blue Devils and won by four points, 83-79. It was an important victory but there was still one more game to play, against lightly-regarded Texas Western (now the University of Texas, El Paso).

Harry Lancaster admitted in an interview that "when we beat Duke on Friday night we thought we had it won." The Cats watched Texas Western defeat Utah and, according to LeMaster, were not impressed. At that time the semifinal and final games were played on successive days, and UK was drained emotionally from the Duke game, which it had regarded as the more important contest. Physical weakness also affected the players. Joining flu-sufferers Kron and Conley on the ailing list was Pat Riley, who turned up on game day, March 18, with a badly infected foot which apparently was treated incorrectly. Despite the physical problems, the Wildcats still seemed to have too much talent and experience for Texas Western, the underdog, to overcome. Almost no one thought the Texas team had any chance of defeating the mighty Wildcats with their proud tradition and experienced coaches.

Once the game started, the Big Blue found that their rivals were neither intimidated by the pressure nor overwhelmed by press clippings. After about five minutes of play in the first half, and with the score tied at 9, Texas Western guard Bobby Joe Hill twice stole the ball from UK dribblers at midcourt. Texas Western was never behind after that. The steals, although they had a devastating effect on the Cats, were not the only reason for the upset. Riley, for example, relates that he "can still see 'Big Daddy' Lattin dunking over our one-three-one zone and Neville Shed stuffing home a thunder dunk." UK lost 72-65.

UK partisans emphasize the role of overconfidence and illness in the game's outcome, but these are probably not the most important reasons. *Courier-Journal* Sports Editor Billy Reed's emphasis on the role of race seems to be more accurate. In a March 2, 1982, article, Reed observed, "In retrospect, that was a historic game. It told everyone, in case the point had been missed, that the game had changed, never to be the same again. The five black starters for Texas Western were too quick for Rupp's all-white team." According to Reed, the only consolation that could be found was the statement of an unidentified sports editor at the annual team banquet that "at least we're still the best white team in the country." Reed hastened to add that "the statement offended the sensibilities not only of anti-racists, but of UK followers who understood the lesson of the Texas Western game." Perhaps that lesson was learned, but one thing the game results did not change during the remainder of Rupp's tenure was recruiting. At that time the coaching staff included one of the finest recruiters in the college game, Joe B. Hall, who had joined the staff that season with the primary responsibility for recruiting. During Rupp's last years at UK, Hall recruited several talented players but, with the exception of Tom Payne, all were white. The responsibility for this exclusive attitude obviously was not Hall's. As he had proved before he joined the Wildcat staff as well as since he became UK head coach, Hall is concerned about talent rather than color.

The Wildcats' biggest need during the 1960s probably was a dominating center. Ironically the state produced two during the decade but neither one attended UK. Both were black. Wes Unseld, twice named an All-American at the University of Louisville, was a high school senior in 1964. One can only wonder about how great the 1966 UK team would have been with Unseld at center, and whether the 1967 season would have turned out differently. Later in the decade 7' Jim McDaniels led Western Kentucky to a three-year record of sixty-five wins, nineteen losses, two Ohio Valley Conference championships, and a third-place finish in the 1971 NCAA tournament. UK was Western's victim in the opening game of the 1971 Mideast Regionals in Athens, Georgia, the first time the two ever met. All five of Western's starters were native Kentuckians and all were black.

Forward Pat Riley's gesture epitomizes the frustration of the Cats as they go down to a 72-65 defeat in the 1966 NCAA tournament against an all-black team from Texas Western.

Louie Dampier evades two Illinois defenders, while Thad Jaracz (55) awaits a possible rebound. Illinois won the December 5, 1966, game 98-97 in overtime.

If 1966 with its glittering won-lost record and second-place finish in the NCAA was a pleasant surprise for the Wildcat faithful, the following season was a crushing disappointment. Despite the presence of Riley and Dampier, UK limped to a 13-13 record, the worst in Rupp's long career. But help was on the way. In 1966, his first season as recruiter, Joe Hall signed a large and talented group of players to scholarships. Led by 6'8" Dan Issel, 6'4" Mike Casey, and 6'4" Mike Pratt, coach Harry Lancaster's freshman team stormed to an 18-2 record. The frosh were so talented and successful that they attracted more fan interest and support than the varsity team.

For the varsity, 1966/67 was a long and miserable

season made more difficult by an injury to Pat Riley and a run-in between Rupp and starting guard Bob Tallent. Because of back problems growing out of a water skiing accident suffered in the summer of 1966, Riley, who had been a superb rebounder and prolific scorer during the preceding season, was below par the entire season. Tallent, a fine outside shooter with excellent range, was faulted by Rupp for making too many mistakes and for not being the ballhandler and playmaker that his predecessor Tommy Kron had been. In his own way, Rupp made Tallent, the team, the media, and through them the UK fans fully aware of his feelings. In a February 13 game against Tennessee in Knoxville, the drama came to an unfortunate but perhaps inevitable conclusion. During the contest, in which UK was badly outplayed and lost 76-57, Tallent made a mistake and was immediately pulled from the game. When he reached the bench, the junior guard and Rupp "exchanged bitter words." In the locker room after the conclusion of the game the two exchanged more words. When the team returned to Lexington, Rupp had the equipment manager inform Tallent that his services would no longer be needed. The Baron then informed the press that, among other things, Tallent could not play well under game pressure. Probably because of the team's poor season performance, this behavior by Rupp was widely criticized. The university newspaper suggested that perhaps it was Rupp who was "choking," while UK President Oswald reprimanded the coach for his treatment of Tallent.

At the end of the season UK not only had a 13-13 record but its performance within the SEC was a disaster. The Cats won only eight of eighteen conference games and tied for fifth place in the final standings. Hated Tennessee won the SEC championship. Furthermore, the Vols as well as Vanderbilt and Florida swept their two-game series with the Wildcats. During the season UK was routed by Cornell (92-77), Florida (89-72), Tennessee (76-57), Alabama (81-71), Auburn (60-49), and Vanderbilt (110-94).

Serious suggestions were advanced that it might be time for the Man in the Brown Suit to consider retiring. The sixty-six-year-old Rupp, of course, would hear none of it. He was well aware that Hall had collected an excellent crop of players. It was not beyond the realm of possibility that the Issel-Casey-Pratt group could bring Rupp his fifth NCAA title before they completed their eligibility at UK, especially if Hall continued to stock the UK team with choice athletes. And Hall certainly fulfilled that responsibility. In the 1968/69 season forward Larry Steele, a future NBA star, and guard Bob McCowan joined the varsity. The

Part of Rupp's refusal to retire after the disastrous 1966/67 season was the large crop of talented players garnered by Joe Hall's recruiting efforts, and the hope of a fifth NCAA championship. *Left,* Rupp with (l-r) Mike Casey, Dan Issel, and Mike Pratt, all signed by Hall in his first year as recruiter. *Below,* more of Hall's recruits in a December 5, 1970, win against Michigan: Tom Parker (12), Tom Payne (54), Larry Steele (25), and Mike Casey (34). Payne was UK's first black player.

next season brought forwards Randy Noll and Tom Parker, the latter with his deadly left-handed outside jump shot, and two tall and talented guards, Stan Key and Kent Hollenbeck, along with 6′ 8 1/2″ center Mark Soderberg. In 1970/71 began the varsity careers of 6′11″ Jim Andrews and 7′ Tom Payne as well as two powerful forwards, Dan Perry and Larry Stamper.

Unfortunately for the team's hopes, injuries and defections depleted the Wildcat ranks. While Issel, Casey, and Pratt started together at UK, they did not finish together. Casey, a fiery competitor and excellent offensive player, suffered a broken leg in an auto accident during the summer between his junior and senior years and had to sit out the 1969/70 season. Although he returned to the starting lineup the following season, he was unable to regain the quickness and speed that had distinguished his play and made him a virtual one-man fastbreak before the accident.

The 1969/70 UK team was talented. The usual starting lineup was Pratt and Steele at the forwards, Issel at center, and senior Terry Mills and junior Jim Dinwiddie at guards. Reserves included forwards Tom Parker and Randy Noll, center Mark Soderberg, and guards Bob McCowan, Bill Busey, Stan Key, and Kent Hollenbeck. The Cats compiled a 25-1 regular season record but lost to Jacksonville and its 7′ center Artis Gilmore by a score of 106-100 in the NCAA regionals. It is fascinating to contemplate (as Issel did in a June 1983 interview) the possible results if Casey, a great clutch performer, had been available and in top con-

Dan Issel, who played from 1967/68 through 1969/70, holds the men's career scoring record as well as the single-game scoring record for UK. Here he shoots against the LSU Tigers.

Right, Stan Key (30) dribbles and Mike Pratt (22) watches as UK trounces Georgia 116-86 on February 16, 1970.

dition. But Casey, of course, was not available. One of the hazards of big-time athletics is injury. A number of other key performers were lost for varying periods during this and other seasons because of injuries. Obviously the purpose of dependable reserves is to fill in for injured regulars. Hence a serious drain on UK was the loss of several talented reserve players, including Noll and Soderberg, who transferred to other schools. One other player, Tom Payne, made himself available for the NBA draft after only one varsity season at UK and was drafted by the Atlanta Hawks.

During the 1969/70 season Issel broke the UK career scoring record set by Cotton Nash in 1964. Before the season began, Issel recalled in an interview, Rupp promised that he would do everything he could to help break Nash's record if Issel would participate in the conditioning program that Assistant Coach Joe Hall had introduced at UK. The grueling program was very unpopular with the team, and Issel's cooperation was essential to head off a rebellion. This story has been recounted before but the aftermath of his record-setting performance at Oxford, Mississippi, on February 7, 1970, has not. During the season Rupp had been true to his word and had left Issel in games even after the outcome was decided in favor of UK. Finally, in the February 7 game against the University of Mississippi, which the Wildcats won 120-85, Issel broke the UK single-game record as well as the career record. "After the game," Issel related, "Coach Rupp came up to me

Above, high-flying Larry Steele helped UK whip Michigan 104-93 on December 5, 1970. Steele went on to a long and successful career in the NBA. Left, Ronnie Lyons executes a layup hook, a shot made necessary by his 5'9" height, to boost UK to an 85-69 victory over Marquette on March 16, 1972. This was the last victory of Adolph Rupp's career.

and said: 'I was kind of sorry to see you break [Cliff] Hagan's record but I'm glad you beat Nash's record.'" Apparently Rupp felt this way because the independent-minded Nash had been outspoken in expressing opinions to and about the Baron. Because Nash was so crucial to the team's success Rupp had been unable to retaliate at the time. Issel's single-game record of 53 points still stands, but a member of the UK Lady Cats team, Valerie Still, now holds the school career mark. She scored 2,763 points in 119 games (from 1978/79 to 1982/83), while Issel scored 2,138 in 83 contests. It might be noted, however, that while Issel's record was set in three seasons of varsity competition, Still played four varsity seasons.

During his last four years as coach, Rupp suffered from a variety of serious physical ailments. In February 1971 he checked into the University Medical Center for treatment of an ulcerated foot which had been bothering him for more than a year. When he returned to the team he had to sit with his foot resting on a stool. Rupp was back in time for the final game of the season at the Coliseum against arch rival Tennessee. It was not a crucial game. The title had been decided five days before at Auburn when the Wildcats scored a nineteen-point victory over the Tigers (102-83). Nevertheless, the Tennessee game, which UK won 84-78, was a "welcome back" for coach Rupp and a tune-up for the upcoming NCAA regionals in Athens, Georgia. At the regionals, despite the presence of 7' Tom Payne and 6'11" Jim Andrews as well as sharpshooting Tom Parker and Larry Steele, the Wildcats were no match for an excellent Western Kentucky team. They suffered a humiliating twenty-four point defeat. The next night, in the consolation game of the regionals, the Blue and White were routed for the second straight game, 91-74, by coach Al McGuire's Marquette Warriors. Tom Parker has recalled that this, his junior season, was a very difficult time because "although we had a lot of talent

UK President Otis Singletary congratulates Adolph Rupp on the achievements of his long and distinguished career in a ceremony marking the Baron of Basketball's retirement, March 6, 1972.

and had a winning year, we never really got it all together. That was the year Coach Rupp was fighting to keep his job and a lot of the things that occurred off the floor had an effect on the way the team performed."

When the Wildcat squad assembled the following October for preseason practice, it was still uncertain whether this would be Rupp's final campaign as coach. The uncertainty persisted throughout the season although university regulations specified seventy as retirement age. Rupp made it very clear that he did not want to retire and applied pressure through the media as well as friends on the Athletics Board to obtain an exemption.

Although no one could be certain at the time that it would be the Baron's "last hurrah," former players, including Tom Parker and Jim Andrews, recall it as a special experience. "Every place we went during my senior year," Parker related, "people gave him a standing ovation. In a way it helped UK because out of respect for Coach Rupp the crowds were a little more mellow than in other years. It was really good to see that at Auburn, Florida, and even Tennessee because it showed they respected the man for what he had done."

At the end of the season Rupp's fate was still in doubt. The UK administration was still waiting, as it had all season, for the Baron to take the initiative and announce his retirement. Rupp refused to do so. Finally, nine days after UK's elimination in the NCAA regionals, the Athletics Board met and voted not to waive the mandatory retirement rule. Rupp was forced into retirement. He received the news with bitterness.

As Tev Laudeman observed in the conclusion to *The Rupp Years*, the Man in the Brown Suit was gone "but he had left a mark of excellence on basketball which could never be erased."

Part III
Joe Hall: Keeper of the Flame

The Passing of the Torch

Joe B. Hall has been head basketball coach at UK since 1972. During that time, he has become one of the most successful coaches in the country. Hall's teams have averaged more than twenty-two victories a season, have won or shared the SEC championship eight times, won the NIT in 1976, and were runners-up in the NCAA tournament in 1975 and national champions in 1978. Yet it is not unusual for callers-in to Hall's radio show to demand of him, as one did recently, "Why don't you just forget your lame excuses and admit you can't coach." Nor is it unusual for newspapers to contain letters from fans similar to one printed in the January 26, 1983, *Herald-Leader*. After describing Hall's numerous shortcomings as a coach and a molder of young men the writer bitterly concluded: "As far as I am concerned, the only real mistake Adolph Rupp ever made was convincing Hall to stay at Kentucky when he might otherwise have gone to St. Louis to build his dynasty. If Joe Hall really cares about the University of Kentucky he will step aside after this year and give the school the chance it needs to be great again."

Like comedian Rodney Dangerfield, Hall often "gets no respect." Yet Hall told reporter Mark Bradley (*Lexington Leader*, February 19, 1982), "I don't care what people say about me as long as they keep the Kentucky program in perspective." Hall's mission, Bradley observed, is "to guard the flame" of UK's basketball tradition, and that means the program. "The important thing to me," Hall has often stated, "is the program, that's Number 1." The program, Reporter Bradley maintained, is "bigger than any player, any

coach. Bigger than the ghost of Adolph Rupp, than the flesh of Joe B. Hall. The Program. Joe Hall says it lovingly, as a priest might speak of The Lord."

A native of Cynthiana in north central Kentucky, where he was born in 1928, Joe Beasman Hall absorbed the Wildcat tradition as he grew up. In a 1980 interview Hall recalled that he and his brother "never missed the radio broadcasts of the UK games" and he still has some of the statistics he compiled while listening. Hall attended Cynthiana High School, earning three letters each in basketball and football and captaining both teams in his senior year. One of the greatest thrills of his life was being invited by Adolph Rupp to try out for a place on the UK squad and being chosen from a group of approximately 150 for a scholarship. Unfortunately for Hall this was the era of the "Fabulous Five," a group he still regards as the greatest team of its era, just as he considers John Wooden's UCLA squads the greatest teams of their era. With little chance to play at UK, Hall transferred after his sophomore season, and with Rupp's help, to Sewanee. After completing his eligibility Hall returned to UK to finish his degree.

Hall's coaching career began in 1956 at Shepherdsville High School in Bullitt County as both basketball and football coach. During his second season the basketball squad compiled a 22-6 record and went to the district finals, winning conference "Coach of the Year" honors for Hall. On the strength of this record Hall was offered, and accepted, a position as assistant coach at Regis College, a small Jesuit institution in Denver. After only one season he was named head

Victory is sweet as the Wildcats hoist Coach Joe Hall aloft after winning the University of Kentucky Invitational Tournament trophy on December 21, 1974.

93

coach and athletic director, and in his five seasons as head coach at Regis he built a powerhouse. Although nominally operating on the small-college level, Hall's teams defeated such schools as Arizona State, Oklahoma State, Oklahoma City, Air Force Academy, Denver, Colorado State, Creighton, Idaho State, and Montana State. Just as he was gaining national prominence for Regis the school's leaders decided to deemphasize basketball by cutting financial support and reducing the number of athletic scholarships awarded. To remain at Regis under these circumstances would have meant professional suicide so Hall moved on, accepting a head coaching position at Central Missouri State College. In his one season there Hall's team had a 19-6 record, won the conference championship, and represented the league in the NCAA tournament.

During the years Hall coached at Regis and Central Missoui he kept in contact with Rupp, and in 1965 accepted an offer to return to his alma mater as an assistant coach with the primary responsibility of recruiting. "Of course, Coach Rupp wanted me for recruiting purposes once before," Hall recalled at a later date, "and I told him I wasn't interested in being on the road all the time. That was while I was at Regis. When I turned him down, I told him if he ever needed a full-time coaching assistant, to call me. Well," Hall

continued, "this time he said if I would take the job that I would be a regular assistant and the whole staff would be involved in recruiting."

Whether or not Rupp and Lancaster participated in the recruiting, the major burden fell on Hall's shoulders, and he performed these duties so effectively that in a short time he earned a reputation as a master recruiter. In his first season on the job Hall collected an excellent group of high school stars from Kentucky, Illinois, Ohio, Alabama, and Tennessee. In addition to Dan Issel the new Wildcats included Kentucky's "Mr. Basketball," Mike Casey; Mike Pratt, one of Ohio's top scorers; Randy Pool, Tennessee's top high school prospect; and Travis Butler, widely regarded as "Alabama's top schoolboy cager in history"; as well as Bill Busey, Jim Dinwiddie, Terry Mills, Benny Spears, and Mort Fraley from Kentucky. In the following years Hall continued to find and sign for UK an excellent collection of prospects, including Larry Steele, Greg Starrick, Bob McCowan, Larry Stamper, Jim Andrews, Ronnie Lyons, Tom Payne, Tom Parker, Randy Noll, Stan Key, Mark Soderberg, and Kent Hollenbeck.

Although he was earning a reputation around the nation as an outstanding prospect for a head coaching position, Hall was, according to Russell Rice, a frustrated and insecure man. A dedicated family man,

In 1948, Joe Hall was a sophomore and in his only varsity season of Wildcat play. Here, Adolph Rupp poses with his eventual successor and Hall's teammates, l-r: Garland Townes, Walt Hirsch, Bob Henne, and Roger Day.

A crew-cut Joe Hall, then an assistant coach and principal recruiter for the Cats, signs Stan Key to an athletic scholarship. Key starred at guard for UK from 1969/70 through 1971/72 and was co-captain of Rupp's last team.

"Hall's worst fears came to roost as he found himself more and more on the road in search of basketball players," Rice maintained in his *Big Blue Machine*. "In addition there was an element of frustration in a job that seemed to hold no future for him." Although Rupp was nearing the mandatory retirement age of seventy, "the Baron showed no signs of accepting retirement unless it was forced on him. It was generally assumed that Harry Lancaster would become head coach when and if Rupp retired." All this changed, however, when Athletic Director Bernie Shively died in December 1967 and Lancaster eventually was named his successor. "Joe was suddenly first in line to succeed Rupp. The problem," Rice noted, "was that Joe had no guarantee that he would even be on the UK basketball staff after Rupp retired." Hall sought assurance that he would be named Rupp's successor but received "nothing concrete," and on April 2, 1969, he forced UK's hand by accepting the head coaching position at St. Louis University.

What happened next is open to dispute. Rupp later claimed that Hall asked if he could have his old job back. According to Hall, Rupp asked through an intermediary that the two meet one more time to discuss the situation. Hall told Oscar Combs (*Kentucky Basketball: A New Beginning*) that he had agreed to the meeting because he "wanted to hear just what Coach Rupp had to say. He told me," Hall recalled, "if I would return to UK that he would personally endorse me for the head job when he retired. Before, no one had assured me of that. Other UK officials also promised me their support. That's when I decided to return." Whatever the real reason, just a week after accepting the coaching position at St. Louis, Hall was back on the job at the University of Kentucky.

If Hall thought this settled the question of Rupp's retirement he was wrong. The Baron had no intention of bowing out gracefully and in his last three years on the job did everything he could to postpone the dreaded retirement. Rupp supporters, led by former basketball star Dan Issel, urged university officials to waive the mandatory age limit and permit Rupp to coach as long as he wanted. Others, including many former players, argued that it was time for Rupp to step aside. "For one of the few times in history," Oscar Combs noted, "Kentucky fans divided and chose sides."

Further complicating the situation in 1972, Rupp's last season at UK, was the presence of one of the greatest freshman groups in Wildcat history. The "Super Kittens," recruited by Hall, included Kevin Grevey, Jimmy Dan Conner, Mike Flynn, Bob Guyette, Steve Lockmueller, Jerry Hale, and G.J. Smith. Under Hall's direction the freshman team (freshmen were not permitted to play varsity ball at the time) compiled a perfect 22-0 record and the Kentucky faithful talked seriously of another NCAA championship. If the Wildcats were to win their fifth national title, Rupp adherents argued, the honor should go to Uncle Adolph. Because of all he had done over the years for the university, Rupp deserved the privilege of coaching the "Super Kittens."

Two days before the end of the 1972 regular season the Baron made a final public bid for sympathy. "If they force me to retire," Rupp told a newspaper reporter, "then they might as well take me out to the Lexington Cemetery." The UK administration did not budge. Later that spring the Athletics Board announced the mandatory retirement of Adolph Rupp and the hiring of Joe B. Hall. Rupp refused to attend the ceremony celebrating Hall's promotion. Instead he reportedly stalked from his office, announcing curtly that he was "going to the farm."

The Rupp era was ended but comparisons between the Baron of the Bluegrass and his successor have continued to the present, generally to the disadvantage

of Hall. The main reason for this, claimed Caywood Ledford in an interview published in the June 7, 1983, *Lexington Herald-Leader*, is the difference in personality between the two men. "There couldn't be two men more different," maintained Ledford, who knew both Rupp and Hall well. "Adolph was always on stage, you know. He was one of the great colorful characters I've known in my life." Yet ironically Rupp was not the person he appeared to be in public. "He just wasn't a real warm person, really," Ledford recalled. "I don't think he had a close friend. . . . I don't think anyone outside his family got to know him very well."

Other knowledgeable people have made similar observations about Rupp. UK Sports Information Director Russell Rice noted in his book *Joe B. Hall: My Own Kentucky Home* that "although a camera or microphone would turn Rupp on automatically, he would try to avoid the limelight in his private life." Despite, or perhaps because of, his aversion to the masses in his private life, people tended to gravitate toward Rupp. By contrast, Rice noted, Hall gravitates to people. Hall is "the mainstream type; when he is dining in a restaurant, he talks to the waitresses, the busboys, the folks seated at the next table." In his daily life Hall "touches an amazing number of people in all walks of life, but he seems to enjoy most those types that he encounters in the small groceries or on the

farms during his hunting and fishing trips." Caywood Ledford has also noted that Hall is much more socially inclined than the Baron was. As a result Ledford has grown to know Hall much better than he ever did Rupp. His personal friendship with Hall has made it difficult for Ledford to understand or explain the contrast between Rupp's cordial and close relations with the press and Hall's, which are adversarial and often strained.

The fact is that both Rupp and Hall wanted the same thing, a favorable press, and both tried to control treatment of the UK basketball program and of themselves in the newspapers. Rupp was successful. Hall's efforts have boomeranged and merely increased suspicions on both sides. In contrast to Hall, who often seems heavy-handed and blunt in his demand for favorable copy, Rupp's control of the press was subtle and indirect but very effective. Unlike his successor the Baron instinctively knew how to manipulate the press and later radio and television. With an offhand joke or a colorful quote he was able to present himself in a favorable light as a warm and likeable person while providing reporters with what they in turn desperately needed—interesting stories that would appeal to readers or viewers. Hall, a much more bland personality, is unable or unwilling to do this. Even Ledford has admitted that Hall seems to

Hall puts his players through their paces in the UK strength and conditioning program.

"have the knack of saying the wrong thing sometimes" and then of compounding his problems by reacting angrily when his statements and actions are reported in the press.

Billy Reed, the *Courier-Journal's* sports editor and one of Hall's fiercest critics, in a January 29, 1981, article compared UK's basketball program as directed by Hall to a totalitarian state. "Inside the Program," Reed maintained, "Hall rules supreme. He decides everything. . . . A bunker mentality, an us-against-them kind of thing, prevails within The Program. 'Them,' of course, includes rival coaches, recruiters and referees. It also includes the press, particularly the print media. Inside The Program," asserted Reed, "the press is distrusted, even despised." At UK, he concluded, "The Program is all-powerful and all-pervasive" and in fact "has become virtually autonomous, with only the barest of ties to the rest of the athletic department." Although this is an extreme and emotional attack, even Russell Rice has admitted that Hall monitors his players so closely that they nicknamed him "Papa Bear" after he fell asleep on Kevin Grevey's bed while waiting into the wee hours of the morning for his star forward to return to his room.

Hall wants to know everything about his players and, Rice noted, generally does. He keeps in close personal touch with the players, has them to his house for meals, takes them fishing, lets them help with work around his farm, keeps a close check on their academic progress, and has set up classes on how to deal with the media. This is in sharp contrast to Rupp, who remained aloof from his players and left discipline, class attendance, and anything else that was needed to others. In the Rupp era, Hall recalled, "you showed up for practice on October 15 and that was the first time you would see Coach Rupp. You stayed at a distance and he kept his distance. It left you with a fear and respect for him. You never got to a point where you felt comfortable around Coach Rupp." Hall wanted to change that atmosphere.

Players and coaches who have worked with Hall tend to disagree with the essentially negative assessment by sportswriters. Although Dan Issel still reveres the memory of Adolph Rupp, he stated in a June 1983 interview that he believes "Joe Hall is becoming a legend in his own right."

Former UK Assistant Coach Joe Dean discussed Hall and the UK program before he left Lexington in late July 1983 to assume his duties as head coach at Birmingham Southern College. In a wide-ranging discussion, Dean maintained that "working with Coach Hall for the last six years has been a tremendous learning experience for me. I feel he is not only a great basket-

An off-court workout. Kyle Macy and Rick Robey help Hall hang tobacco on his Harrison County farm in the fall of 1977.

ball coach but also a fine person. He really cares about his people and does everything he can to help them. Most people outside the program don't understand that." Hall is, Dean continued, "a down-home, sincere, honest person who cares about one thing and that is the success of University of Kentucky basketball. I honestly don't think he receives the credit he deserves for the job he has done during the last eleven years as UK head coach. When he was hired I doubt there were many people who expected him to last eleven years but he has. I hope," Dean concluded, "that Coach Hall can continue to coach here as long as he wants and that he wins at least another national championship along the way."

Even critics admit that Hall is a great recruiter but they fault him for not getting the best and the most from the talented players he brings to the UK campus. This is ironic because not only does Hall have a winning percentage of better than .750 but his teams have won or shared the SEC championship eight of the twelve seasons he has been at UK.

Unfortunately for Hall this period has witnessed the emergence of the SEC as one of the strongest conferences in the nation. No longer is the SEC the football conference which Rupp could so easily dominate. Those days "when Kentucky made a monkey out of the other conference opponents are over," Jock Sutherland wrote in a January 20, 1983 *Herald-Leader* article. "All of the other SEC schools have built beautiful arenas, and the basketball program is now important to all of the conference teams." Another indication of the increased strength of the SEC, Sutherland noted, was its record against non-conference foes during the 1983 season. Through January 16, 1983, conference teams had a 27-17 record against non-SEC teams. Alabama had an 8-0 record, including a twenty-three-point victory over powerful Georgetown, before the conference season began but only a 1-5 record in its first six SEC games. Later in the season Alabama took time out from its regular succession of drubbings at the hands of conference foes to play and soundly defeat UCLA, which at the time was ranked Number 1 in the nation. Georgia, another conference doormat in the 1983 season, caught fire in the SEC and later the NCAA tournament and was one of the final four teams in the playoff for the national championship. One SEC coach who is familiar with the parity in the conference expressed amazement to a Lexington reporter during the 1980 season at the lack of appreciation for Hall's accomplishments. "I don't know why," he began, Hall "has his detractors here in Lexington, because the man has done a job that's the envy of practically every school in the country,

not only in recruiting and promoting, but in coaching. Kentucky may get knocked" by other coaches, he continued, "but it's just envy. . . . Joe does a very good job with his talent."

Hall, for his part, knew when he inherited the Rupp throne in 1972 that for him it would be a hot seat unless he won soon, won often, and won big. Unfortunately, Hall did not begin his tenure the way Big Blue fans wanted and expected—that is, with an NCAA championship in his first season as head coach. All his team did was compile a 20-8 record and win the SEC championship. But this team boasted the "Super Kittens" who were supposed to bring UK its fifth national title. Jim Andrews, who was the starting center and team captain, recalled that "after they went 22-0 as freshmen everybody assumed they were going to go out the next year and win the title. But it isn't that easy." Steve Lockmueller, one of the "Super Kittens," reminisced about his sophomore season in a February 1983 interview. "It was really a pressure-filled year. Not only for us but more especially for Coach Hall and his staff because here they were following a legend. If we didn't succeed in some fashion," he noted, "it would be easy for people to say that Coach Hall doesn't have it like Coach Rupp did, that the players just don't do as well as they did under Coach Rupp." Fellow "Super Kitten" Bob Guyette emphasized the same point. "Coach Hall had a lot of pressure on him. It was a very intense year. In fact, the first couple of years were tough, until 1975 when we got to the finals of the NCAA. That took some of the pressure off Coach Hall."

The usual starting lineup in the 1972/73 season consisted of sophomores Kevin Grevey and Jimmy Dan Conner at the forwards, senior Jim Andrews at center, and sophomore Mike Flynn and junior Ronnie Lyons at guards, although sophomore Bob Guyette started several games at forward and Conner often switched to guard when the Wildcats needed a big guard. With his height and good scoring touch Andrews was vitally important to the team's success. The 6'11" Ohio native had come a long way from his sophomore season when he was a backup center, along with 6' 8 1/2" junior Mark Soderberg, to fellow sophomore Tom Payne. The 7' Payne, who was UK's first black player, left after the end of the season to play pro ball. Soderberg also departed leaving Andrews to carry the load at center. Although Andrews was the team's leading scorer in 1973, with an average of 20.1 points per game, the Big Blue also depended heavily on the contributions of sophomore starters Grevey, Conner, and Flynn, who combined for an average of nearly forty points a game, as well as the solid bench strength

provided by sophomores Guyette and Lockmueller.

The "Super Kittens" were a multitalented group and they knew it. When the season started, Jim Andrews noted in a January 1983 interview, "they figured all the teams we played would be afraid of us. We started the season with a great game against Michigan State, up there. Just beat the tar out of them." Unfortunately, he continued, "the sophs were young, inexperienced kids. They didn't know enough yet to keep their mouths shut. 'We can't wait until Iowa comes in here,' they told reporters. 'We're just going to tear Iowa up.' Well, it didn't work out that way. Iowa just whipped us. And then we played Indiana and North Carolina and they beat us. Well the kids learned some valuable early lessons."

After suffering these early-season shocks the Wildcats rebounded with two easy victories to capture the UK Invitational Tournament and followed that up with victories over intersectional rivals Kansas and Notre Dame to end December. In January the Blue and White entered the important part of the season, the eighteen-game home-and-home schedule against the other teams of the SEC. This second season did not get off to a good start. In the period between January 6 and February 3 UK lost four conference games. Perennial nemesis Tennessee beat the Big Blue in an exciting 65-64 contest in Knoxville while Vanderbilt swept the season series with a one-point victory in Nashville and an impressive seven-point win in Lexington. Perhaps the most difficult defeat for the Wildcats to accept, Steve Lockmueller noted, was a 61-58 decision to lightly regarded Mississippi. It was UK's first loss to Old Miss in forty-five years, and coach Cob Jarvis proudly proclaimed it the greatest victory in Reb basketball history.

On February 3, 1973, with four conference defeats and only five victories on their record, the highly touted Wildcats looked very vulnerable but showed great character by fighting back in February and winning seven straight games. With two games left on the regular schedule UK, which a month before appeared to be out of the race, was in a position to win the league championship. With the title on the line the Big Blue turned a pressure-packed away game against Auburn on March 3 into a 91-79 rout.

Everything came down to the final game of the season, a home contest with Tennessee which would decide the SEC championship. The day before the game, students began camping on the sidewalk in front of Memorial Coliseum to assure themselves of good seats. At game time the Coliseum was packed to overflowing, with an estimated crowd of 13,000. The Vols, led by their 7' center, Len Kosmalski, led 65-61

Jim Andrews sinks Tennessee with his last-second shot on January 22, 1973. UK won 72-70 and Hall ended his first season as head coach with the SEC championship, but the fans blamed him for not bagging the NCAA title.

with 11:07 left in the game. Then Kevin Grevey took over. He hit four jump shots in a row to put UK ahead 69-67. Grevey finished the game with a total of twenty-eight points to pace the Big Blue to an 86-81 victory and give Hall the SEC championship in his first season as head coach.

The Wildcats departed for the Mideast Regionals in Nashville with high hopes. In the opening round they faced Ohio Valley Conference champion Austin Peay and its scoring sensation "Fly" Williams. Austin Peay was coached by Lake Kelly and Leonard Hamilton, now members of the Wildcat coaching staff. UK had much more trouble with their small but quick rivals than Big Blue fans had anticipated, but finally prevailed in overtime, 106-100. This set up a return match with Big Ten champion Indiana, winners of a regular-season contest between the two teams.

The young Wildcats impressed Indiana Coach Bobby Knight with their sticky defense and tenacious play but again lost to the Hoosiers, 72-65. Jim Andrews finished his varsity career in spectacular fashion, scoring twenty-three points, pulling down ten rebounds

Steve Lockmueller shoots a hookshot during the 1973/74 season.

and rejecting six Indiana shots. The Wildcat players and fans were broken-hearted. After trailing through most of the game the Big Blue fought its way back and finally, with 7:35 left, gained the lead 61-59. Then disaster struck. UK took four successive shots that banged around the rim but refused to fall in. "If they had only gone in," Hall lamented after the game. "They were good shots, but they just wouldn't drop. After our comeback, it was kind of a disappointment." The Wildcats consoled themselves with the thought that with a little luck they would have gained a place in the NCAA final four.

If their sophomore season ended on a disheartening note for the "Super Kittens," their entire junior season was a disaster. Despite the great expectations of coaches, players, fans, and press the Big Blue limped to a 13-13 season record, matching Rupp's 1967 mark. Not since 1927, when the season totals were 3-13, had UK had a worse record, Bob Guyette ruefully noted in an interview that his junior season stands out in his

mind "for the losses and the pressure from the fans and the press for our poor record. There was just a lot of pressure on Coach Hall and on us. We fought like crazy all season but we just couldn't quite make it. It was not an enjoyable experience." The major problem, both Guyette and Coach Hall believe, was a lack of size and muscle. Hall stated that with 6'3" Conner at forward, 6'8" Guyette at center, 5'9" Ronnie Lyons at guard, and 6'6" Steve Lockmueller as backup center, "there was no way we could match some opponents physically. We were just too small a team."

The 1973/74 season got off to a typical good UK start with a resounding 81-68 victory over Miami of Ohio in the opening game, but immediately after that everything fell apart. The Wildcats lost the next three games by decisive margins to Kansas (71-63), Indiana (77-68), and North Carolina (101-84). In the Indiana game, played in Louisville, the Big Blue actually led by five points at halftime but during the intermission Indiana Coach Bobby Knight decided on an adjustment in personnel that other UK rivals during the season would also make. In the second half 6'5" substitute guard John Laskowski was placed in the lineup against UK's 5'9" Ronnie Lyons. Laskowski took his shorter opponent inside with devastating effect. Although he had scored only six points in the Hoosier's previous two games against the Wildcats, Laskowski hit eleven of fifteen shots and led the Indiana squad to a nine-point victory. Hall's worries about lack of team size were borne out in this and numerous other games during the season.

UK bounced back from its three-game losing streak to win the next three games against Iowa (88-80), Dartmouth (102-77), and Stanford (78-77). The latter two were UKIT contests. The Blue and White finished the intersectional schedule on a losing note, however, when they met Notre Dame at Freedom Hall in Louisville on December 29. With 6'9" center John Shumate contributing twenty-five points and fourteen rebounds, the Fighting Irish destroyed UK, 94-79. Thus the intersectional schedule ended on an inconclusive note with four victories and four defeats. Hopes for a better fate against SEC rivals were immediately dashed when, on January 5, 1974, the Wildcats traveled to Baton Rouge to play LSU. Eddie Palubinskas, Collis Temple, and Glenn Hansen combined for seventy-four points to lead the Tigers to a 95-84 victory. The Wildcats staggered through the remainder of the SEC campaign winning nine games but losing the same number.

Joe Hall, his staff, and members of the team departed almost gratefully in May on a month-long exhibition tour of Tahiti and Australia. Both Hall and

the players maintained in interviews that this trip, on which the Wildcats played a total of nineteen games in twenty-six days, was one of two major factors responsible for the team's turnabout in 1974/75. The other key was the arrival of an excellent group of freshmen who provided the combination of size and depth that had been lacking in the previous two seasons.

Bob Guyette maintained that the State Department-sponsored Australian tour was very important in helping the team make a turnaround from the disastrous 1973/74 season. "The chance to be together and to play a lot of games under adverse conditions really helped us the next season," Guyette stated. After playing one game in Tahiti, against the National team, the UK squad flew to Australia for a series of contests all across the country. "We travelled by car," Guyette continued, "six of us to a station wagon plus luggage. We would drive all day and arrive in the town where we were scheduled to play just in time to suit up for the game. We would stay the night in private homes and then be off early the next morning for the next

game. So," he concluded, "playing the games while we were so tired helped us get ready for our final season."

If the Australian trip was an unqualified success, so was the vitally important job of recruiting. Before departing on the foreign trip Hall put the finishing touches on a recruiting campaign that yielded a group that rivaled the famous "Super Kittens," both in numbers and in quality. Realizing that the team's major weakness was lack of size and bulk in the front line, Hall signed three 6'10" centers—Rick Robey, 235 pounds, from New Orleans; Mike Phillips, 240 pounds, from Manchester High School in Ohio; and Dan Hall, 220 pounds, from Kentucky's Betsy Lane. Hall also recruited two of the most talented ever to come out of central Kentucky: 6'4" forward Jack Givens from Bryan Station High School, and Henry Clay High School product James Lee, a 6'5" forward. In Lexington high school circles they were known respectively as "Mr. Silk" and "Mr. Steel."

The signing of Givens and Lee to basketball scholarships underlined a radical and basic change that was

Jimmy Dan Conner's hustling brand of ball helped the Cats to an NCAA runner-up spot in 1974/75. Here he dribbles around a Northwestern player in the season opener, which UK won 97-70.

freshman season had been the lone and often lonely black on the squad, would jokingly remark as he walked through the locker room: "Man, it sure was different when I first came here." Years later, Warford related to D.G. FitzMaurice (*Lexington Herald*, May 24, 1979) some of the experiences he had had as a freshman on the otherwise all-white Wildcats. The tone of the year was perhaps set during the first week of practice when, Warford recalled, one of the players "called me to his room. I was a freshman, and I thought I should go, so I did. This guy and two other players were sitting around a table chewing tobacco and playing Rook. I figured they wanted another player, and even though I didn't know how to play Rook, I was going to fake it. Instead," Warford said, "this guy looks up, and in a very soft voice, tells me he doesn't like colored boys and for me to stay out of his way. I told him that was fine with me, and today we get along all right." Warford's four years at UK were, FitzMaurice observed, "one bizarre incident after another." Through them all Warford managed to retain his sense of humor, but it must have been a trying experience for the young man. As FitzMaurice noted, "Warford, certainly not the most gifted guard to wear the basketball Wildcats' blue and white, nevertheless conducted himself with style and grace during

Reggie Warford, Hall's first black recruit as head coach, helped UK drub Mississippi State, 112-79, on February 1, 1975. Warford was a major factor in the Cats' conquest of the 1976 NIT title.

Right, the coaching staff in action during a time-out. Dick Parsons kneels to Hall's right, while Leonard Hamilton leans over Parsons.

taking place in UK recruiting. By the 1974/75 season the racial composition of the Wildcat squad was completely and permanently changed. In only three seasons as coach, Joe Hall accomplished something Rupp had found almost impossible to do, recruit blacks. In his first season Hall signed one black, guard Reggie Warford, a hard-working and intelligent player. The following season two talented guards, Larry Johnson and Merion Haskins, joined the team, and in 1974 Hall added forwards Givens and Lee. By the following season, when Warford was a senior and Hall was in his fourth year as head coach the transformation was complete. With the addition of guards Dwane Casey and Truman Claytor in the 1975/76 season, the Wildcats had a team composed of seven blacks and six whites.

By his senior year Warford, who during his

his career at Kentucky despite circumstances that at times would have distressed a man of lesser character."

Although Hall may be open to criticism on other points, where recruiting is concerned it is clear that he was and is color blind. He wants players with athletic talent, regardless of color. Even more important to him than talent, however, is what he regards as a good attitude and willingness and ability to fit into the UK system and to abide by Hall's standards of behavior. With regard to the use of narcotics, for example, Hall maintains "If any of my players smoke pot, they're gone. For good. No suspension. Gone." No compromise with permissiveness. "Life's too short to be putting up with illegal behavior," Hall points out. "I'd get out of coaching first." From all indications, Hall has stuck to his principles.

In 1975 UK had a superabundance of talent with the Givens-Robey group joining the Grevey-Conner contingent. The team was an excellent combination of size, speed, shooting ability, rebounding, solid man-to-man defense, and depth. Hall and his assistant coaches—Dick Parsons, Leonard Hamilton, and Lynn Nance—used the talent very effectively. The usual starting lineup consisted of Grevey and Guyette at forwards, Robey, the only nonsenior, at center, and Conner and Mike Flynn at guards. Grevey, a two-time All-American and three-time All-SEC selection, and Conner carried most of the scoring load while Guyette, at power forward, and Robey, who was also the third leading scorer on the team, handled the rebounding. Playmaking duties fell to Flynn, who had to sacrifice his own scoring for the good of the team. UK's strong bench included forwards Givens and Lee, 6'10" center Mike Phillips, and speedy sophomore Larry Johnson and senior Jerry Hale at guards.

Although the team got off to a good start with victories over Northwestern and Miami of Ohio, in the next game, against Indiana in Bloomington, the Wildcats seemed to return to the losing ways of the previous season. The game was a humiliating experience for the Big Blue not only because of the score, 98-74, but because of the manner in which the Hoosier center, Kent Benson, initiated UK's freshman pivotmen, Rick Robey and Mike Phillips, to the rough and tumble of big-time college basketball. Knight's offense involved a lot of movement and setting of picks, moving picks, to free players for open shots at the basket. Benson was particularly vigorous in setting picks, and UK's players responded with elbows or forearms to the face or chest. The Wildcats complained bitterly because the referees seemed to ignore Indiana's illegal picks but called penalties on UK players trying to fight through the picks.

Finally, with just a couple of minutes left in the game and the Hoosiers enjoying a commanding lead, an incident took place that seemed to add the final measure of humiliation. It was precipitated by a foul called against Indiana substitute Steve Ahlfield for charging into UK's Jerry Hale. IU coach Bobby Knight became particularly incensed over the call, feeling that too many fouls were being called against the Hoosiers, a view which Hall, of course, did not share. Knight walked in front of the Wildcat bench to talk to the official, and Hall left the bench to join in the argument. As the UK coach turned away Knight cuffed him on the back of the head. Although Knight immediately claimed it was a playful gesture, the Wildcat bench interpreted it as a symbol of contempt. Assistant Coach Lynn Nance, who had once been a member of the FBI and knew some karate, started to take off his coat and go after Knight but was restrained. Eventually everyone calmed down and the game was permitted to continue and—finally and mercifully—to end.

The Big Blue would not forget the valuable lessons learned in Bloomington. Hall maintained later that it

Tempers still flare on the court. Here, Indiana coach Bobby Knight (right) has just hit (or patted) Hall on the back of the head during a December 7, 1974, game, and assistant coach Lynn Nance has to be restrained by Hall. To add to the insult, Indiana trounced the Cats 98-74.

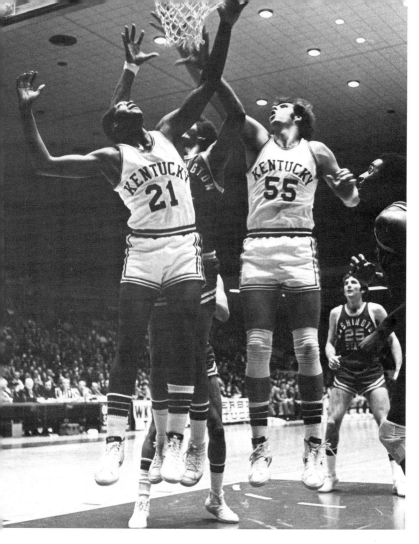

Jack Givens (21) and Mike Phillips (55) fight a Washington State player for a rebound in the 1974 UKIT.

excellent Tar Heel team that included Phil Ford, Mitch Kupchek, and Walt Davis, all future stars in the NBA.

The Wildcats followed up the North Carolina victory with impressive wins over Washington State and Oklahoma State to take the UKIT championship, as well as traditional rivals Kansas and Notre Dame. The average margin of victory in the four games was twenty-five points, with Kansas going down to a thirty-seven-point defeat, 100-63. What a stunning reversal from the previous season, when the Big Blue had had a difficult time against intersectional foes. UK was not to have as easy a time in its SEC schedule as against intersectional foes (after the loss to Indiana) but, as Guyette has noted, "Our senior year seemed overall to be the reverse of the previous season when so much was expected of us and we just didn't deliver. In 1975 not as much was expected of us but we got better and better as the season progressed." Jack Givens, who was a freshman reserve in 1975, observed in an unpublished autobiography that "success in basketball is a strange thing. It seems to build on itself. It only takes one or two good games to get things going right. The momentum carries over into practice and you have some great practices and you're even more up for the next game." Except for occasional lapses which Hall did not accept with good grace, that was the story of 1975. UK lost only three regular games after the Indiana defeat and all were to SEC opponents—to Auburn, Tennessee, and Florida. Although the Wildcats defeated Alabama both times they played, the Tide was in the race for the conference title all season. In fact, the championship wasn't decided until March 8, the final day of the regular season.

UK was in Starkville for an evening game against Mississippi State, while the Alabama-Auburn game was the SEC game of the week on television that afternoon. It would take a combination of a UK victory and an Alabama defeat for the Big Blue to tie the Tide for the conference championship. Against all odds that is exactly what happened. The Wildcats thoroughly dominated their game to win by thirty-eight points, 118-80, to set the stage for Hall's second appearance in the NCAA in three years. The UK team was placed in the Mideast Regionals, where it would face Marquette and Indiana, two of the top squads in the nation, as well as Central Michigan, which featured two future NBA stars, Dan Roundfield and Rory Sparrow. The Wildcats disposed of Marquette by twenty-two points, 76-54, at Tuscaloosa on March 15, and Central Michigan by seventeen points, 90-73, on March 20 at Dayton. This set the stage for a return match with Knight and the Hoosiers for the regional championship and a trip to the final four in San Diego. It

was "a pivotal game. It woke us up to the physical type of play that we were going to face throughout the season and the fact that we had to give the same kind of effort if we were to win." In the early stages of the following game, against powerful North Carolina in Louisville, there were no signs that the lesson had been learned. Hall acknowledged that "going into the next game, against North Carolina, we were still a little stunned from the loss to Indiana. It took about fifteen minutes for us to find out where we were and what style of ball we were to play the rest of the season." With the Blue and White down 31-16, Hall called time-out and employed a tactic to wake the team up that he would put to good use under similar circumstances in the future. He benched four starters. When they finally were permitted to return to the contest they responded with inspired play. Guard Jimmy Dan Conner, in particular, played like a man possessed. He finished the game with thirty-five points and led the Wildcats to a 90-78 victory over an

was, Jack Givens maintained, "probably the best college game I've ever seen or been involved in, even though I didn't play that much."

Indiana entered the game as the number-one team in the nation and the odds-on favorite to win the national championship. The Hoosiers had suffered a serious blow late in the season when forward Scott May, the team's leading scorer, broke a wrist. Indiana was so strong and so deep that despite the loss of May the Hoosiers were able to finish the regular season undefeated. With a special cast to protect his wrist May started the UK game but did not play up to his usual brilliant standards. Nevertheless, the two teams were evenly matched and the game was hard-fought. The Wildcats had learned in the first Indiana game how to play tough, aggressive, and physical basketball and how to make effective use of a deep and talented bench. They had learned their lesson so well that reporter Robert Marcus of the *Chicago Tribune* dubbed them the "Slaughterhouse Five." In analyzing the game, which the Big Blue won 92-90, Marcus wrote: "The Kentucky Wildcats played like five guys who make their living sledge hammering steers in a stockyard Saturday to earn their greatest basketball victory in a decade."

After the game came another thrill for Givens and his teammates. The squad boarded a bus for the return trip to Lexington. "A police escort met the bus as it crossed the Ohio River," he recalled, "and we rolled down the interstate at about seventy miles per hour

Above, 6'9" power forward Bob Guyette scores against Mississippi State en route to the 1975 NCAA finals in San Diego.

Left, Mike Flynn displays his fastbreak technique for fans at Memorial Coliseum.

105

to the Coliseum. We were leading a long caravan of supporters. For miles behind us cars with their lights on were honking their horns. People were standing on the expressway overpasses with signs, waving at us. You'd look over in a field," he continued, "and a farmer and his family who had watched the game on TV or listened on the radio would be standing with a big homemade sign waving at us. It was great. Of all my experiences, I'll probably remember that one longer than any of them." When the team arrived in Lexington and the bus pulled up in front of the Coliseum "it seemed there were a million people there. All the seats were filled and the floor was packed with people. They were chanting 'San Diego here we come.' "

After that game, Givens noted, the Wildcats' playing went downhill. The tension of the Indiana game and "the fact that we were up so high made it seem like an NCAA final game. We wanted to beat Indiana so badly and got up so high for the game that it was hard to get up again after that. The seniors especially seemed to be flat or emotionally exhausted after the Indiana game."

An additional problem was that the finals were played in San Diego, far from friends and fans. None of the Wildcats had been to California, and playing basketball almost seemed like a secondary consideration. "We had a great time sightseeing," Givens re-

called. "We went to Sea World and to the zoo and Easter morning we had an Easter egg hunt outside the hotel where we were staying." The coaching staff and the freshmen would learn from the mistakes made in 1975. When they returned to the NCAA finals in 1978 they would be all business.

The Big Blue played poorly in the semifinal game against Syracuse but because of a sparkling performance from reserve forward Jack Givens, UK proved too strong for the easterners and won by sixteen points. In the other semifinal game perennial national champion UCLA met the Louisville Cardinals, whose coach, Denny Crum, had played and later coached under John Wooden. UCLA won an exciting and hard-fought contest in overtime, 75-74, to set up a meeting between UK, winner of four NCAA titles, and UCLA, national champions nine of the previous eleven seasons. In addition to whatever advantage UCLA might enjoy from its phenomenal success in NCAA tournament competition, the Bruins would be playing close to home and would have the full and vocal support of their fans. As if all this was not enough, Wooden announced his retirement on the day before the championship game.

The effect of Wooden's announcement was electrifying and immediate, as the Bruins' coach undoubtedly had anticipated. The UK coaches and players realized

Kevin Grevey shovels an underhanded layup with his right hand as he shoots against the entire Mississippi starting lineup. Grevey, a southpaw, had a left-handed outside jump shot with tremendous range.

the psychological impact the announcement would have on the UCLA players and supporters but, as Bob Guyette noted, there was little they could do about it. As game time approached it was clear that Wooden's words were having the desired effect on his players and, when the game got under way, on the fans. The announcement may also have had an effect on the referees because, Guyette maintained, "Wooden did get away with some things, like walking out on the floor and some other things, that were out of character for him, I thought. For example, he got up and scolded the officials a few times." Givens also believes the referees were affected "because they made some calls in critical situations differently than they would have under other circumstances." And still, Guyette noted, "it was a close game."

The Wildcats finally lost 92-85 but, as Hall later stated, there could be no doubt "about the tremendous effort our players gave and after we viewed the game on film, we saw what a tremendous game they played, and we can only say that UCLA played a better game. They had a great motivation to win, and it was one of the finest games that we had seen them play that season."

The Wildcats returned to Lexington and a rousing welcome from the faithful at the Coliseum. The "Super Kittens" had grown up. They had vindicated themselves and Hall in the eyes of UK's legion of fans. The pressure on Hall was not ended, however. In the view of many of the Wildcat faithful he had not won "the big game." It would now be up to Givens, Robey, and associates to carry the banner of the Blue and White forces to the promised land and bring UK its first national championship in nearly twenty years—not an easy goal.

Freshman center Rick Robey muscles a rebound against Notre Dame in Louisville's Freedom Hall on January 28, 1975, as the Cats down the Irish 113-95. Merion Haskins is at left.

Return to Glory

If the 1975 team began UK's return to its former glory, the 1978 squad completed the journey. The road was not an easy one to travel. In fact, through much of the 1975/76 season it appeared that the Wildcats were trapped in a living replay of the 1973/74 debacle. After the first twenty games the won-lost record was 10-10. The conference record to that date, February 14, was even worse. The Big Blue was able to win only five games while dropping seven. There appeared to be little hope for improvement in the six remaining SEC contests.

Through graduation UK had lost the nucleus of the 1975 NCAA runners-up and was left with an untested group of underclassmen. Gone from the team were four of the five starters from the 1975 team—Grevey, Guyette, Conner, and Flynn—plus valuable reserves G.J. Smith and Jerry Hale.

The only senior on the 1976 squad was guard Reggie Warford, who had not played enough in the previous three seasons to qualify for a single varsity letter. Fortunately for the Big Blue, when he finally got a chance to play Warford proved to be a pleasant surprise. Along with junior Larry Johnson, Warford would provide the Wildcats with strong play at guard, especially late in the season and during tournament play. Taking over Grevey's forward slot and scoring load was Jack Givens. The Lexington native's leadership qualities were recognized when he was chosen team captain, even though at the time he was only a sophomore. Rick Robey, the only returning starter from the 1975 team, was moved from center to power forward. The New Orleanian averaged 15.6 points per game but because of injuries played in only twelve games, including four SEC contests. In Robey's absence fellow sophomore James Lee moved into the starting lineup. At center was still another sophomore, Mike Phillips.

A potentially excellent recruiting crop was ruined when a New Jersey high school sensation, Bill Willoughby, decided, after accepting a scholarship, to forgo college in order to enter the NBA draft. Another promising recruit, guard Pat Foschi, enrolled at UK but left school before the basketball season started, while Bob Fowler, a jumping jack 6'4" forward, was at the university for just one season before transferring to Iowa State. The only freshmen who remained the entire four seasons were guards Truman Claytor and Dwane Casey.

The 1976 season began on a sour note. The Big Blue travelled to Evanston, Illinois, for their opening game against the Northwestern University Wildcats only to lose by twelve points, 89-77. UK also lost the next game, to the North Carolina Tar Heels in Charlotte, but evened their record with victories over Miami of Ohio and Kansas. The Wildcats went down to their third defeat of the season when they met the Indiana Hoosiers in Louisville on December 15. Led by All-Americans Scott May and Kent Benson, the Hoosiers were on their way to an undefeated season and the NCAA championship but were pushed to the limit by a scrappy Wildcat team before finally prevailing in overtime, 77-68. The Blue and White completed their intersectional schedule on a positive note with victories over Georgia Tech and Oregon State to win the UK

Rick Robey, James Lee, and Jack Givens savor the ultimate victory, the NCAA championship, on March 27, 1978—the end of a long, tough season for the Cats.

Invitational Tournament, and the traditional late December meeting with the Notre Dame Fighting Irish in Louisville. With their intersectional schedule finally behind them, recalled Truman Claytor in an interview, the Wildcats turned with high hopes to the conference race. But their hopes were to be dashed immediately as they opened their SEC schedule with three straight losses—to Mississippi State, Alabama, and Tennessee. To add to UK's problems Rick Robey suffered a thigh bruise during the first conference game, with Mississippi State, and a knee sprain two nights later against Alabama. After missing the next three games Robey returned to the lineup for two games but reinjured the knee in practice and was sidelined for the rest of the season.

On February 14, with the SEC season two-thirds completed and disaster seemingly in the offing, the Wildcats suddenly changed direction and ended the regular season with six straight conference victories. Jack Givens recalled the frustrations of his sophomore season, "It appeared that we were going nowhere but we kept on trying and working and it paid off. We won our last six conference games and in the next to the last game we beat Alabama, the league champs that year, in a nationally televised game from the Coliseum. That victory got us an invitation to the NIT in New York and we felt lucky to be invited." Even with the strong finish the Big Blue could do no better than tie for fourth place in the conference. Givens was right. UK was lucky to be invited to the NIT.

The ten-day trip to New York for the NIT was UK's first appearance in the "Big Apple" since the basketball scandal of the early fifties. According to Claytor, Lee, Givens, and Dwane Casey, the players were frequently asked how it felt to be the first UK team to appear in Madison Square Garden in twenty-six years. The Wildcat players' response was succinct and to the point: "That was long before our time and we don't think much about it."

The Big Blue peaked at just the right time. To win the tournament UK had to play and win four games in nine days. In close and exciting games they defeated Niagara, Kansas State, Providence, and, for the title, the University of North Carolina at Charlotte. The

A preseason photo of the 1976/77 Wildcats shows the team's changing racial composition. Seated, l-r, Mike Phillips and Rick Robey. Standing, Kyle Macy (a red shirt who did not play that season), Jay Shidler, Tim Stephens, James Lee, LaVon Williams, Jack Givens, Merion Haskins, Larry Johnson, Dwane Casey, and Truman Claytor.

strong UNC Charlotte team was coached by Lee Rose, previously of Lexington's Transylvania University, and led by future NBA star Cedric "Cornbread" Maxwell. Powered by a fourteen-point performance by Reggie Warford in his final appearance in a Wildcat uniform, UK overcame second-half foul trouble and another outstanding game from Maxwell, who was voted the most valuable player in the tournament, to win 71-67.

With the season-ending ten-game winning streak and the NIT championship, the Wildcats converted a potentially disastrous season into a memorable one. In another respect 1976 was a milestone in UK basketball annals: for the first time a majority of both the starting players and the reserves were black. The ratio was in stark contrast to the situation just a couple of years before, when UK had a bad reputation among blacks. Jack Givens, a highly recruited senior at Lexington's Bryan Station High School, recalled that in 1974 "some blacks, especially some older people, would come up to me and tell me I shouldn't go to UK. They would tell me that UK didn't like blacks, that I wouldn't get to play, that they would have me locked up, amazing things like that." Typical of Kentucky blacks, Givens had never followed Wildcat basketball so "I didn't really notice that UK didn't have any black starters until people started pointing it out. UK only had one black player, Reggie Warford, on the varsity and he was sitting on the bench. There were two other blacks, Larry Johnson and Merion Haskins, on the freshman team."

Fortunately for the Wildcats, when Givens talked with Warford, Johnson, and Haskins "they told me they really liked UK, that everything was great." Givens acknowledged that if Adolph Rupp had still been coach he probably would not have attended UK, in large part because he doubted Rupp would have been interested in him. But Joe Hall and Dick Parsons made a very favorable impression on Givens and his mother, and they seemed to be genuinely interested in the "Goose" and his well-being. The UK coaching staff impressed James Lee and the other blacks they recruited in the same positive way, and they continued to attract blue-chip white athletes, as well. Two other master recruiters joined the UK staff, Leonard Hamilton in 1974 and Joe Dean in 1977.

In the 1976/77 season everyone from the NIT championship team returned except Reggie Warford, and the Wildcats had another excellent group of freshman recruits. Joining the squad were sharpshooters Jay Shidler and Tim Stephens and rugged rebounder LaVon Williams. Shidler, who arrived at UK with bleached hair and was promptly nicknamed "White Lightning" by an adoring public, had an excellent long-

The 1976/77 squad try to relax and loosen up before a game.

range jump shot and played hustling defense. The Lawrenceville, Illinois, native became a starting guard as a freshman, scoring in double figures in twelve games and registering a game and career high of twenty points against Indiana. Stephens's contributions were limited because of injuries in 1977 and 1978 and he decided to transfer from UK after his sophomore season. Williams also served as a substitute in 1977 and 1978 but became a starting forward in his junior and senior seasons with the Wildcats. In addition to the freshmen, Purdue transfer Kyle Macy arrived on the Lexington campus. Although he was ineligible to play in 1976/77, it was obvious that Macy, who had been Purdue's third leading scorer as a freshman with a single-game high of thirty-eight points against Minnesota, would be a valuable addition to the team in 1977/78.

With a young and inexperienced team UK had played inspired ball in the last third of the 1975/76 season and capped a dazzling comeback with the NIT

championship. After the Big Blue won the NIT on March 21, 1976, Joe Hall told his team, as Jack Givens reported, that "some people would say and write that it was a great ending but that they were wrong because, as he put it, 'the NIT championship is only the beginning for you.' "

UK's prospects for the 1976/77 season appeared to be excellent. The Cats had an experienced and deep squad with juniors Jack Givens, Rick Robey, and Mike Phillips and senior playmaker Larry Johnson. Joining them in the starting lineup was the sensational freshman prospect Jay Shidler. Hall also made full and effective use of his talented reserves, who included James Lee, LaVon Williams, Truman Claytor, Merion Haskins, and Dwane Casey.

The Big Blue won twenty-six games and lost only four but each of the four defeats was crucial. The first, to Utah, cost the Wildcats the championship in their invitational tournament. In the grueling eighteen-game conference schedule UK suffered only two defeats, both at the hands of Tennessee, who tied the Cats for the SEC championship. By virtue of holding the series edge the Vols won the right to represent the conference in the Mideast Regionals at Baton Rouge, with the regional finals at Rupp Arena in Lexington, while UK was placed in the East Regionals with games first in Philadelphia and then in College Park, Maryland.

After impressive victories over Princeton and Virginia Military Institute the Big Blue met North Carolina in the regional finals for the opportunity to move on to the finals of the national championship. The Cats fell behind early in the game but worked their way back to trail by only one point, 71-70, with 1:32 left in the game. That was as close as they came, as the Tar Heels pulled away to win 79-72. UK hit five more field goals than North Carolina but lost the game at the free-throw line. Because they were behind through most of the game the Wildcats were forced to commit fouls and the Tar Heels cashed in on thirty-three of their thirty-six free throws, while UK, with only eighteen free throws, converted on sixteen of them. In an interview Kyle Macy recalled the North Carolina contest as "one of those games where they [the Wildcats] just never got the big break or they could have won the championship that year because it was an outstanding team."

In analyzing the season Hall blamed midseason disciplinary problems for the Wildcats falling short of his goal, and the team's, of an NCAA title in 1977. In December, on the eve of the UKIT, Hall had suspended Mike Phillips, Jay Shidler, and Truman Claytor for a curfew violation. Without them the Wildcats struggled before pulling away from a weak Bowling Green team. In the tournament finals, however, they had problems with Utah, a disciplined and balanced squad, and fell by two points, 70-68. Looking back on the events Hall was convinced that the incident created a division within the team. "I don't think we ever completely recovered from that," Hall maintained. He was determined not to let anything similar happen the next season.

Adding a sense of urgency to this determination was the anticipated impact of penalites imposed by the NCAA on the UK football and basketball programs. In December 1976 the NCAA, college sports' governing body, announced the results of its investigation of UK. The report documented violations of the NCAA code by UK recruiters, staff members, and alumni. Although most of the violations had been committed by or in the interests of the football team, the basket-

Senior Larry Johnson was playmaker for the Cats in 1976/77.

ball program was also penalized. The football team was prohibited from appearing on NCAA telecasts and its postseason bowl games for one year, although it was permitted to appear in an already scheduled Peach Bowl Game in Atlanta. In addition, the number of recruits UK was allowed to sign was limited for the next two years to twenty-five in football and three in basketball. Because recruitment is the lifeblood of a successful college athletic program, such a restriction could adversely affect Wildcat basketball and football for years to come. Thus pressure to win in 1977/78 started early.

The football team responded with a glittering 10-1 season. Pressure was intense on Hall and the basketball team to win not only the conference title but the national championship. Indeed, nothing less than an NCAA title would satisfy sportswriters and fans. The specter of possible failure haunted Hall during the entire season. Although the Big Blue was ranked Number 1 for all but two weeks, Hall criticized, cursed, and chastised his squad throughout the season and even suggested, after a loss to LSU in February, that they might be immortalized in Wildcat annals as the "Folding Five" or the "Quitting Quintet."

After UK completed the season with a victory over Duke in the finals of the NCAA to win their first national championship in twenty years, *Sports Illustrated* reporter Larry Keith observed that "it was never easy for Kentucky. There was never any time to sit and smile. From the very first game this season, the Wildcats were haunted by their tradition, pressured by their opponents and driven mercilessly by their coach. All the joys of winning had to wait until they had won it all."

Jack Givens recalled that "the pressure of my senior season [1977/78] actually started during my junior year right after we lost to North Carolina in the East Regionals of the NCAA at College Park, Maryland." After that defeat "we moved to dedicate ourselves to win it all the next year. We worked hard all summer and looked forward with great excitement and anticipation to the coming season but we knew we had lost two quality people in Larry Johnson and Merion Haskins. We knew we had our work cut out for us."

Even with the graduation of Johnson (a vastly underrated player) and Haskins, UK appeared to have a deep and talented squad. Returning were four starters from the 1977 team plus all of the top reserves, including forward James Lee, who was good enough to start and even star on most college teams. At UK he was the first reserve off the bench. The front court starters were the sharp-shooting 6'4" left-hander Jack Givens and two powerful 6'10" inside players, Rick

Jay Shidler demonstrates the style that earned him the nickname "White Lightning" during his sensational freshman season, 1976/77.

Robey and Mike Phillips. Back at one guard position was crowd favorite Jay Shidler, who had started twenty-eight of UK's thirty games as a freshman. Shidler's main problem had been a lack of consistency, which he hoped to improve in his sophomore season. But on the second day of practice he broke a bone in his right foot and was sidelined for five weeks. In Shidler's absence junior Truman Claytor got an opportunity to display his talents as a shooter, ball handler, and defensive player. By the time Shidler was ready to return to action Claytor had won a starting guard position. This replacement meant that the Illinois native was relegated to a reserve role because the other guard, the playmaker, was Kyle Macy.

For Shidler or anyone else to displace Macy was unthinkable. Even before Macy played his first varsity game for the Wildcats, Hall was lavish in his predictions of greatness for the young man. During Macy's

Reserve guard Dwane Casey (20), besides playing solid man-to-man defense, made invaluable contributions to team morale in the 1977/78 championship season.

cellent outside shooting and, along with reserve guard Dwane Casey, solid man-to-man defense.

Casey was acknowledged by his teammates to be one of the keys to UK's success in 1978. Jack Givens maintained that Casey was "one of the most important people on the team that year. . . . Everyday in practice and every minute he was in a game he showed more heart and desire than any guy I have ever seen. Considering the limited amount of time he got to play he could have complained and caused dissension. Instead he was always the happiest and most optimistic member of the team."

Co-captains Jack Givens and Rick Robey were team leaders. Macy put all these talents together and contributed some of his own. He became UK's floor leader on both offense and defense. In addition he possessed an accurate jump shot and was probably the best free-throw shooter on the team as well as a smart, if not very quick, defensive player. As Macy noted in an interview, the year he spent as a redshirt was invaluable because it provided an opportunity to observe. He wasn't "thrown right into the fire. I had that year to learn the program and get to know the other players, the coaching philosophy, and to build up my motivation."

Both Macy and Joe Hall agreed that another important ingredient in Macy's excellent play in 1977/78 was the strength and endurance he gained during his redshirt year. In fact, all of the players for the 1978 team that I interviewed gave a full measure of credit to the conditioning program for UK's outstanding success that season. Even Dan Issel credited the conditioning program, which Hall introduced when he joined the UK coaching staff in the mid-1960s, with helping to improve his play during his four years at UK (1966/67-1969/70).

The formal preseason conditioning program begins shortly after the start of classes in the fall semester and continues until basketball practices start on October 15. Players are also expected, but not required, to follow a strict regimen throughout the summer and also to play informal basketball games two or three nights a week at Alumni Gym. The conditioning program includes work on the running track as well as in the weight room. Pat Etcheberry, who is strength coach for the football and basketball teams and former track and cross country coach, has said that "the basketball program stresses development of the lower body more than the upper body as well as work to develop and maintain flexibility." The result, if the player works to the limit of his capabilities (and Etcheberry is famous for making sure he does), is a strong, agile athlete with great endurance.

redshirt season, 1976/77, Hall maintained that "we have not had a guard with the leadership qualities of Macy. The closest was Jimmy Dan Conner, who had the leadership but not the skills Macy has. Kyle is an excellent outside shooter, passer, penetrator. He's a quarterback, a coach on the floor." Heady praise indeed for a college sophomore with just one year of varsity playing experience at Purdue, but it was fully justified. Seldom has a college player lived up to his advance billing as rapidly or as completely as Kyle Macy did. The 6'3" guard from Peru, Indiana, was the final ingredient in Joe Hall's formula for success. The Wildcats had an abundance of size and strength. In addition to Robey, Phillips, and Lee, Hall could call on 6'6" sophomore forward LaVon Williams and three freshman giants: 6'10" center Chuck Aleksinas, 6'10" forward-center Scott Courts, and 6'8" forward Fred Cowan. Givens, Claytor, and Shidler provided ex-

Following very successful conditioning and practice sessions, the 1977/78 basketball season began with a solid thumping of a touring Russian team in an exhibition on November 11 in Memorial Coliseum. In that contest the "Fysical Five," as the 1978 team came to be called, handled a big, strong, and talented Soviet squad with ease and cruised to a thirty-four-point victory, 109-75.

During the regular season, which began with a 110-86 victory over Southern Methodist, the Big Blue suffered only two losses, neither to an intersectional foe. The Wildcats defeated SMU, Indiana, Kansas, South Carolina, Portland State, St. John's, Iowa, Notre Dame, Nevada Las Vegas, and sixteen of eighteen SEC opponents. After the December 12 game against South Carolina at Rupp Arena, which UK won

Hot-shooting Truman Claytor won a starting position as guard when Shidler was injured before the start of the 1977/78 season.

by nineteen points, 84-65, Gamecock Coach Frank McGuire marvelled that the Wildcats "were like a pro team, with the kinds of bodies they've got out there."

UK's only losses were away games against conference foes Alabama and LSU. The memory of those games is still fresh in Jack Givens's mind. "We were undefeated at the time and the press and our fans expected us to continue that way. Alabama had a good team but no one expected us to lose, even though we hadn't played well the previous few games." He noted that Hall "warned us before the game that Bama was playing well and that we would get killed if we didn't play a great game. To say that we played badly would be an understatement. Alabama played with more enthusiasm, more desire, more pride, more heart, more everything than we did and whipped us by a score of 78 to 62." Hall was furious. He blasted the team, especially the stars, in the press, singling out Givens, who he knew could take the criticism and would understand the motivation, which was to blast the team out of its sense of complacency. "He said I played scared and with no heart," Givens recalled. "He threatened to remove me from the starting lineup. And those were the nice things he said about me."

The Wildcats returned home after the Alabama loss and, with the faithful roaring their approval, defeated Georgia, Florida, and Auburn by wide margins. The "Fysical Five" seemed to be back to playing their game. Then the Big Blue travelled to Baton Rouge to play the LSU Tigers on February 11. As Givens observed, "everything fell apart again." UK lost its second conference game by one point, 95-94, in overtime. "What made it so bad," the Goose noted, "was that their entire starting team fouled out in regulation time to only two of our starters. So in the overtime period it was our first team against their second team. Once again Coach Hall ripped us apart in the press and I came in for my share of the criticism. As a team he referred to us as the 'Quitting Quintet' and the 'Folding Five.' "

The Wildcats played at Mississippi State two days later and, although they won by twelve points, did not play particularly well. Things did not get back to normal until the following weekend when UK, now at home, thoroughly outclassed Tennessee to win by thirteen points. "This was an especially sweet victory," recalled Givens, "because not only was Tennessee our most hated rival but they had beaten us five straight times over the preceding three seasons. As if by magic the Alabama and LSU games were all but forgotten. Instead of the excessive criticism from the sportswriters and the fans there was excessive praise." The rest of the season was clear sailing for the Wildcats but the NCAA tournament brought new crises.

As the top-ranked team in the nation, according to all the polls, UK was seeded Number 1 in the Mideast Regionals. In their very first tournament game, a March 11 encounter with Florida State in Knoxville, the Big Blue found themselves in serious trouble. Throughout the season quick teams like Alabama had given the Wildcats problems and Florida State was a much quicker and more talented squad than Alabama. At halftime Florida State was ahead by seven points and Hall was furious. "He lectured us on all the things we were doing wrong and predicted that if things continued the same way in the second half we would end up the same as we did at Alabama." And that, noted Givens, would be a bitter fate. "He finally told us that if we were going to lose we would lose with people who wanted to play and who wanted to win. So at the start of the second half he put in Dwane Casey, LaVon Williams and Fred Cowan. For the first time in three years I wasn't starting a second half. The move totally surprised everyone, players, media, fans." It also surprised Coach Hugh Durham and his Florida State Seminoles. Givens continued:

Fortunately for Hall the move worked because if it hadn't the second guessers would have been all over him and the Adolph Rupp diehards would have been after his scalp. At any rate, Dwane and the others came out playing as though there was no tomorrow and, since one loss eliminates you in the NCAA, there was no tomorrow for us. They played great defense, fought like demons for rebounds, and dove for loose balls and they had Florida State completely off balance. If they hadn't gotten tired and could have shot better I might never have returned to the game. But I did get back in. When Rick [Robey], Truman [Claytor] and I reentered the game we played inspired basketball and UK won. Coach Hall's move was a real gutsy one and in the end he looked great because it proved to be the turning point in the game. I think the decision exemplified the way Coach Hall handled pressure all season. His job was to win games but he intended to do it his way. He was going to make his own decisions regardless of whether or not the fans, the press, or even his own players agreed. If his career at UK was to come to an end he was going to go down fighting.

Givens confessed to having "a great deal of respect and admiration for Coach Hall."

The Wildcats came back in the second half of the Florida State game to win by nine points, 85-76, but they still had four more games to play to win the national championship. The next opponent, Miami of Ohio, was no match for UK's size, skill, and experience and fell 91-69. The regional finals, against the Michigan State Spartans and their freshman sensation, "Magic" Johnson, was another matter, but the Cats were able to make adjustments and win the game. In a May 1983 interview Kyle Macy recalled that "Michigan State was in a zone that was giving us a lot of trouble in the first half. As we came out of the locker room at the end of the half, Coach Hamilton stopped

James Lee, a powerful forward, moves downcourt on a fastbreak against Arkansas in the semifinals of the 1978 NCAA tournament. UK won 64-59 in a tougher game than the final one against Duke.

Coach Hall and suggested trying an offense that he had in mind." Hall agreed to the plan and "called Rick Robey and me over and explained what he wanted us to do. Basically what it involved was for Rick to come up and set a pick on the zone, which is a little unusual. Fortunately," Macy laughed, "it worked." Robey's picks freed Macy for outside jump shots. "I would either hit the shot or be fouled and hit the free throws." Hamilton's offensive adjustment and Macy's shooting skill brought the Wildcats back in the second half and UK eked out a three-point victory, 52-49.

The Michigan State game underlined a point Macy made about the Wildcats' success in 1978. "I've always felt a major reason we won the championship that year was because we had the ability to adjust to every situation. If a team tried to stop Jack or Rick inside we had other players in the starting lineup or on the bench who could pick up the slack. There wasn't any one thing a team could do to stop our offense. And at the same time we did play pretty good defense."

By defeating Michigan State the Big Blue won the Mideast Regionals and qualified for the finals in St. Louis. In their first game, against an excellent Arkansas Razorback team, the Cats had still another chance to show their adaptability. "I'd say the Arkansas game was really the toughest game of the entire tournament," Macy stated. "That was because they presented some problems as far as matchups were concerned. They were a little shorter team than we were and quicker, and they had some outstanding shooters in Sidney Moncrief, Ron Brewer, and Melvin Delph. I think we did a good job of keeping our composure," he maintained, "and not making too many unforced errors, and then, with about a minute to play, made a big play when we had a run out with Jack [Givens] against their press." Givens also recalls the Arkansas contest as the "best game of the five we played in the whole tournament. Arkansas had a much better team than Duke. In fact, they were definitely one of the best teams we played all season."

The UK players had no doubts about winning the championship game against Duke. "We went into the Duke game prepared for anything they were going to do," noted Givens. "We were so excited and fired up about playing that we didn't even need Coach Hall to get us prepared. Everybody's attitude was just great." Kyle Macy pointed out that "before the game we had a team meeting, even before the coaches got there, and everybody just looked at each other and said: 'Hey, we've worked this hard to get here, let's just go out and do it.' " The Cats were a serious and dedicated band of veterans in 1978. As freshmen in San Diego

for the 1975 NCAA finals they had learned, in Givens's words, "that there was plenty of time for partying and having a good time after it's all over. So when we went to St. Louis my senior year we were strictly business. We went to St. Louis to win. We knew the only way we were going to be satisfied was to win."

In the Duke game the Wildcats were powered by one of the outstanding individual efforts in the history of the NCAA Championship game. As the April 3, 1978, issue of *Sports Illustrated* proclaimed in recounting UK's success: "The Goose was Golden." Jack Givens scored forty-one points in leading the Big Blue to a 94-88 victory over the outclassed Blue Devils. The smooth-shooting southpaw's point total was just three short of Bill Walton's record for the championship game. Givens is still amazed by his performance. "In fact," he noted, "when the game started out, I think I missed a couple or three shots. I certainly didn't expect to get the shots I did. I took twenty-seven shots from the field in that game and hit eighteen. I hadn't taken that many shots in any other game my four years at UK but the shots were there against Duke. We were a lot quicker than Duke was and I got a lot of points on fastbreaks but I got a lot more against their zone."

"Inexplicably," *Sports Illustrated* reported, "the Blue Devils did not come out of their zone defense until it was too late, and Givens just kept pouring in sweet jumpers, along with a selection of tips, layins and free throws." According to James Lee, this lack of strategy simply reflected the fact that Duke was a young and inexperienced team. "We would never have permitted a player to get so many open shots right in the middle of our zone," observed Lee. "After he hit a couple, we would have made an adjustment in our zone. The Duke players just didn't know what to do and, being a veteran team, we took full advantage of their mistakes. What most people didn't realize, and still don't realize," he emphasized, "is how versatile a team we were. We were able to adjust to any style of play or any situation. It was a real pleasure to be on that team."

Hall recounted after the game that "when we saw how open Duke was leaving the middle, we junked our game plan and just tried to get it to Jack." Characteristically, Givens saved his best performance for his most important game as a Wildcat. Also characteristically, he maintains that he played "a better all-around game [against Arkansas] than I did against Duke."

After twenty years in the wilderness UK was again college basketball's national champion. In the euphoria following the Duke game even *Courier-Journal* sports

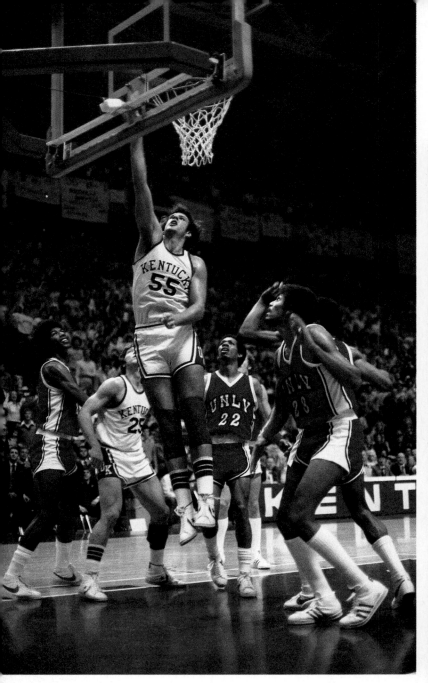

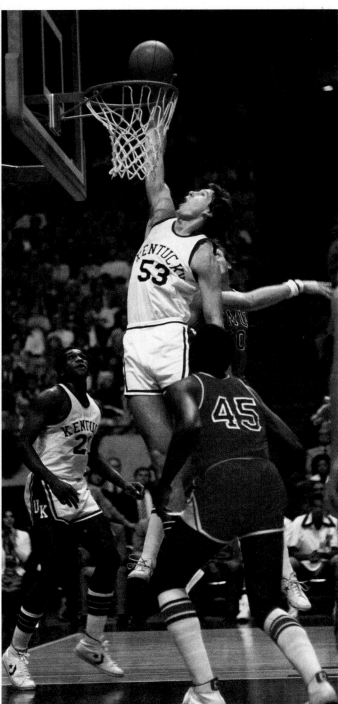

Above, Mike Phillips sinks the ball as the Cats run away from the Runnin' Rebels of the University of Nevada Las Vegas, 92-70, on March 4, 1978.

Right, the Wildcats roared off to a fast start for the 1977/78 season as they corralled the SMU Mustangs in the season opener. Rick Robey lays it in. Jack Givens is ready in case of a rebound.

Above, Truman Claytor prepares to sink two from long range against the Duke Blue Devils in the 1978 NCAA championship game in St. Louis. Two keys to winning the championship were reserve forward James Lee *(below left),* shown here driving against the University of Nevada Las Vegas on March 4, and stellar playmaker Kyle Macy *(below right),* the Cats' "coach on the floor."

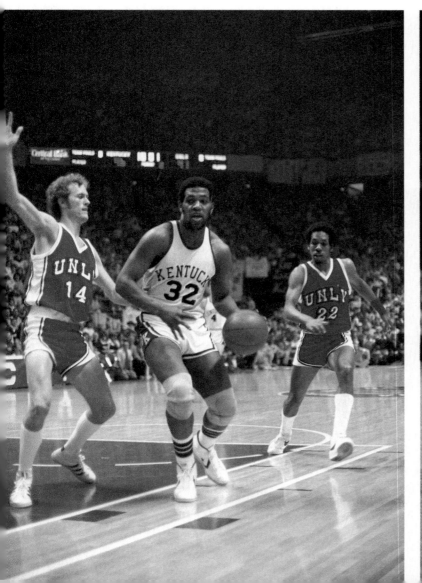

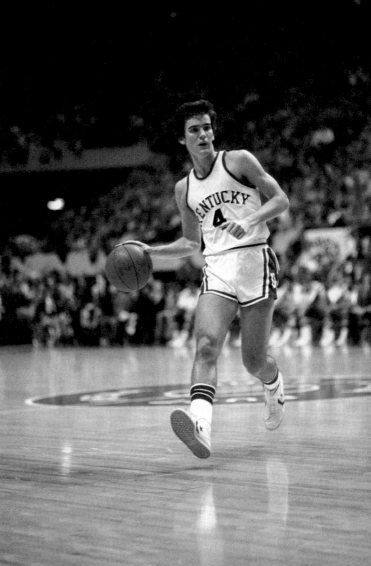

The sweet taste of victory. *Upper left,* "The Goose Was Golden!" Jack Givens shoots for 2 of his 41 points against the Duke University Blue Devils in the NCAA finals, his last—and best—Wildcat performance. *Upper right,* Rick Robey's victory roar says it all. *Below,* the Wildcat faithful, awaiting the team's return from St. Louis, revel in UK's first NCAA championship in twenty years.

editor Billy Reed found words of praise to shower on Hall. "Invariably," Reed maintained in a special post-tournament issue, Hall "doesn't get nearly as much credit or attention as slick-talking, media-oriented coaches such as Digger Phelps of Notre Dame. . . . Hall has earned the right to be respected by the press, the public and his peers. That, and the right to a little peace of mind." This was only a temporary truce, however. An end to hostilities was not in the offing—either from the press or from Hall.

With the victory over Duke in the 1978 national championship game, UK regained the glory of the Rupp era, but that enviable situation lasted only a short time. The NCAA-imposed restrictions on the number of basketball scholarships had an immediate impact on UK's basketball fortunes. Only because of the brilliant play of Kyle Macy and freshman Dwight Anderson, an all-out effort by the other members of the team, and a fine coaching job by Hall and his staff, were the Wildcats able to stave off potential disaster in 1979. Nevertheless, victory in the 1978 NCAA tournament marked a major turning point in the coaching career of Joe B. Hall.

Following the 1978 season Hall and Ernst Jokl, a retired UK professor of physical education and a widely respected authority on sports medicine, collected statistics from the 1948, 1958, 1968, and 1978 seasons to compare physiques and performance of the current national champions with earlier Wildcat teams (Tables 5 and 6). Not only did the Wildcat teams of 1958, 1968, and 1978 have higher scoring averages than the 1948

NCAA champions, but so did UK's opponents in 1968 and 1978. Neither the "Fabulous Five" nor the "Fiddlin' Five" were able to score 100 points in a game. The high scoring Issel-Casey-Pratt group, which ranked fourth in the nation in 1968, totaled 100 or more points seven times during the season, while the 1978 team, which had a reputation for playing a more deliberate, ball-control game, scored 100 points six times. The 1968 and 1978 teams not only scored more points than their predecessors but were also more accurate, both from the field and from the free throw line. Although fans and even sportswriters tend to believe that the Wildcats were better in the "good old days" of Rupp than under Joe Hall, the evidence seems to prove otherwise. In size and shooting ability, even on free throws, the 1978 team was superior to the other squads examined.

Table 5. UK Team Records, Selected Years, 1947/48-1977/78

Season	Average Points Scored per Game		No. of Games UK Scored 100 Points
	UK	Opponent	UK
1947/48	69.0	44.0	0
1957/58	74.5	62.6	0
1967/68	88.9	77.9	7
1977/78	84.2	69.8	6

Table 6. Comparison of UK Players, Selected Years, 1947/48-1977/78

	Starters				Substitutes			
	1947/48	1957/58	1967/68	1977/78	1947/48	1957/58	1967/68	1977/78
Height	6'2 1/6"	6'3 1/3"	6'4 3/4"	6'5 1/2"	6'1 1/2"	6'3 1/3"	6'4 1/3"	6'5 1/6"
Weight (lbs.)	192.0	183.8	209.2	206.6	177.9	188.2	196.0	206.1
Field goal percentage	33.47	37.88	46.51	55.97	27.54	34.05	48.87	49.55
Free throw percentage	63.08	75.22	70.76	77.85	61.59	67.47	70.58	70.86

10

Building a New Tradition

For Joe Hall and his Wildcats the 1978/79 season was a series of problems, including injuries and defections. Finally, in the SEC tournament, exhaustion and lack of players—UK was down to seven experienced players for the championship game—caught up with the Big Blue to prevent a Cinderella finish to a frustrating season. Nevertheless, at least one rabid UK supporter was hopeful. At the end of the season Oscar Combs, who in 1976 sold two weekly newspapers he published in Eastern Kentucky to move to Lexington and launch *The Cats' Pause*, a weekly sports magazine devoted to UK sports, published a book entitled *Kentucky Basketball: A New Beginning*. The optimism reflected in the subtitle seemed fully justified. Hall, finally freed after two seasons of NCAA-imposed restrictions on recruitment, had signed five of the top high school seniors in the country to scholarships—Sam Bowie, Dirk Minniefield, Derrick Hord, Charles Hurt, and Tom Heitz—while a sixth, Melvin Turpin, had announced that after a year in prep school to improve his academic record, he also would enroll at UK.

Bo Lanter, who walked on as a redshirt at UK in 1978/79 after an excellent season at Midwestern State University at Wichita Falls, Texas, stated in an interview that "if someone had told me when I transferred that I was going to be at Kentucky four years and that we would not win a national championship, I would have told him he was crazy. There were no doubts in my mind. After all," he pointed out, "we were coming off a national championship and that means good recruiting. Then [for the 1979/80 season] we signed four superstars in Bowie, Minniefield, Hord, and Hurt. Matter of fact, I was counting on two or three

[championship] rings before I got out of school." Although UK has yet to win its sixth NCAA title, the program has been successful in the seasons since 1977. It is also building a new tradition, one that is racially integrated.

The venerable Wildcat tradition is safe and secure in the hands of Joe B. Hall, and now it is a tradition for black Kentuckians as well as for whites. A recent UK signee was quoted in the press as saying that to play for the Blue and White was "a dream come true." This black athlete was happy to join the Wildcat tradition, but for him it is not the tradition of Beard and Groza, Hagan and Ramsey, or Nash and Issel, but of Givens and Minniefield, two black stars from Lexington. As he put it, "Playing at UK is something I've always wanted to do. I've grown up watching Jack Givens and Dirk Minniefield play at UK, and I really look up to them." This attitude is a welcome and healthy change from the racially exclusive tradition of the Rupp era.

The Wildcats began the 1978/79 season with six black and six white players. Among the three freshmen recruits on the squad was 6'3" guard Dwight Anderson of Dayton, Ohio, one of the most exciting and talented players in UK basketball history. Although he remained less than a season and a half, his stay was memorable. Anderson was a multitalented player who possessed blinding speed, lightning quickness, uncanny moves, and outstanding leaping ability. In only his seventh game as a member of the Big Blue, against a strong Notre Dame team on national television, Anderson scored seventeen second-half points to lead the Wildcats from a twelve-point deficit, with only

Although he played less than two seasons at UK, flashy and versatile Dwight Anderson *(above)* left an indelible imprint on Wildcat basketball. *Below,* he and Hall are interviewed on national television after his brilliant performance against Notre Dame, December 30, 1978.

eight minutes left in the game, to an 81-76 win. His play was so outstanding that NBC color man and former Marquette coach Al McGuire was moved to proclaim on the air: "A new star was born tonight in college basketball." And Anderson, the game's Most Valuable Player, was not even playing his normal position of guard. Because UK was so short-handed throughout the season, Anderson had to play at forward. Although just a substitute in UK's first thirteen games, and forced to play opponents several inches taller, "Dwight Lightning" finished the season as the team's second leading scorer.

From the beginning of the 1979 season the Wildcats lacked depth and size, the cumulative effect of the recruiting restrictions imposed in 1977. In 1977/78 the Big Blue had added 6'8" forward Fred Cowan and 6'10" centers Chuck Aleksinas and Scott Courts as well as walk-on guard Chris Gettelfinger. The 1978/79 season brought the arrival of 6'7" forward Clarence Tillman, 6'6" Chuck Verderber, Dwight Anderson and walk-on Bo Lanter. Of the six scholarship players recruited during those two seasons only two—Cowan and Verderber—completed their careers at UK. Courts departed the team at the end of his freshman season, leaving the 6'10" 258-pound Aleksinas as UK's biggest player. Aleksinas became dissatisfied with the Wildcat style of play, unfortunately, and quit the team in January 1979. In a June 1983 reunion of the 1978 NCAA championship team, Aleksinas admitted he had made a mistake in quitting and regretted his decision. But that admission did not help the 1979 team. Neither did it help that another member of the championship team, 6'3" junior forward Tim Stephens left the squad at the beginning of January 1979. With the departure of Stephens and Aleksinas, UK was left with only ten scholarship players and without a natural center. With a front court consisting of 6'3" 175-pounder Dwight Anderson, 6'7" 220-pound LaVon Williams, and 6'8" 210-pound Fred Cowan, and with 6'3" 188-pound Kyle Macy and 6'1" 180-pound Truman Claytor at the guards, the Cats could not be mistaken for the "Fysical Five," but they were quick and rugged.

The 1978/79 team had a poor regular-season record by UK standards, winning sixteen and losing ten, including eight losses to SEC rivals. The Wildcats were saved by the fact that the conference had returned to the postseason tournament format for the first time since 1952. With the flashy and often brilliant Anderson, streak-shooting Claytor, and smart, steady Macy leading the way, the Big Blue upended Mississippi, Alabama, and LSU in SEC tournament play to qualify for the championship game and an automatic bid to the NCAA tournament. Unfortunately for the Cats,

Anderson, who had averaged twenty points in the previous eight games, suffered a fractured wrist in the first minute of the LSU game and was lost for the championship game against Tennessee.

Joe Dean considers the UK-Alabama game, which the Wildcats won 101-100, to be "one of the greatest games I have ever seen. We were shorthanded, we were playing Bama in Birmingham, and their star, Reggie King, had a great game but we still won because Claytor, Macy, and Anderson were just absolutely incredible that night shooting the ball. Then, against LSU," Dean's story continues, "Anderson broke his wrist and we had to play with a makeshift lineup." With only seven experienced players, plus the seldom used Lanter and Gettelfinger, the Big Blue were simply outmanned by Tennessee, but forced the game into overtime before finally falling, 75-69. "It was tough to lose to the Vols," Dean acknowledges, "but our players were just so worn out."

UK's late-season heroics brought an invitation to participate in the NIT, but without the spectacular Anderson to ignite them the exhausted Wildcats ran out of miracles. Although they played their first tournament game before their wildly cheering fans at Rupp Arena, the Big Blue lost in overtime to Clemson of the Atlantic Coast Conference by one point, 68-67.

Considering the variety of problems UK faced during the season, 1979 has to be reckoned a successful season. The four seasons that followed were in many respects less satisfying.

Before the start of the 1979/80 season, yet another highly touted player, forward Clarence Tillman, quit the team and school, leaving only six returning lettermen. Before the end of December, Anderson also would depart and, as in 1978/79, the Wildcats would again be short on experience. Hall never explained the real reasons for Anderson's departure, but in a February 13, 1980, *Courier-Journal* article, Billy Reed claimed that a rift between the coach and his enormously talented but undisciplined star was inevitable. "It wasn't that I doubted Anderson's ability," Reed maintained. "It was just that, judging by what I had seen and heard of Anderson, I didn't think he would be unselfish enough to fit into Hall's disciplined, team-oriented system." In 1979 UK had been "so thin," especially after Chuck Aleksinas quit the team, that "Hall had to sit there and let him [Anderson] do things. He had no choice." In 1980 the situation was different. With five excellent freshman prospects joining the team, Hall was less dependent on the highly individualistic Anderson. The basic problem, in Reed's opinion was that Hall and Anderson "defined 'fun' differently. To Hall, fun means success through hard

LaVon Williams puts up a rebound against LaSalle on December 2, 1978. Chuck Aleksinas (50) quit the team in mid-season, and forward Fred Cowan (right) moved to center.

work, sacrifice, discipline and selflessness. To Anderson fun means success through doing your own thing both on and off the floor."

My conversations with former UK players underscore the point that Hall subscribes to essentially the same theories of motivation as Adolph Rupp did. Like his predecessor, Hall believes there are two types of players—those who have to be driven hard to perform their best and those who need encouragement and special treatment. Like Rupp, Hall prefers the former type and insists that players with sensitive egos either adjust to his hard-driving style of coaching or leave. Over the years many talented players have left while many others who decided to stick it out at

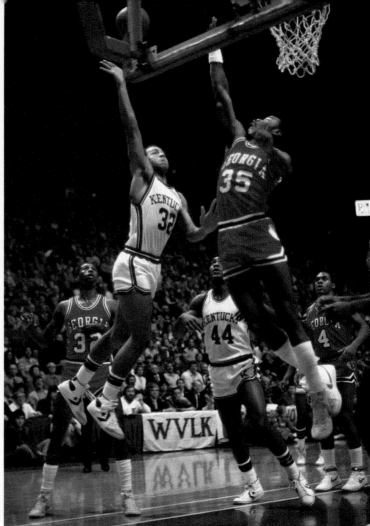

More fast and furious Wildcat action. *Above left,* Melvin Turpin muscles the ball in over an Alabama defender. *Right,* Derrick Hord leaps high against Georgia while Charles Hurt (44) moves into position for a possible rebound.

UK simply shriveled up inside and never played up to their abilities. Players and journalists I have talked with agree that Derrick Hord was a player who needed encouragement and sensitive treatment. But as sportswriter Mark Bradley of the *Herald-Leader* observed in an interview, "that is not Joe Hall's style."

Derrick Hord was one of five very talented high school stars who arrived on the Lexington campus at the start of the 1979/80 season. With recruiting restrictions finally removed by the NCAA, Joe Hall enjoyed a bountiful harvest. In addition to the smooth-shooting Hord, who was generally considered the best basketball player ever from the state of Tennessee, Hall signed to national letters of intent 7'1" Sam Bowie, outstanding guard prospect Dirk Minniefield, and high school All-American forwards Charles Hurt and Tom Heitz. The Wildcats just missed signing the most highly regarded of all the college prospects, 7'4" Ralph Sampson, when he chose the University of Virginia over UK, his other final choice, in order to be closer to his fam-

ily. Even without Sampson, the future looked bright for Hall and the Big Blue.

In the seasons since, Hall has added several more blue-chip athletes to the UK roster. The 1980/81 season brought, in addition to 6'11" center Melvin Turpin, Indiana's high school "Mr. Basketball," Jim Master, a guard with an excellent shooting touch; 6'9" forward Bret Bearup from Long Island; and 5'11" Dicky Beal, a lightning quick guard with exceptional jumping ability. Forward Troy McKinley and guard Mike Ballenger arrived for the 1981/82 season and were joined the following season by forwards Kenny Walker, Georgia high school player of the year, and Todd May, Kentucky's "Mr. Basketball," as well as Indiana's "Mr. Basketball," guard Roger Harden. Ballenger and May have since left UK, Ballenger to Western Kentucky while May transferred during his freshman season to Wake Forest. In the spring of 1983, Hall signed four more excellent prospects—6' 7 1/2" forward Winston Bennett of Louisville Male High School, Kentucky's

"Mr. Basketball"; 6'3" guard James Blackmon of Marion, Indiana; 6'3" Laurel County guard Paul Andrews; and Vince Sanford, a 6'5" swingman from Lexington's Lafayette High School.

A new method of recruiting emerged in the late 1970s and early 1980s, and Hall is fully as effective in its practice as Adolph Rupp was in the system used in the 1940s. Although recruiters still spend a great deal of time travelling around the country watching high school games and visiting prospects and their families, the key to locating and capturing the top players, the "Blue Chippers," to use Al McGuire's very descriptive term, is the summer basketball camp. While most summer camps stress instruction in the fundamentals of basketball, the more prestigious ones, like Five-Star, Sportsworld's Superstar, and B/C Basketball Camp, offer competition, pure and simple. In the July 17, 1983, issue of the *Herald-Leader* Sportswriter Mike Fields reported on a visit to the B/C camp, located in Rensselaer, Indiana. Director Bill Cronauer, who along with partner Bill Bolton runs B/C, touts B/C as a "superstars" camp which stresses "saturation basketball" from morning until evening for a solid week. The Rensselaer camp attracted more than 460 young hopefuls, each paying $220 to attend. Part of the attraction is the opportunity to test one's talent against high-level competition. Undoubtedly of much greater importance is the presence of more than 300 college coaches. "One observer," Fields noted, "compared the

B/C Camp to a horse sale, right down to the players wearing hip numbers as identification. The college coaches, strictly prohibited by NCAA rules from making any contact with campers, are the buyers in the scenario," the reporter continued. "They consult player catalogs, which are sold at the door for $10 a clip. The coaches don't bid on the players, but they do evaluate them and decide whether to ante up scholarships." The college coaches, Fields learned, "certainly benefit from this congregation of basketball talent. Instead of spending months crisscrossing the nation in search of prospects, the coaches can book a motel room in Rensselaer for a week and evaluate hundreds of kids." Bolton and Cronauer also hold two camps in Milledgeville, Georgia, and one in Bowie, Maryland. "All together this summer they will draw some 1,300 players and almost as many coaches."

Incoming UK freshman forward Winston Bennett underscored the importance of summer camps for high school players in a July 1983 interview, acknowledging that he gained "a lot of valuable experience from the summer camps." Tagged a can't-miss prospect while still a ninth grader, the 6' 7 1/2" Louisville native maintained that "the opportunity to play against some of the best players in the United States really helped me a lot to improve my game. When you go up against guys who are bigger and stronger than you are it makes you either get stronger or learn techniques to overcome their advantages."

The summer basketball camp has become an important scouting and recruiting method. Here, Jack Givens instructs campers in UK's Seaton Center.

Chuck Verderber's rebound helped UK to an 86-80 victory over Notre Dame on December 29, 1979.

In addition to the camps run by talent scouts like Bolton and Cronauer, many coaches, including Joe Hall, offer their own camps. The Joe B. Hall Wildcat Basketball Summer Camp attracts the cream of the high school basketball crop. This offers Hall and his staff a marvelous opportunity to observe the best talent available competing against one another every day for a week. In many respects this is an even more valuable opportunity to judge ability than the tryouts Rupp used so effectively in the 1940s to build his great teams. The camps are not, it must be emphasized, the end-all of recruiting, but they are invaluable for pinpointing the most likely prospects for intensive recruiting before the start of their senior year in high school. As Leonard Hamilton noted in an interview, "Recruiting is a year-round job," but the various summer camps are crucial "for evaluating talent."

The UK coaching staff did an excellent job of "evaluating talent" in preparation for the 1979/80 season. Going into the season the Big Blue appeared to have the same mixture of talented and battle-tested veterans and brilliant freshmen that propelled the 1975 team to the NCAA finals. The Wildcats started the season with six returning lettermen (the seventh, sophomore Clarence Tillman, left school in October), five freshmen, and walk-on guards Chris Gettelfinger and Bo Lanter, who won scholarships through hard work and solid performance in practice and occasional game appearances. The veterans included forwards Fred Cowan, Chuck Verderber, and LaVon Williams and guards Kyle Macy, Jay Shidler, and Dwight Anderson. Macy was the brains of the team while Anderson was the catalyst.

Unfortunately Anderson also proved to be a disruptive influence. Before the December 29 game with Notre Dame, Anderson, Sam Bowie, and Dirk Minniefield were caught violating team rules and were disciplined. According to a team press release, Anderson decided to leave the team for, as Hall put it, "personal reasons," while Bowie, who although only a freshman was the team's starting center, and Minniefield, a substitute guard at the time, were suspended for the Notre Dame game "for violation of well-established training rules." The coaching staff never divulged the real reasons for Anderson's departure, despite heavy pressure from D.G. FitzMaurice of the *Herald-Leader*, Billy Reed, and other sportswriters. In an article in the December 30 *Herald-Leader* FitzMaurice maintained that as "Richard Nixon had his Watergate" so too did Joe Hall "have a Wildcatgate on his hands." The reason for the accusation was Hall's refusal to confirm or deny a report made by Lexington television sports director Tom Hammond that Anderson was discovered with a "controlled substance, a narcotic," that is, marijuana, in his possession. "It is time," FitzMaurice stated with indignation, "for Joe Hall to level with the fans, and to quit playing cute word games with the press. It's time for Coach Hall to set the record straight. It's time for the complete truth to emerge. Anything less is an insult to Kentucky fans everywhere."

Hall did not respond, however, and the campaign to pressure him into "setting the record straight" eventually died because it finally became clear that Hall would not budge. The incident had the unfortunate result of increasing the already existing antagonism between the press and UK's coaching staff. Hall, for

his part, felt the press should concentrate on the team's on-court performance which, considering the lack of experienced players was surprisingly good in 1980. After Anderson's departure in December 1979, UK was down to five scholarship players. Through much of the rest of the season the Big Blue started two freshmen—Bowie and Minniefield—along with veterans Cowan, Williams, and Macy.

After a season-opening loss to Duke in overtime, 82-76, in the 1979 Hall of Fame Game in Springfield, Massachusetts, the Wildcats played brilliant ball throughout December culminating an eleven-game winning streak with an 86-80 victory over Notre Dame on December 29 in Louisville. In the nationally televised game the Cats, playing without the suspended Anderson, Bowie, and Minniefield, defeated a strong Fighting Irish team that entered the contest with a 6-0 record and a Number 3 ranking in the national polls. The Big Blue faltered in January—the "January Swoon," as the press terms what seems to be an annual occurrence for Hall's teams—losing three of ten conference matches. UK rebounded in February to win nine straight games and the SEC championship for the thirty-second time in the league's history. The Cats were knocked out of the SEC tournament in Birmingham by an inspired LSU team but, as regular season champions, were placed in the NCAA Mideast regionals with games scheduled for Bowling Green and Lexington. With the advantage of playing before the home crowds the Big Blue seemed a shoo-in as regional champions. After a strong performance against Florida State the Cats returned home to Rupp Arena for a return match with Duke. But even with the full support of their loyal fans, the Big Blue had no more luck in this game than in the Hall of Fame game. Once again UK lost by one point, 55-54, when Macy missed a long jump shot at the buzzer. "It was," Bo Lanter maintains, "the only key shot I can recall Kyle missing in the time I was at UK. You could always depend on Kyle to hit the pressure shot or free throw. Even on that one [Duke guard] Vince Taylor admitted after the game that he had hit Kyle." With the loss to Duke, Kyle Macy's brilliant career at UK came to an end. Macy noted in an interview "with a break here or there we could have won the Duke game and made it to the Final Four, and with a young team. Even with the loss, though, it was a very good season."

With Macy gone, a lot of responsibility fell to Dirk Minniefield in the 1980/81 season, especially since his running mate through much of the season was converted forward Derrick Hord. Backups included very promising freshman prospects Jim Master and Dicky Beal as well as junior Bo Lanter and senior Chris

Jim Master demonstrates his impeccable free-throw technique.

Gettelfinger. Hord never did fully adjust to the guard position and the following season was moved back to forward, his natural position. Hord's conversion to guard was made necessary in part by the lack of experienced players at that position. Another factor was the abundance of talent available at forward where, in addition to starters Fred Cowan, a senior, and sophomore Charles Hurt, the Cats had team captain Chuck Verderber and 6'9" freshman Bret Bearup. At center UK had even more talent available with Sam Bowie, who would become an All-American that season as a sophomore, and freshman Melvin Turpin, who proved to be a capable backup.

The Big Blue lost only four regular-season games in 1980/81, but three of these defeats were to SEC teams, thus denying UK its thirty-third SEC championship, at least for a year. The Wildcats were nevertheless invited to the NCAA Mideast Regionals at Tuscaloosa, where they played small, quick Alabama-Birmingham for the second time in the season. The Big Blue had defeated Alabama-Birmingham in the championship game of the UKIT at Rupp Arena in December but in the return match UK fell short by seven points, 69-62. The groundwork for a very suc-

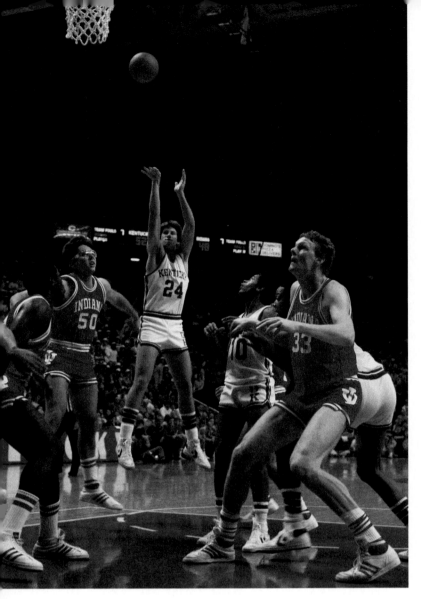

New York native Bret Bearup scores as the Cats top Indiana on December 3, 1983. James Blackmon is no. 10.

even though he is a great athlete, just had to do too much."

Dirk Minniefield also stressed Bowie's importance. "When we lost Sam," he stated in an interview, "we definitely lost our inside punch because all of a sudden we were a team without a proven inside player. Now Melvin [Turpin], who had little playing experience, had to step in and try to take over. This meant the guards had to make a big adjustment. I had to take on more of a scoring load early in the season but once Melvin got settled in we went more to an inside-oriented style of play." The Wildcats had to adjust to the loss of Bowie, and to a great extent they did.

UK's resilience and overall talent is evident from the fact that the team did not fold, despite the unexpected loss of its leading scorer and rebounder and the heart of its man-to-man defense. Bowie's place in the starting lineup was taken by untried sophomore Melvin Turpin, who led the team in rebounding and blocked shots and was third in scoring. The team's leading scorer in 1982 was Derrick Hord, who returned to his familiar forward position. Senior Chuck Verderber usually started at the other forward position although Charles Hurt started eight games and was generally the first player off the bench in the other games. Dirk Minniefield, the team's assist leader, returned as playmaking guard while sophomore Jim Master, an outstanding outside shooter, started twenty-nine of UK's thirty games in 1981/82. The Big Blue proved to have a deep and talented bench even without Bret Bearup, 6'9" 230-pound power forward who chose to red-shirt in 1982 after playing in twenty-six of UK's twenty-eight games in his freshman season. In addition to Hurt, reserves included Tom Heitz, who had red-shirted in 1981, and freshman Troy McKinley in the front court, while speedy sophomore Dicky Beal, freshman Mike Ballenger, and senior Bo Lanter contributed at guard.

UK completed the 1981/82 season with an overall record of 22-8, including 13-5 in regular SEC play and 2-1 in the post-season conference tournament. The SEC co-champion Wildcats travelled to Nashville and an all but assured NCAA tournament confrontation with the University of Louisville, a game the media had for months been clamoring for. Even the *Sporting News* on December 5, 1981, featured a cover story on "The Bitter Fight for Kentucky" between UK and the Louisville Cardinals and an eagerly anticipated "Louisville-Kentucky matchup in March." The NCAA selection committee obliged by placing the Wildcats and Cardinals in the same regional.

All that stood in the way of "the game" was for the Big Blue to defeat lightly regarded Ohio Valley cham-

cessful 1981/82 season, and even for an NCAA title, seemed to be laid, however. UK would lose only Fred Cowan and Chris Gettelfinger through graduation. Back would be UK's most experienced team since the 1978 national champions. But then disaster struck.

Before the start of the 1981/82 season Joe Hall announced that All-American and twice All-SEC center Sam Bowie was suffering from a small, incomplete fracture of his left tibia, or shin bone. Bowie missed the entire season, a loss that dealt a crippling blow to UK's title hopes. In an interview Bo Lanter maintained that "when you have a player like Bowie you have a franchise. I feel it was a big step for the UK program to get a player like Bowie. So his loss was a very serious blow. For one thing not having him in the middle hurt Minniefield. With Bowie out, Dirk,

pion Middle Tennessee. But instead of going on to meet Louisville for the championship of Kentucky and advancing to the NCAA Final Four, the Wildcats suffered a humiliating 50-44 defeat. Derrick Hord admitted in an interview that "I'd be lying if I said we weren't looking ahead but we didn't take Middle Tennessee for granted. It was just one of those nights where we couldn't do anything right and they couldn't do anything wrong. They were really pumped up because they wanted to knock off Kentucky and we couldn't get our shots to fall. I know I was something like two for sixteen and normally I'm a 50 percent shooter. So they outscored us and that's the name of the game." Middle Tennessee was a small, quick team and Bo Lanter noted that UK adjusted its game to combat Middle Tennessee's quickness "rather than having them adjust to our height." Lanter compared the Middle Tennessee game with the 1981 NCAA tournament loss to Alabama-Birmingham. "Alabama-Birmingham had a better team then we thought they had and they played extremely well against us and I give them a lot of credit. I also give Middle Tennessee credit but I just feel like the loss to Middle Tennessee was more of a fluke than the one to Alabama-Birmingham was. We just plain old didn't play them," he acknowledged.

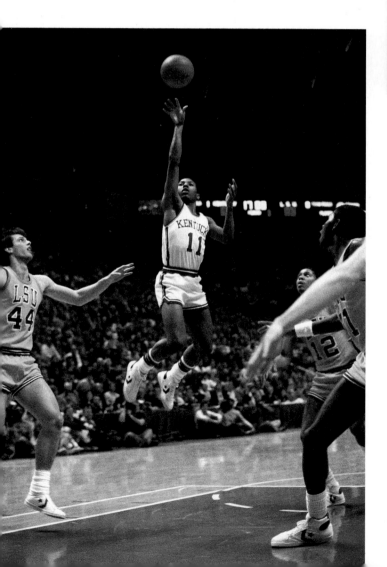

Above, Kenny Walker plays rock-ribbed defense against Georgia, while guard Jim Master waits in the background.

Left, Dicky Beal (5'11") lays the ball up as UK closes its 1983/84 regular season with a victory over LSU. Beal's inspired playing sparked the Cats to the SEC championship.

"We made a lot of mistakes, stupid mistakes. It really killed me because it was my last game at UK. I wanted a national championship so bad and that was the end. I'll never forget the feeling that night. I was so upset I cried like a baby after the game." For departing seniors Lanter and Verderber that was the end of their dream of winning a national championship. For the returning members of the team, the 1982/83 season would prove equally frustrating.

UK had a winning season in 1982/83, won the SEC championship, and played in the NCAA tournament. By normal standards that should qualify as a successful season. But for Wildcat fans and for the press it was *not* a successful season for two reasons: the Big Blue

The 1982/83 season was disappointing for many, including senior Derrick Hord, who came under intense criticism from Hall and the local press when his game began to deteriorate at mid-season.

lost to Louisville and that defeat knocked the team out of contention for UK's sixth NCAA championship. Without exception, the players and coaches I interviewed saw the 1982/83 season in a more favorable light. They felt the team overcame problems and adversities to end the season on a positive note. Dirk Minniefield maintained that what stood out in his mind about his senior year was "the way the team put aside all the outside distractions, the newspapers and all, and came together and played great down the stretch. I thought that by the end of the year we got to be a total team. All things considered," Minniefield observed, "we went pretty far. In fact, we probably went a lot farther than some people thought we could go." To Minniefield, the Louisville game "was great from all aspects. I think that once the game started we were more than they expected. They came back and beat us but that's what you expect a great team to do."

For Derrick Hord, 1982/83 was "an up-and-down season." "Jim [Master], Melvin [Turpin], and Dirk [Minniefield] and the rest of the guys really looked great," Hord acknowledged in a July 1983 interview. During the previous season the Bristol, Tennessee, native had led the Cats in scoring with a 16.3 points per game average. At the end of that season Hord was named All-SEC and honorable mention All-American. On the basis of his tremendous potential and his performance in 1981/82, a lot was expected of him in his senior year. Ironically, Hord "had the best opening

season since I got here," but for reasons he cannot fully understand his play soon became inconsistent. "There I was, averaging nearly seventeen points and getting about thirty minutes a game" during the preceding season "and I came into the latter part of the season this year and the coaches are looking around me to put somebody else in. They don't want to put me in. It does something to your confidence. It's a learning experience anyway," he noted grimly.

When Hord's game started falling apart, Hall added to his inner anguish by ripping him apart in practice, during and after games and in the press. Although the player recognized that an integral part of Hall's coaching philosophy is picking on his players, especially seniors who seem not to be performing up to their potential, in order to force them to play better, it apparently had the opposite effect on Hord. A very intelligent, thoughtful, and sensitive young man, Hord reacted by withdrawing even further within himself. He acknowledged that during the season "a lot of people" had told him that he let "a lot of things bother me that I probably should have ignored but," he noted, "that's the way I am. I'm usually a sensitive person in that respect and I like to perform for somebody who thinks I can do the job. If I go into the game and feel that they don't think I can do the job then I'm thinking, Why did they put me in?" In addition, he continued, Kenny Walker "was having a great freshman year and he [Hall] knew that he could put Kenny in and Kenny would excite the crowd and get the team going while I'm kind of a silent player. In my junior year I'd go out there and people wouldn't know I was there. I'd usually get the job done pretty well without a lot of excitement." What this meant was that when things went wrong for Hord, Hall apparently felt there was no reason for keeping him in the game.

Hord emphasized that he understood Hall's motivation in openly criticizing his play and that of others on the team. He maintained that "all of us really knew that it wasn't personal." But the treatment accorded coaches and players in the media, especially in the local press, was something he could not comprehend. "The Louisville papers like to jump on Coach Hall but the Lexington papers jump on everybody. 'Piranha Press,' that's what I call them. They build you up to break you down. Not all the reporters though, just a couple." Apparently other members of the team felt the same way because, Hord maintained, "there was a time" during the middle of the season "when we just didn't go in and talk with the press." It would begin early in the season, he went on. "They'd start talking 'January slump' in October when we had press con-

ferences. They'd bring on a lot of stuff. I know that is part of the game, but nowhere else in our conference do they write stories like they do here."

Despite the problems, Hord stated emphatically that if he had it to do all over he definitely would come to UK. "I would probably do things a lot differently but it has been a great experience."

Derrick Hord undoubtedly received and accepted more blame than he deserved for UK's failure to fulfill its promise during the four years he was on the team. The major problem with the team in that period, maintained Jack Givens in an August 1983 interview, was a lack of consistency, especially after the loss of Sam Bowie. "All the guys looked super in some games," Givens noted, "but in others they wouldn't be looking for their shots. It only takes a few bad games to get your confidence down and you start wondering whether you can do it at all." Givens, who observed the team at close range as a television commentator for UK home games, continued his description. "It seemed as though each member of the team was waiting for someone else to come out and do things. After Sam, who was their leader, was lost they never did establish another leader. No one else played as consistently, both on offense and defense, as Sam did." Givens thought Dicky Beal "might have become the leader if he had stayed healthy. When he was in the game you could see the difference in the team. Everyone was more alert and involved with Dicky in there."

Others, including sportswriters and some players, believe that the loss of assistant coach Dick Parsons after the 1980 season was a major factor in UK's problems in the following years. Parsons left because of a change in NCAA regulations which reduced the size of coaching staffs. Hall wanted all of his coaches to help with recruiting, something Parsons reportedly no longer enjoyed. *Courier-Journal* veteran sportswriter Earl Cox regarded the departure of Parsons as a great loss for the Wildcat program. "The little guy with the quiet demeanor," Cox wrote on January 18, 1983, "had a strong influence on Hall. He was the one who tugged at Hall's coat to keep him away from referees. He was the one who soothed players' feelings after tongue-lashings by Hall. Joe listened to Dicky's suggestions. They were a team, on and off the floor, fishing buddies even." One of the players with whom I talked also lamented the loss of Parsons. "We all hated to see Coach Parsons go," he maintained. "Coach Parsons was close to the players and we all liked him a lot. He also played an important part in the preparation for games and coaching during the games. We've all missed him since he left."

Dirk Minniefield was one of four high school All-Americans who arrived at UK for the 1979/80 season, raising hopes for another national title, but it eluded the Cats.

The Wildcats finished the 1982/83 season with a 23-8 record. Six of the losses were suffered within the tough and highly competitive SEC. The Big Blue avenged an early season loss to Indiana with a 64-59 victory in the semifinals of the NCAA Mideast Regionals in Knoxville to set up the long-awaited confrontation with Louisville on March 26. The eagerly anticipated "Dream Game" was the first meeting between the two schools in twenty-four years. Although UK lost in overtime, 80-68, it was a more hotly contested and well-played game than the final score might indicate. Jack Givens also acknowledged that the Wildcats played a much stronger game than he had expected. "I really expected Louisville to win by about eight in regulation time. I thought the Louisville forwards would pretty much have their own way but Derrick started out hot and Charles [Hurt] had a good game. I felt Kenny would give UK strength coming off the bench, and I expected Melvin to have a great game.

And he did. Jim Master played just super. He had a much better all around game than I expected. You just can't do anything about an overtime period if you start off bad. That five-minute overtime period feels awful short when you get four or five points behind right away. But I thought UK overall played a good game."

Minniefield and the other players had good feelings about the Louisville game. "I knew they had a great team," Minniefield said about the Cardinals, "but I think we were more than they expected. I don't feel Louisville expected us to play as well as we did." In an interview with Billy Reed printed in the July 20, 1983 *Courier-Journal*, Jim Master recalled that by the Louisville game UK had developed into "a great team" that was "only a play or two from going to the Final Four. That's the first year we've done that since I've been at Kentucky. It was positive—very positive." Sportswriters also expressed great enthusiasm over the game. Noting that the final score was deceiving, one reporter observed to me that "the game had

Right, Charles Hurt, a high school All-American, was a top-notch rebounder and defensive player who never showed his good shooting touch while at UK. Behind him is Tom Heitz (33). *Below*, Fred Cowan dodges the Vanderbilt defense.

everything, steals, dunks, comebacks; it was truly a basketball fan's 'Dream Game.' "

In the aftermath of the March 26 "Dream Game," Louisville and Lexington sportswriters continued their demands for an annual meeting between the two schools. Joe Hall, for his part, maintained his adamant opposition to regular-season games with state schools. Cliff Hagan, as UK athletics director, had fully supported Hall's position on this issue. But as university officials, trustees, a growing number of fans, and even the governor indicated a growing interest in—or at least, a willingness to discuss—the possibility of a UK-U of L series, Hagan altered his position. According to Reporter Jerry Tipton in an April 3, 1983, *Herald-Leader* article, "Hagan and others in the UK hierarchy" who supported Hall and his policy in the past had by this time "lessened that support." Hagan's posi-

tion, as quoted by Tipton, now was that "if the coach wants to play, we'll play." According to Hagan, "It's always the coaches who decide whom they want to play, where they want to play and if they're going to play." Referring specifically to Hall, he said, "He's continuing a practice. If he wanted to change it, I'm sure we'd change it." Thus very clearly the point was made that a major, perhaps the only, stumbling block remaining in the way of the series was Joe B. Hall.

Just a couple of days later the UK Board of Trustees underlined Hall's growing isolation on the issue by voting that the Athletics Board formally consider a request for the Wildcat basketball team to schedule games with other state schools, especially the University of Louisville. The Athletics Board met on April 14. On the eve of the meeting Hall reiterated his position in an exclusive front-page article published in the university newspaper, the *Kentucky Kernel*. According to *Kernel* sports editor Mickey Patterson, the UK coach maintained that the policy he inherited was "evidently initiated for a reason." In addition, Hall went on, "the policy or tradition of not playing state schools has been very good to the University of Kentucky." Among other things, it has confirmed UK's status within the state "with border-to-border support," has made and maintained the Wildcats "as a national power," and has even brought "international prominence." If, Hall continued, "I felt that we would be benefitted by playing state schools I would have scheduled them a long time ago, but from where I sit

it's never been explained to me how it would help our program here at Kentucky to play state schools, and all the arguments for playing games have not been arguments that would be beneficial to the University of Kentucky." Hall blamed "the state's media" for misinforming the public about the need for and benefits to be gained from playing U of L and other state schools. "I think it's a crusade by the *Courier-Journal*," Hall bluntly stated, "to bring about a schedule between Louisville and Kentucky." Furthermore, "I think it's definitely a desire of the University of Louisville to be on our schedule and our local [Lexington] press has picked it up as a way to sell newspapers, and I think once the fire dies down, the interest will die down." That prediction proved almost immediately to be inaccurate.

The day after Hall's interview appeared in the *Kernel*, the Athletics Board convened to discuss the question and Hall made a final bid for support. When the meeting opened he handed each board member a copy of a printed statement opposing the proposal before the body. He then spoke to the board, asking the members to ignore "external pressures that are not in the best interest of the University of Kentucky and its basketball program" and allow him to maintain the practice started by his predecessor, Adolph Rupp, "of not playing state schools during the regular season." Hall then left the meeting to allow board members to analyze the proposal and his statement.

After a spirited and wide-ranging debate the board

Joe Hall and his staff plot strategy during a 1983/84 game; l-r, Lake Kelly, Hall, Leonard Hamilton, and Jim Hatfield.

voted 12-6 to ask Hagan and Hall to make an exception to long-standing practice and "ascertain if mutually acceptable terms and conditions" existed for a UK-U of L game. The resolution directed the negotiators to be sure that "such negotiations should not only be mutually acceptable to the parties but also should result in no financial loss to either program."

After nearly two months of negotiations between Hagan and U of L Athletics Director Bill Olsen the fans got their wish. Hagan and Olsen finally agreed on a four-year pact which would alternate games between Lexington and Louisville, with the first game at Rupp Arena.

Entering the 1983/84 season, UK possessed a team that was awesome, at least on paper. Sam Bowie, "the franchise," was back after two seasons of injuries, and was joined in the front court by Kenny Walker, Bret Bearup, Tom Heitz, Troy McKinley, and freshman Winston Bennett. Melvin Turpin, a potential All-American, was back at center for his senior season, while the guards included sharpshooting Jim Master, Dicky Beal, and Roger Harden, as well as freshmen James Blackmon and Paul Andrews.

Helping to coach this group were associate coach and master recruiter Leonard Hamilton and two newcomers, Lake Kelly and Jim Hatfield. Both Kelly and Hatfield brought to their new jobs considerable experience as head coaches on the major college level, Kelly at Austin Peay and Oral Roberts, and Hatfield at Mississippi State, Southwestern Louisiana, and Hardin-Simmons, where he also served as athletics director. According to sportswriter Jerry Tipton, Hall was pleased with his coaches, both old and new. Writing in the December 1, 1983, *Herald-Leader*, Tipton maintained that "Hall has gone on record as saying this year's staff is the best he has worked with." Although all the coaches made contributions in practice, during games, and in recruiting, there was a division of labor. Kelly was assigned primary responsibility for overseeing defense, and Hatfield concentrated on the UK offense and helped with recruiting, while Hamilton continued to add to his reputation as one of college basketball's outstanding recruiters. There was no question, however, that Hall was boss. As Kelly emphasized to Tipton, Hall is "the hammer. He makes it [the program] go."

The Wildcats were a talented and deep squad, one apparently capable of getting to the NCAA championship game in Seattle, but only if a number of questions could be resolved. The most important was whether Sam Bowie and Dicky Beal, the keys to a successful season, could come back from serious injuries. Bowie, the former All-American, had not played for

The prospect of reaching the 1984 NCAA finals in Seattle depended heavily on whether Sam Bowie (31) and Dicky Beal (11) could snap back from serious injuries. Bowie had been sidelined for two seasons with a shinbone stress fracture; Beal had had knee surgery.

two seasons because of a stress fracture of his left shinbone, while Beal had undergone three arthroscopic knee operations as well as enduring an assortment of other injuries during his first three years at UK. At the beginning of the 1983/84 season Beal was still in pain from the latest surgery, and serious doubts were expressed by Hall and others as to whether he would ever again play for UK.

Discussing his problems at a November 24 press conference, just three days before the Wildcats would open the regular season against Louisville, Joe Hall ruefully observed: "I'm optimistic about the future but concerned about the present." The concern was based in large part on the play of Bowie and Beal in UK's 73-55 victory over the Netherlands National Team in an exhibition game in Rupp Arena on November 22. Bowie had appeared to be confused, tentative, and tired through much of that contest, while Beal, whom Hall was counting on to start at point guard, was able to play only four minutes.

Adding to Hall's worries were the back spasms that sophomore forward Kenny Walker began to suffer toward the end of the exhibition game. This ailment continued to plague Walker in the following weeks, hampering his practice time and limiting his performance during games, while various therapies were tried. Doctors finally settled on the use of stretching exercises and whirlpool treatments. The reason for this approach, Hall reported to the press on December 9, was that "the doctors think his muscles are so tight that they never relax. They're like rocks." This diagnosis evidently was correct because soon after the treatments were begun Walker returned to full effectiveness. Bowie and Beal also finally overcame the effects of their injuries and inactivity, and by the last third of the season the Wildcats were at full strength.

At the beginning of the season, however, with serious questions about the health and effectiveness of three of UK's five starters, the Wildcat bench became increasingly important. There was good reserve strength on the front line, with 6'9" senior Tom Heitz, 6'9" junior Bret Bearup, and 6'6" junior Troy McKinley available, along with highly touted freshman Winston Bennett, a powerfully built 6'7" Louisville native. The backcourt replacements were less numerous but might prove to be talented. In the absence of Dicky Beal, who had started only eight games during his first three years at UK, the Big Blue would have to depend on sophomore Roger Harden to direct the offense. The only other guards on the squad were untested freshmen James Blackmon and Paul Andrews. Help arrived in mid-season when 5'5" (some claimed he was really 5'2") Lexington native Leroy Byrd, a transfer from the University of Nevada at Las Vegas, joined the team in time to take part in a 64-40 blowout of a strong Georgia team on January 29, 1984, at Rupp Arena. The shortage of players at guard never really became a problem. Harden filled in admirably for Beal at point guard while the quick and multitalented Blackmon contributed at both point guard and shooting guard throughout the season.

The season opener, a November 26 game with Louisville, was billed as "the Battle of the Blue Grass." It more than lived up to its billing—at least for Wildcat partisans, for whom it was a glorious evening. A UK victory was generally anticipated, but the margin of victory, twenty-one points, was not. With Harden starting his first college game and Bowie his first since the 1980/81 season, the Big Blue began the game tight and uncertain but quickly recovered their composure. UK led by as many as three points four times early in the game (the last time at 12-9) but, as *Herald-Leader* sportswriter Jerry Tipton observed, "Louisville seemed

to come unglued because of Kentucky's defensive pressure." The Cardinals seemed confused by Hall's decision to play man-to-man defense from the opening tipoff. Turpin and Bowie, the "Twin Towers," intimidated the Cards inside, while veteran guards Lancaster Gordon and Milt Wagner, U of L's top scorers, were unable to hit their outside shots. But the game's turning point came near the end of the first half when James Blackmon, playing in his first college game, came up with two steals in the space of ten seconds and converted both into baskets. Such plays were supposed to be a U of L, not a UK, trademark. The Cards never got over the shock. During the second half the Cats led by as many as twenty-nine points, and during his postgame press conference Hall expressed his pleasure at the ease with which UK had won the contest.

With the victory over Louisville the Wildcats embarked on what their supporters and the press expected

Freshman guard James Blackmon (10) stunned the U of L Cardinals with two quick steals near the end of the first half. Louisville never recovered and the Cats went on to win "the Battle of the Blue Grass" 65-44 on November 26, 1983. Jim Master is no. 20.

to be the "Road to Seattle" and a sixth NCAA title. The euphoria of the Louisville victory lasted a week—until UK's December 3 meeting with an inexperienced and supposedly outmanned Indiana Hoosier team. Coach Bobby Knight's strategy exposed the Wildcats' lack of team quickness (especially in Beal's absence) and questionable outside game. Even Jim Master, the team's most dependable outside shooter, had trouble hitting his twenty-footers when guarded closely. UK entered the game as seventeen-point favorites, but the Hoosiers, led by freshmen Marty Simmons and Steve Alford and junior Uwe Blab, a 7'2" native of West Germany, fought their taller and more experienced opponents to a standstill throughout the first half, which ended with IU ahead 32-31.

Indiana continued to frustrate the Cats in the second half until, with seven minutes left in the game, Hall turned to freshman guard James Blackmon, who proved to make the difference, as he would in UK's December 24 meeting with Illinois. In the closing minutes of both games the Big Blue cleared one side and let the Marion, Indiana, native go one-on-one. The result in both games was victory for the Wildcats. After the Indiana game, Hall confided to the press that "Blackmon was super. He was the only guy we had who played." Blackmon's offensive play began to tail off in January but he made valuable contributions in a number of early-season games and his speed and quickness helped to break the press throughout the season.

UK swept through its December intersectional schedule with victories over Kansas, Wyoming, Brigham Young (to capture the UK Invitational Tournament championship), Cincinnati, Illinois, and Purdue, for a perfect 8-0 record and high hopes and great expectations for the upcoming SEC schedule. The Wild-

Kenny Walker battles for a rebound in the November 26, 1983, UK–U of L game. UK's 65-44 victory avenged the Cats' defeat by the Cardinals at the close of the previous season.

A triumphant trio of Wildcats celebrate UK's win over U of L at Rupp Arena. Left to right, Jim Master, Melvin Turpin, and Sam Bowie. For Bowie it was the first regular-season game in two years.

cats started off the "second season," against conference opponents, with another strong showing by Blackmon in his first starting assignment for UK against Mississippi. The Big Blue won the January 2 game at Rupp Arena, 68-55, without Jim Master who, along with Troy McKinley, had violated a team curfew and been benched by Hall.

Master returned to the starting lineup in the next game, against LSU in Baton Rouge on January 7, but he soon seemed to lose his shooting eye, hitting four of ten shots against LSU, four of twelve against Mississippi State, and one of five against Auburn, and missing all four shots taken in the January 22 game against Houston. Although Master began to regain his touch in February, he was unable to regain the shooting form of his previous seasons, and UK's overall play suffered as a result. No one else on the team seemed able to hit the outside jumper consistently to loosen up an opponent's defense and open up the inside for Walker and the "Twin Towers." Fortunately Turpin's shooting throughout the season, with the exception of games against Auburn and Georgetown, was exceptional. In UK's 96-80 trouncing of LSU, for example, Turpin hit fifteen of seventeen field goal attempts as well as five free throws, for a total of thirty-five points. In the words of D.G. FitzMaurice, Turpin "played like an All-Cosmos pick, or maybe better."

Early in the season Bowie shot poorly but compensated with excellent passing, strong rebounding, and solid man-to-man defense. As the season progressed he also regained his shooting eye, and while he never returned to the All-American form of his sophomore season, he did come close. Although Kenny Walker had to play in the long shadow of the "Twin Towers," he was a consistent and valuable contributor on both offense and defense and is clearly a star of the future.

Going into their January 13 meeting with Auburn the Wildcats were riding a thirteen-game winning streak. To many they seemed destined to complete the season with a perfect record as well as the national championship. Although Hall warned that such statements were premature, few listened, especially when it became known that some members of the team had stated, within earshot of the press, that the 1983/84 squad was probably the greatest team in college basketball history. Reality, in the chubby but hugely talented body of Charles Barkley, rudely interrupted such dreams and returned the Cats and their followers to reality. FitzMaurice observed in the January 14 *Herald-Leader* that "it took a 272 pound wrecking ball, but the Twin Towers were finally razed here [at Auburn] last night."

Still recovering from a back injury that limited his play early in the season, the 6'6" Barkley did not even start for the Tigers against UK. Coming off the bench, the "Round Mound of Rebound" (one of Barkley's many nicknames) played thirty minutes, scored twenty-one points, and grabbed ten rebounds as Auburn pulled an 82-63 upset to replace UK atop the SEC standings. The stunning nineteen-point defeat was devastating for the Cats but the worst was to come four days later in Gainesville, when lightly regarded Florida outclassed the Big Blue and won 69-57. The Gators employed a game plan that was being used increasingly against UK. Florida sagged in on defense and forced the Wildcats to take, and hit, the outside shot. The result, sportswriter Bill Weronka wrote in the *Courier-Journal*, was that "the Gators sagged and so did UK's outside shooting, just as it has the last three games. And this time the inside game wasn't any help."

Bruised and demoralized by the road trip to Auburn and Gainesville, the Wildcats returned home, where they rebounded to win all four games convincingly. They roared past Vanderbilt, 67-46; Houston, 74-67; Georgia, 64-40; and Tennessee, 93-74. The Big Blue appeared to have regained their momentum. The victory over Houston was especially sweet. The January 22 game, played on "Super Sunday" on national televi-

Point guard Roger Harden bounces the ball past a Purdue defender on December 28, 1983. Harden was starting guard through much of the 1983/84 season until Dicky Beal recovered from surgery and returned to play.

Freshman Winston Bennett goes up on a shot as UK downs Houston 74-67 on January 22, 1984. Melvin Turpin (54) was another powerhouse in the game.

sion just before pro football's championship game, represented a meeting between college basketball's number three ranked team (UK) and number four ranked Houston. It was also billed as a meeting of the giants—the Cougars' 7' All-American Akeem "the Dream" Olajuwon and UK's "Twin Towers." On this day the Wildcats had too many towers for Houston to handle.

After this strong homestand it appeared that Hall had the team back on track to win the SEC title and build the needed momentum for the league and national championships. With January and its annual slump past, UK took to the road on February 4 for a game against an Alabama team which, up to this point, had not played up to expectations. But the Tide

on this day played an inspired game and handed the visitors their third defeat of the season, all to SEC teams. UK bounced back two nights later to whip Mississippi State 77-58, but with only seven regular-season games left (all with SEC opponents) the Blue and White seemed to be in serious trouble once again.

It was obvious that something had to change to get UK back to the level of intensity and performance that had marked their play in December. Lending a note of urgency was the fact that their next game was against the Auburn Tigers and their powerful but agile center, Charles Barkley, and high-scoring forward Chuck Person. The Tigers entered the February 11 game at Rupp Arena atop the SEC standings, one game ahead of UK. Barkley played his usual strong game against Turpin, but Dicky Beal and Winston Bennett came off the bench to score seventeen points each and lead the Big Blue to an 84-64 runaway victory. Two nights later Beal again came off the bench to ignite the Cats to a hard-fought win over the tough Florida Gators, 67-65. The final ingredient was ready to be added to the UK starting team.

On February 19 against Vanderbilt in Nashville, Dicky Beal finally overcame the various injuries that had plagued him during his UK career and became the starting point guard. Later in the season Sam Bowie explained in simple but direct terms Beal's importance to the team: "Dicky puts us in another gear." Beal's style of play blended well with the usual starters—Bowie, Walker, Turpin, and Master—as well as Bennett and Blackmon, the Cats' principal substitutes. Benefiting especially from Beal's move into the starting lineup was Blackmon, who had been called on during the season to play both the point- and shooting-guard positions. Explaining the effect on Blackmon's play, Hall noted that "It takes a lot of pressure off him, not having the ball-handling responsibilities and not having to guard the other team's quick player." With Beal handling the ball, UK's fastbreak became a more potent weapon and the team was seldom bothered by the full court press. The outside shooting also improved, in part because Bowie finally regained his shooting eye and also because Beal began to display a touch that had not been evident during his first three years of college play.

The Wildcats won four of their last five regular-season games and, with hot-shooting Sam Bowie leading the way, wrapped up their thirty-fifth SEC title with a nineteen-point victory (76-57) over Mississippi at Rupp Arena on March 1. The regular-season finale two nights later against LSU, which at the time was ranked second in the conference standings, was important only as an opportunity for the fans to bid

farewell to the departing seniors and for the Cats to build momentum for post-season competition. In both respects the evening was a success. For the Wildcat faithful it was a golden moment. They had an opportunity to relive happy memories as the five seniors— Beal, Bowie, Heitz, Master, and Turpin—were introduced, along with their parents, before the game, and then to cheer as the entire team participated in the dismemberment of a strong LSU Tiger team, 90-68.

For the first time since the revival of the SEC tournament in 1979, UK entered the postseason competition on a positive note and, for the first time in that period, won the tournament. Building on a late-season emphasis on fundamentals in practice as well as the momentum from the impressive victory over LSU, the Wildcats, led by red-hot shooting Melvin Turpin, whipped Georgia in their first tournament game, 92-79. In that contest Turpin tied the SEC tournament single-game scoring record with forty-two points and

Above, Turpin gets physical with Auburn's "Round Mound of Rebound," Charles Barkley, in a February 11, 1984, meeting. The Cats won 84-64, after losing to Auburn less than a month before. When the teams met in the SEC finals in March, UK slipped past the Tigers 51-49 with a last-second basket by Kenny Walker *(left),* a vital member of UK's brilliant front-court trio. Here, Walker contributes to the Cats' 90-68 rout of LSU on March 3, 1984.

Dicky Beal goes up for a shot against U of L in the 1984 Mideast Regionals. Beal led the Cats to a 72-67 victory in a game that was much closer than their season opener.

broke the field goal record with eighteen two-pointers. (Both records had been set by UK's Cliff Hagan in 1952.) In addition, the Wildcat center pulled down sixteen rebounds, one short of the tournament record set by Alabama's Bobby Lee Hurt in 1983. The Big Blue had a tougher time against their next opponent, Alabama, but with Dicky Beal hitting two pressure-packed free throws with three seconds to play, UK won 48-46 to set up a confrontation with Auburn for the tournament title. Despite excellent performances by Charles Barkley and Chuck Person, the Wildcats won that game at the buzzer as a last-second jump shot by Kenny Walker bounced around the rim and finally fell in. The final score was 51-49, and with the victory UK was assured of being placed in the Mideast Regionals of the NCAA, where, assuming they won,

two of their three games would be played at Rupp Arena.

The Wildcats began their quest for the NCAA title (a record-setting twenty-ninth appearance) on March 17 in Birmingham against the Cougars of Brigham Young, the first of three opponents they had defeated during the regular season that they would face in the Mideast Regionals. The others were Louisville and Illinois. In their earlier meeting, in the UKIT, Brigham Young had proved a tough and tenacious opponent until UK's superior size, speed, and strength wore the Cougars down and the Big Blue broke the game open in the second half to win by thirty-four points. Hall was determined not to give BYU a chance to dictate the pace of the game this time. With Beal leading the charge the Wildcats roared to an early 15-4 lead before BYU's use of a karate defense slowed the pace. UK adapted easily and coasted to a 93-68 victory. It was, Hall admitted in a postgame interview, "the type of game you'd like to open a tournament with." Following the surprisingly easy win over BYU the Cats returned to Lexington to prepare for a March 22 meeting at Rupp Arena with the Louisville Cardinals, UK's opponent in the opening game of the regular season.

In the days before the rematch, the Louisville players expressed their pleasure at getting a chance to redeem their pride. And redeem it they did. The game was not decided until the final thirteen seconds of play. The Cardinals got excellent performances from their guards—Lancaster Gordon with 25 points and Milt Wagner with 23—but "time and again," Billy Reed wrote in the March 23 *Courier-Journal*, "it was the senior from Covington [Dicky Beal] who rallied the Cats when they seemed in danger of faltering." Joe Hall agreed that Beal, the shortest player on the floor, was the key: "Beal just did a super job down the stretch orchestrating for us, both offensively and defensively."

UK turned from its hard-earned 72-67 victory over the Cards to prepare for the regional championship game on March 24 against Illinois, winner in a mild upset over a strong Maryland team. Playing a bruising physical game, the underdog Illini took away the Wildcat fastbreak and, at least in the first half, their inside game as well. Bowie was scoreless in the first half, which was not surprising because he never got a chance to shoot the ball. Fortunately he came alive in the second half to score eleven points and grab ten of his game-high fourteen rebounds. Living up to their nickname, the Fighting Illini refused to wilt and the game was not decided until Beal, the tournament's Most Valuable Player, scored five points in the final forty-three seconds of play. The Wildcats had a 54-51

victory and their first appearance in the Final Four since 1978. But Seattle, where the 1984 NCAA finals were played, proved to be a far less satisfying experience than St. Louis had been in 1978.

The Big Blue entered what was to be their final game of the season as slight underdogs, playing against the powerful Georgetown Hoyas and their great 7' center, Patrick Ewing. The Hoyas came into their March 31 confrontation with UK with Final Four experience, having lost in the final seconds of the 1982 championship game to North Carolina, when Ewing was a freshman. Despite their inexperience in Final Four competition, the Wildcats jumped off to a quick lead in the first half. When the shot-blocking Ewing, the centerpiece of Georgetown's intimidating pressure defense, picked up two fouls in the first seven minutes of play and his third with 8:52 remaining in the first half, UK appeared to be in a commanding position. The Big Blue led throughout the game's first twenty minutes, enjoying as much as a twelve-point lead (27-15) and ending the half with a 29-22 advantage.

This lead melted in the second half as UK had dry shooting spells of truly incredible proportions. The Cats scored not a point in the first ten minutes of the second half and only two in the first sixteen minutes. The starters took twenty-one shots in the half and did not score a single point from the field, although they did hit three free throws. As a team, UK connected on only three of thirty-three shots in the second half for a scoring percentage of 9.1. The half-time lead disappeared and the game ended with the Wildcats on the short end of a 53-40 final score.

In a season packed with achievements, UK had the misfortune to save its worst performance for last. After the debacle, Hall, the players, and Big Blue fans groped for an explanation. How could this happen to a team as talented as the Cats? In the final analysis it is probably impossible to explain UK's second-half shooting, but some reasons can be identified.

For one thing, at halftime Hoyas coach John Thompson made key personnel switches on defense. He put intense and aggressive 6'9" freshman forward Michael Graham on 6'11" Turpin, and assigned Ewing to guard 7'1" Bowie. Bowie played away from the basket and did not drive to the hoop, which saved Ewing from committing additional fouls. These defensive adjustments, as well as guard Gene Smith's tenacious dogging of Dicky Beal out front, played a part in UK's poor shooting percentage in the second half, but they are only part of the story. As Jerry Tipton, who covered the Cats throughout the season, observed in the April 1 *Herald-Leader*, "Kentucky got pretty much the same shots it had shot en route to a 29-4 season

record. Melvin Turpin got his favorite turnaround jumpers in the lane. Jim Master was taking those perimeter jumpers. Sam Bowie got shots from fifteen feet. Dicky Beal popped from the top of the key and drove to the basket. None of it went in the basket." *Kernel* sportswriter Mickey Patterson fully agreed, concluding that it all added up to "a freak happening, an oddity beyond comparison."

Jack Givens, who was in Seattle for the game, had a different view. In a recent interview Givens observed that in the second half UK "came out wanting to protect that lead and not wanting to make any mistakes. They just played too tentatively and when you play that way you are in hot water because the Hoyas are a loose, self-confident team. Kentucky was playing that way in the first half. Just running and playing their game. They missed those shots early in the second half and they thought too much. They started thinking about the shots instead of just shooting them. They became hesitant and it was like no one wanted to shoot—except Winston Bennett." While the game was still in progress CBS television analyst Billy Packer offered a similar explanation for the complete reversal in UK's fortunes. The Wildcats, Packer theorized late

UK earned its first trip to the NCAA Final Four since 1978 with a victory over the Fighting Illini. Here Bret Bearup guards against an Illini shot.

Jim Master and Sam Bowie fight for a rebound against Illinois in the 1984 NCAA Regional. It was to be their last victory. A week later the Wildcats fell to the Georgetown Hoyas in the championship game.

did, and I think that came back to haunt them in the Georgetown game when they had them down in the first half and they had Ewing in foul trouble." What is ironic, he concluded, "is that Georgetown didn't play that well in the second half. If the Cats had just hit 30 percent [of their shots] in the second half they could have won—or at least come really close." To be both fair and accurate I must point out that UK did dominate some teams late in the season, among them Georgia in the SEC tournament and BYU in the Mideast Regionals.

A week after the game, and after viewing game film, Joe Hall had this explanation on his final television show of the season: "In the first half we played tremendous basketball. Georgetown being down at halftime came out and they were unbelievable. They really got physical inside with us. I wouldn't say they intimidated us. I'd say they just physically took us out of the game with their inside play." Hall emphasized the role referees can play in determining a game's outcome. "I'm not talking about bad calls or good calls. I'm talking about the style of play they allow to exist. And they just allowed it to be a very physical game. I think Georgetown had the type athletes that could benefit from that type game more than we could. They just rooted us out inside. They put a lot of pressure on us defensively and we got almost shell shocked. Offensively we got excellent shots," Hall acknowledged, "but we were trying so hard they just wouldn't fall."

Each of the theories has some validity, but a more comprehensive explanation combines elements from various theories, though from a somewhat different perspective. For example, the referees probably did let Georgetown play their type of game and that certainly was not to UK's advantage, especially in the second half. But this underlines the fact that the 1984 Wildcats were not a physical team, in contrast to the 1978 NCAA champions, with their "karate defense." More important, the 1984 squad was not one that could adapt to a different style of play as well as the 1978 team could.

Perhaps of equal importance, the 1984 team lacked experience in Final Four competition. As members of the 1978 team emphasized in interviews, a Final Four game is like no other college basketball contest. No other college game, regular or tournament, is as pressure-packed. Joe Hall had been to the Final Four twice before and knew what was needed to win the national championship, but it is one thing for a coach to tell a team and another for the players to fully understand what he is saying. Georgetown, on the other hand, had been there before. Several of the key Hoya players had participated in the 1982 champion-

in the game, "might have felt like they had the big lead and relaxed a little bit at halftime and just never could get it back in stride."

Another former UK player I recently interviewed offered still another perspective. According to this view UK's play in the second half of the Georgetown game was simply another example of a persistent late-season problem—the Wildcats' inability to "put an opponent away when they had him on the ropes." The Cats "lacked the killer instinct. They just never did really dominate an opponent late in the season the way they did on occasion early in the season. When they had a team down they just never did put them away," he stated emphatically. "They never did physically dominate an opponent the way the 1978 team often

ship game. They knew from experience the pressure involved and the price that has to be paid. From losing in their earlier effort, they were even more determined this time.

Georgetown's experience—and UK's lack of experience—were evident at the end of the first half and the beginning of the second half. In the last three minutes of the first half Georgetown cut the UK lead from twelve points to seven and began to change the game's pattern. Thus the second half merely continued a pattern that had begun to develop in the first. Stated another way, the Wildcats did not score a point in the last 3:06 of the first half. Combine that with the first 2:52 of the second half, when the Hoyas went ahead for good on a Ewing tip-in, 30-29, and the momentum had been completely reversed in Georgetown's favor. During that six minutes the Hoyas established the superiority of their punishing, physical style of play, at least for that day, and the confidence of the UK starters was severely shaken. Stated bluntly, UK just did not exhibit the "killer instinct" that Georgetown did.

I do not claim this is a more accurate explanation of the Georgetown win, but, unlike the game itself, it makes sense to me. For many fans, the problem in the Georgetown game was not the loss but the *way* it was lost. The Wildcats did not suffer an ordinary defeat, fighting all the way to a close finish. They were humiliated. And to attempt to explain that is what makes an analysis of the game so difficult, but also so fascinating.

Whatever the reason or reasons, the "Year of the Twin Towers" (as one popular poster described the 83/84 season) ended on a less than satisfying note. But next season the slate will be wiped clean. The journey will begin again. That is the attraction of sports. With the departure of four starters—Bowie, Turpin, Beal, and Master—and reserve Tom Heitz, the Wildcats will be a different team. And Joe Hall's cupboard of basketball talent will certainly not be bare. Returning will be Kenny Walker, Winston Bennett, James Blackmon, Roger Harden, Bret Bearup, Troy McKinley, Paul Andrews, and Leroy Byrd. In addition, UK will have yet another excellent group of recruits. The incoming freshmen will include Richard "Master Blaster" Madison, a 6'7" forward from Memphis; Todd Ziegler, a 6'7" forward from Louisville; Cedric Jenkins, a 6'8" forward-center from Dawson, Georgia; Robert Lock, a 6'10" center from Reedley, California; and Ed Davender, a 6'2" guard from Brooklyn, New York.

The Kentucky Wildcats have built "the winning tradition" through eighty-one basketball seasons, but the story has not yet ended. Indeed, the story has no ending, because the tradition is still living and growing. UK basketball has given Kentuckians a rich sport heritage, a heritage that is a source of pleasure and pride not only in the state but to basketball fans everywhere. Wildcat basketball is so much a part of Kentucky life that it has become more than just a game. To some, it is a passion; to others, an obsession.

Wildcat Facts

All-Time Leading UK Scorers—Varsity Career

Player (Position)		Years	Points	Games	Ave.
1. Dan Issel (C)	3	(1967/68-1969/70)	2,138	83	25.7
2. Jack Givens (F)	4	(1974/75-1977/78)	2,038	123	16.6
3. Kevin Grevey (F)	3	(1972/73-1974/75)	1,801	84	21.4
4. Cotton Nash (C-F)	3	(1961/62-1963/64)	1,770	78	22.7
5. Alex Groza (C)	4	(1944/45, 1946/47-1948/49)	1,744	120	14.4
6. Louie Dampier (G)	3	(1964/65-1966/67)	1,575	80	19.7
7. Mike Casey (G)	3	(1967/68-1968/69, 1970/71)	1,535	82	18.7
8. Ralph Beard (G)	4	(1945/46-1948/49)	1,517	139	10.8
9. Melvin Turpin (C)	4	(1980/81-1983/84)	1,509	123	12.3
10. Cliff Hagan (C)	3	(1950/51-1951/52, 1953/54)	1,475	77	19.2
11. Pat Riley (F)	3	1964/65-1966/67)	1,464	80	18.3
12. Johnny Cox (F)	3	(1956/57-1958/59)	1,461	84	17.3
13. Kyle Macy (G)	3	(1977/78-1979/80)	1,411	98	14.4
14. Rick Robey (F-C)	4	(1974/75-1977/78)	1,395	105	13.3
15. Mike Phillips (C)	4	(1974/75-1977/78)	1,367	120	11.4
16. Mike Pratt (F)	3	(1967/68-1969/70)	1,359	81	16.8
17. Frank Ramsey (G)	3	(1950/51-1951/52, 1953/54)	1,344	91	14.7
18. Jim Andrews (C)	3	(1970/71-1972/73)	1,320	80	16.5
19. Sam Bowie (C-F)	3	(1979/80-1980/81, 1983/84)	1,285	96	13.4
20. Jim Master (G)	4	(1980/81-1983/84)	1,282	121	10.6

Kentucky All-Americans
(30 Players Chosen 48 Times)

Basil Hayden (F) 1921
Burgess Carey (G) 1925
Carey Spicer (F) 1929, '31
Paul McBrayer (G) 1930
Forest Sale (C-F) 1932, '33
Ellis Johnson (G) 1933
John DeMoisey (C) 1934
LeRoy Edwards (C) 1935
Bernard Opper (G) 1939
Lee Huber (G) 1940, '41
Bob Brannum (C) 1944
Jack Parkinson (G) 1946
Ralph Beard (G) 1947, '48,* '49*
Alex Groza (C) 1947, '48,† '49*
Wallace Jones (F) 1949†
Bill Spivey (C) 1951*
Cliff Hagan (C) 1952,* '54*
Frank Ramsey (G) 1952, '54†
Bob Burrow (C) 1956†
Vernon Hatton (G) 1958
Johnny Cox (F) 1959*
Cotton Nash (C-F) 1962,† '63,† '64*
Pat Riley (F) 1966
Louie Dampier (G) 1966†
Dan Issel (C) 1969, '70*
Kevin Grevey (F) 1974, '75
Jack Givens (F) 1976, '77, '78
Rick Robey (F-C) 1977, '78
Kyle Macy (G) 1979, '80*
Sam Bowie (C-F) 1981, '84

*Consensus; †Second Team Consensus

Tournaments (For Dates, Sites, and Scores See All-Time Record Section)

Sugar Bowl Tournament
(Ten Appearances—Five Championships)

1963 Won 2, Lost 0. Defeated Duke for championship.
1956 Won 2, Lost 0. Defeated Houston for championship.
1951 Won 1, Lost 1. Eliminated in finals by St. Louis.
1950 Won 1, Lost 1. Eliminated in first game by St. Louis. Defeated Syracuse in consolation game.
1949 Won 2, Lost 0. Defeated Bradley for championship.
1948 Won 1, Lost 1. Eliminated in finals by St. Louis.
1946 Won 0, Lost 1. Lost to Oklahoma A&M.
1940 Won 0, Lost 1. Lost to Indiana.
1939 Won 1, Lost 0. Defeated Ohio State for championship.
1937 Won 1, Lost 0. Defeated Pittsburgh for championship.

Southern Intercollegiate Athletic Association (SIAA) Tournament
(Three Appearances—One Championship)

1924 Won 0, Lost 1. Eliminated in first game by North Carolina.
1922 Won 1, Lost 1. Eliminated in second game by Mercer.
1921 Won 4, Lost 0. Defeated Georgia for championship.

Southern Conference Tournament
(Seven Appearances—No Championships)*

1932 Won 1, Lost 1. Eliminated in second game by North Carolina.
1931 Won 3, Lost 1. Eliminated in finals by Maryland.
1930 Won 2, Lost 1. Eliminated in semi-finals by Duke.
1929 Won 1, Lost 1. Eliminated in second game by Georgia.
1928 Won 2, Lost 1. Eliminated in semi-finals by Mississippi.
1926 Won 2, Lost 1. Eliminated in semi-finals by Miss. A&M.
1925 Won 1, Lost 1. Eliminated in second game by Georgia.

*Kentucky joined Southeastern Conference in 1933.

National Invitation Tournament (NIT)
(Seven Appearances—Two Championships)

1979 Won 0, Lost 1. Eliminated in first game by Clemson.
1976 Won 4, Lost 0. Defeated UNCC for championship.
1950 Won 0, Lost 1. Eliminated in first game by CCNY.
1949 Won 0, Lost 1. Eliminated in first game by Loyola (Chicago).
1947 Won 2, Lost 1. Eliminated in third game by Utah.
1946 Won 3, Lost 0. Defeated Rhode Island for championship.
1944 Won 2, Lost 1. Eliminated in second game by St. John's. Defeated Oklahoma A&M in consolation.

Olympic Trials Tournament
(One Appearance—Champions College Bracket)

1948 Won 2, Lost 1. Qualified as NCAA Champion. Defeated Louisville and Baylor for championship College Bracket. (Lost to AAU Champion Phillips Oilers in National Finals.)

Olympic Games
(One Appearance—One World Championship)

1948 Won 8, Lost 0. Kentucky participated along with the Phillips Oilers as the United States' basketball entry. Defeated France for the championship.

Southeastern Conference (SEC) Tournament
(25 Appearances—Record 14 Championships)*

1984 Won 3, Lost 0. Defeated Auburn for championship.
1983 Won 0, Lost 1. Eliminated in quarterfinals by Alabama.
1982 Won 2, Lost 1. Eliminated in finals by Alabama.
1981 Won 0, Lost 1. Eliminated in quarterfinals by Vanderbilt.
1980 Won 2, Lost 1. Eliminated in finals by LSU.
1979 Won 3, Lost 1. Eliminated in finals by Tennessee.
1952 Won 4, Lost 0. Defeated LSU for championship.
1951 Won 3, Lost 1. Eliminated in finals by Vanderbilt.
1950 Won 3, Lost 0. Defeated Tennessee for championship.
1949 Won 4, Lost 0. Defeated Tulane for championship.
1948 Won 4, Lost 0. Defeated Georgia Tech for championship.
1947 Won 4, Lost 0. Defeated Tulane for championship.
1946 Won 4, Lost 0. Defeated LSU for championship.
1945 Won 4, Lost 0. Defeated Tennessee for championship.
1944 Won 3, Lost 0. Defeated Tulane for championship.
1943 Won 3, Lost 1. Eliminated in finals by Tennessee.
1942 Won 4, Lost 0. Defeated Alabama for championship.
1941 Won 3, Lost 1. Eliminated in finals by Tennessee.
1940 Won 3, Lost 0. Defeated Georgia for championship.
1939 Won 3, Lost 0. Defeated Tennessee for championship.
1938 Won 0, Lost 1. Eliminated in first game by Tulane.
1937 Won 3, Lost 0. Defeated Tennessee for championship.
1936 Won 1, Lost 1. Eliminated in second game by Tennessee.
1935   No tournament held.
1934 Won 0, Lost 1. Eliminated in first game by Florida.
1933 Won 4, Lost 0. Defeated Mississippi State for championship.

*Tournament resumed in 1979 for first time since 1952.

N.C.A.A. Tournament
(Record 29 Appearances—5 Championships)

1984 Won 3, Lost 1. Lost to Gerogetown in semifinal game.
1983 Won 2, Lost 1. Eliminated by Louisville in Mideast Regional Finals.
1982 Won 0, Lost 1. Eliminated by Middle Tennessee in Mideast First Round.
1981 Won 0, Lost 1. Eliminated by Alabama-Birmingham in Mideast First Round.
1980 Won 1, Lost 1. Eliminated by Duke in Mideast Regional Semi-Finals.
1978 NATIONAL CHAMPIONS
     Won 5, Lost 0. Defeated Duke for title.
1977 Won 2, Lost 1. Eliminated by North Carolina in East Regional Finals.
1975 Won 4, Lost 1. Lost to UCLA in Championship Game.
1973 Won 1, Lost 1. Eliminated by Indiana in Mideast Regional Finals.
1972 Won 1, Lost 1. Eliminated by Florida State in Mideast Regional Finals.
1971 Won 0, Lost 2. Eliminated by Western Kentucky in Mideast Regional first game.
1970 Won 1, Lost 1. Eliminated by Jacksonville in Mideast Regional finals.
1969 Won 1, Lost 1. Eliminated by Marquette in Mideast Regional first game.
1968 Won 1, Lost 1. Eliminated by Ohio State in Regional finals.
1966 Won 3, Lost 1. Lost to Texas Western in championship game.
1964 Won 0, Lost 2. Eliminated by Ohio University in Mideast Regional first game.
1962 Won 1, Lost 1. Eliminated by Ohio State in Mideast Regional Finals.
1961 Won 1, Lost 1. Eliminated by Ohio State in Mideast Regional Finals.
1959 Won 1, Lost 1. Eliminated by Louisville in Mideast Regional first round.
1958 NATIONAL CHAMPIONS
     Won 4, Lost 0. Defeated Seattle for title.
1957 Won 1, Lost 1. Eliminated by Michigan State in Midwest Regional Finals.
1956 Won 1, Lost 1. Eliminated by Iowa in Eastern Regional Finals.
1955 Won 1, Lost 1. Eliminated by Marquette in Eastern Regional first round.
1954   Withdrew after winning automatic berth as SEC champion.
1952 Won 1, Lost 1. Eliminated by St. John's in Eastern Regional finals.
1951 NATIONAL CHAMPIONS
     Won 4, Lost 0. Defeated Kansas State for title.
1949 NATIONAL CHAMPIONS
     Won 3, Lost 0. Defeated Oklahoma A&M for title.
1948 NATIONAL CHAMPIONS
     Won 3, Lost 0. Defeated Baylor for title.
1945 Won 1, Lost 1. Eliminated by Ohio State in first round.
1942 Won 1, Lost 1. Eliminated by Dartmouth in second game.

(For Dates, Sites and Scores See All-Time Record Section)

Kentucky's All-Time Record, 1903-1984

(81 Seasons—Won 1,358, Lost 423, Tied 1)   Home: Won 756, Lost 120
(No Schedule Played in 1952/53)   **(Losses in Bold Face)**

1903—Won 1, Lost 2.
COACH: Unnamed
STARTERS: (A. C. Bush, B. W. Bush, Houlihan, Smith and Carter)

Date	Team	Site	UK	Opp.
Feb. 6	**Georgetown**	**(H)**	**6**	**15**
Feb. 18	Lexington YMCA	(H)	11	10
Feb. 20	**Kentucky U.**	**(H)**	**2**	**42**
			19	67

1904—Won 1, Lost 4.
COACH: Leander E. Andrus, Mgr.
CAPTAIN: St. John (Guyn, Arnett, St. John, Wurtele, Coons)

Date	Team	Site	UK	Opp.
Feb. 4	**Georgetown**	**(A)**	**11**	**26**
Feb. 11	**Kentucky U.***	**(A)**	**5**	**12**
Feb. 13	**Georgetown**	**(H)**	**10**	**22**
Feb. 26	**Kentucky U.**	**(A)**	**12**	**14**
Mar. 4	Cincinnati	(H)	25	21
			63	95

* Kentucky University (Transylvania) and Georgetown game at UK was called off because of failure to agree on a referee. State College (University of Kntucky) team was present and agreed to play. The offer was accepted and KU won, 12-5.

1905—Won 1, Lost 4.
COACH:
CAPTAIN: J. M. Coons

Date	Team	Site	UK	Opp.
Jan. 13	**Georgetown**	**(H)**	**9**	**14**
Jan. 21	Cincinnati YMCA	(H)	22	43
Jan. 27	Kentucky U.	(H)	30	19
Feb. 4	**Kentucky U.**	**(H)**	**1**	**22**
Feb. 22	**Kentucky U.**	**(H)**	**23**	**33**
			85	141

1906—Won 5, Lost 9.
COACH: W. B. Wendt (Mgr.)
CAPTAIN: D. P. Branson (Baer, Donan, Barbee, Wilson, Herman)

Date	Team	Site	UK	Opp.
Jan. 11	Lexington YMCA*	(H)	....	....
Jan. 12	**Miami (Ohio)**	**(H)**	**10**	**15**
Jan. 19	Central U.	(H)	15	14
Jan. 20	**Georgetown**	**(A)**	**9**	**34**
Jan. 26	Central U.	(A)	17	15
Jan. 27	**Cincinnati YMCA**	**(H)**	**16**	**29**
Feb. 3	**Christ Church, Cin.**	**(H)**	**24**	**38**
Feb. 9	Georgetown	(H)	22	28
Feb. 12	**New Albany YMCA**	**(A)**	**12**	**29**
Feb. 13	Vernon College	(A)	34	14
Feb. 14	Moores Hill	(A)	32	11
Feb. 15	**Christ Church, Cin.**	**(A)**	**17**	**54**
Feb. 16	**Cincinnati YMCA**	**(A)**	**9**	**38**
Feb. 17	**Miami (Ohio)**	**(A)**	**19**	**29**
			236	328

* W. B. Wendt on Jan. 9, 1969 verified that State College opened the 1906 season against Kentucky U. in the YMCA. Athletic committees of the two schools had cancelled all games after a fight at a football game in November, 1905. Wendt and the Kentucky U. manager agreed to play at the YMCA and list the State College foe as YMCA instead of Kentucky U. State College won but Mr. Wendt didn't remember the score, which he hadn't listed.

1907—Won 3, Lost 6.
COACH: A. M. Kirby (Mgr.)
CAPTAIN: J. M. Wilson (Shanklin, Baer, Bryant, Barbee)

Date	Team	Site	UK	Opp.
Jan. 16	**Lexington YMCA**	**(H)**	**17**	**25**
Jan. 19	Georgetown	(H)	16	15
Jan. 25	Central U.	(H)	22	9
Feb. 12	**Central U.**	**(A)**	**23**	**25**
Feb. 15	Kentucky U.	(H)	16	14
Feb. 21	**Georgetown**	**(A)**	**8**	**19**
Mar. 1	Lexington YMCA	(A)	22	41
Mar. 7	**Kentucky U.**	**(H)**	**5**	**19**
Mar. 9	**Central U.**	**(H)**	**13**	**15**
			142	182

1907-08—Won 5, Lost 6.
COACH: J. S. Chambers (Mgr.)
CAPTAIN: Richard Barbee

Date	Team	Site	UK	Opp.
Jan. 10	**Lexington YMCA**	**(H)**	**19**	**29**
Jan. 21	Kentucky U.	(H)	20	15
Jan. 25	**Central U.**	**(A)**	**21**	**32**
Feb. 4	Kentucky U.	(H)	20	15
Feb. 8	**Louisville Coliseum**	**(H)**	**29**	**28**
Feb. 11	**Georgetown**	**(A)**	**22**	**30**
Feb. 13	Central U.	(H)	31	20
Feb. 15	**Lexington YMCA**	**(H)**	**19**	**23**
Feb. 22	**Louisville Coliseum**	**(A)**	**18**	**30**
Mar. 3	Georgetown		18	13
Mar. 7	**Central U.**	**(A)**	**10**	**29**
			227	264

1908-09—Won 5, Lost 4.
MGR.: J. S. Chambers
CAPTAIN: W. C. Fox

Date	Team	Site	UK	Opp.
Jan. 9	Lexington High	(H)	29	9
Jan. 18	**Advent Mem. Club**	**(A)**	**27**	**41**
Jan. 19	**Cincinnati**	**(H)**	**25**	**41**
Jan. 27	Central U.	(H)	24	23
Feb. 6	**Central U.**	**(A)**	**20**	**35**
Feb. 8	Georgetown	(H)	45	32
Feb. 15	Georgetown	(A)	48	19
Feb. 19	Cincinnati	(H)	28	23
Feb. 26	**Central U.**	**H)**	**20**	**26**
			266	249

1909-10—Won 4, Lost 8.
COACH: R. E. Spahr and E. R. Sweetland
CAPTAIN: Bill Rodes

Date	Team	Site	UK	Opp.
Jan. 8	Kentucky Wesleyan	(H)	14	*12
Jan. 22	Georgetown	(H)	31	11
Jan. 24	**DePauw**	**(H)**	**11**	**24**
Jan. 28	**Central**	**(A)**	**17**	**87**
Feb. 4	**Georgetown**	**(A)**	**16**	**34**
Feb. 7	**Cincinnati**	**(A)**	**17**	**47**
Feb. 9	**DePauw**	**(A)**	**10**	**28**
Feb. 10	**Rose Poly**	**(A)**	**11**	**52**
Feb. 16	Tennessee	(H)	20	5
Mar. 5	**Central U.**	**(H)**	**13**	**31**
Mar. 8	Georgetown	(H)	24	23
Mar. 11	**Central**	**(A)**	**9**	**51**
			193	405

* Denotes one overtime period.

1910-11—Won 5, Lost 6.
COACH: H. J. Iddings
CAPTAIN: J. H. Gaiser

Date	Team	Site	UK	Opp.
Jan. 13	Lexington High	(H)	29	36
Jan. 20	**Transylvania**	**(H)**	**18**	**23**
Jan. 27	**Ky. Wesleyan**	**(A)**	**19**	**21**
Feb. 4	Bethany	(H)	24	11
Feb. 9	**Ohio Wesleyan**	**(A)**	**19**	**37**
Feb. 10	**Otterbein**	**(A)**	**27**	**41**
Feb. 11	**Cin. Christ's Church**	**(A)**	**21**	**32**
Feb. 17	Georgetown	(H)	47	22
Feb. 23	Butler	(H)	21	16
Feb. 28	**Transylvania**	**(A)**	**22**	**19**
Mar. 3	Transylvania	(H)	30	24
			277	282

1911-12—Won 9, Lost 0.
COACH: E. R. Sweetland
CAPTAIN: W. C. Harrison

Date	Team	Site	UK	Opp.
Jan. 5	Georgetown	(H)	38	12
Jan. 12	Central U.	(A)	32	13
Jan. 19	Miami (Ohio) U.	(H)	31	14
Feb. 1	Central U.	(H)	52	10
Feb. 7	Tennessee	(H)	27	15
Feb. 16	Lexington YMCA	(H)	32	20
Feb. 22	Vanderbilt	(H)	28	17
Feb. 23	Vanderbilt	(H)	22	18
Mar. 1	Georgetown	(A)	19	18
			281	137

SOUTHERN CHAMPIONS

1912-13—Won 5, Lost 3.
COACH: J. J. Tigert
CAPTAIN: B. Barnett

Date	Team	Site	UK	Opp.
Jan. 24	**Lexington YMCA**	**(H)**	**25**	**27**
Feb. 8	Cincinnati	(H)	20	18
Feb. 13	Marietta	(H)	42	16
Feb. 15	Louisville	(H)	34	10
Feb. 19	**Vanderbilt**	**(H)**	**17**	**24**
Feb. 20	Vanderbilt	(H)	42	29
Feb. 27	Miami (Ohio) U.	(H)	24	16
Mar. 1	**Cin. Christ's Church**	**(H)**	**19**	**30**
			223	170

1913-14—Won 11, Lost 2.
COACH: Alpha Brumage
CAPTAIN: William Tuttle

Date	Team	Site	UK	Opp.
Jan. 10	Ashland YMCA	(H)	28	15
Jan. 17	Louisville YMCA	(H)	30	21
Jan. 21	Marshall	(A)	46	6
Jan. 20	Ashland YMCA	(A)	30	19
Jan. 22	**Virginia U.**	**(A)**	**23**	**39**
Jan. 24	**Va. Military Inst.**	**(A)**	**18**	**32**
Jan. 31	Louisville YMHA	(A)	59	12
Feb. 7	Louisville	(H)	22	17
Feb. 11	Tennessee	(H)	20	14
Feb. 12	Tennessee	(H)	20	18
Feb. 21	Cincinnati	(H)	20	18
Feb. 23	Chattanooga	(H)	40	7
Feb. 28	Marietta	(H)	19	17
			375	235

1914-15—Won 7, Lost 5.
COACH: Alpha Brumage
CAPTAIN: Ralph Morgan

Date	Team	Site	UK	Opp.
Jan. 16	Maryville	(H)	37	17
Jan. 22	Louisville	(H)	18	14
Jan. 30	St. Andrews	(H)	35	15
Feb. 4	Maryville	(A)	23	22
Feb. 5	**Tennessee**	**(A)**	**21**	**36**
Feb. 6	**Tennessee**	**(A)**	**22**	**27**
Feb. 12	**Vanderbilt**	**(H)**	**34**	**39**
Feb. 13	Vanderbilt	(H)	36	24
Feb. 17	Tennessee	(H)	22	13
Feb. 18	Tennessee	(H)	20	18
Feb. 26	**St. Andrews**	**(A)**	**25**	**50**
Feb. 27	Louisville	(A)	15	26
			308	301

1915-16—Won 8, Lost 6.
COACH: James Park
CAPTAIN: K. P. Zerfoss

Date	Team	Site	UK	Opp.
Jan. 14	Cincinnati	(A)	39	24
Jan. 18	Georgetown	(A)	29	22
Jan. 31	Georgetown	(H)	30	22
Feb. 4	**Vanderbilt**	**(H)**	**25**	**39**
Feb. 5	**Vanderbilt**	**(H)**	**20**	**23**
Feb. 12	**Louisville**	**(H)**	**22**	**28**
Feb. 15	Centre	(A)	38	5
Feb. 19	Cincinnati	(H)	34	10
Feb. 22	Louisville	(A)	32	24
Feb. 23	**Tennessee**	**(H)**	**17**	**28**
Feb. 26	Maryville	(H)	36	25
Feb. 29	Centre	(H)	38	14
Mar. 3	**Marietta**	**(H)**	**22**	**27**
Mar. 4	**Marietta**	**(H)**	**23**	**27**
			405	318

1916-17—Won 4, Lost 6.
COACH: W. P. Tuttle
CAPTAIN: Robert Y. Ireland

Date	Team	Site	UK	Opp.
Jan. 17	Centre	(H)	31	21
Jan. 27	**Georgetown**	**(A)**	**19**	**22**
Jan. 30	Rose Polytechnic	(H)	33	12
Feb. 9	**Tennessee**	**(H)**	**20**	**23**
Feb. 10	**Tennessee**	**(H)**	**19**	**22**
Feb. 16	**Centre**	**(A)**	**24**	**28**
Feb. 21	Georgetown	(H)	32	18
Mar. 1	Cumberland	(H)	48	20
Mar. 2	**Tennessee**	**(A)**	**26**	**27**
Mar. 3	**Tennessee**	**(A)**	**10**	**30**
			262	223

1917-18—Won 9, Lost 2, Tied 1.

COACH: S. A. Boles
CAPTAIN: Patrick Campbell

Date	Team	Site	UK	Opp.
Jan. 9	Ky. Wesleyan	(H)	23	13
Jan. 17	**Centre**	**(A)**	**21**	**29**
Jan. 24	Georgetown	(H)	22	18
Feb. 7	Tennessee	(H)	33	26
Feb. 8	Tennessee	(H)	40	12
Feb. 9	Ky. Wesleyan	(A)	21	21

(This unique tie game resulted from scorer's error which was not discovered until after teams' departures. The contest was re-scheduled but never played for unknown reasons.)

Date	Team	Site	UK	Opp.
Feb. 14	Georgetown	(A)	25	16
Feb. 21	Centre	(H)	22***	20
Feb. 28	Cumberland	(A)	42	21
Mar. 1	Tennessee	(A)	29	18
Mar. 2	Tennessee	(A)	32	20
	POST-SEASON GAME (For State Championship)			
Mar. 9	**Centre**	**(N1)**	**12**	**22**
			322	236

*** Denotes 3 overtime periods.
(N1) Louisville

1918-19—Won 6, Lost 8.

COACH: Andrew Gill
CAPTAIN: J. A. Dishman

Date	Team	Site	UK	Opp.
Jan. 13	Ky. Wesleyan	(H)	46	5
Jan. 18	**Georgetown**	**(H)**	**30**	**32**
Jan. 25	**Centre**	**(A)**	**30**	**38**
Jan. 31	**Cincinnati**	**(A)**	**18**	**28**
Feb. 6	Chattanooga	(A)	28	25
Feb. 7	**Tennessee**	**(A)**	**22**	**40**
Feb. 8	Cumberland	(A)	22	21
Feb. 14	**Vanderbilt**	**(H)**	**26**	**36**
Feb. 15	**Georgetown**	**(A)**	**18**	**22**
Feb. 21	Cincinnati	(H)	34	21
Feb. 22	Ky. Wesleyan	(H)	18	13
Feb. 24	**Centre**	**(H)**	**10**	**21**
Feb. 28	Tennessee	(H)	30	14
Mar. 8	**Miami (Ohio) U.**	**(H)**	**14**	**38**
			346	354

1919-20—Won 5, Lost 7.

COACH: George C. Buchheit
CAPTAIN: J. C. Everett

Date	Team	Site	UK	Opp.
Jan. 17	**Cincinnati**	**(A)**	**11**	**13**
Jan. 22	Maryville	(H)	27	16
Jan. 31	Georgetown	(H)	25	14
Feb. 5	**Tennessee**	**(H)**	**24**	**29**
Feb. 7	**Tennessee**	**(H)**	**26**	**27**
Feb. 14	**Centre**	**(A)**	**15**	**44**
Feb. 17	Georgetown	(A)	28	16
Feb. 21	Ky. Wesleyan	(H)	43	13
Feb. 26	**Cumberland**	**(A)**	**21**	**30**
Feb. 27	**Tennessee**	**(A)**	**25**	**28**
Feb. 28	Tennessee	(A)	36	25
Mar. 6	**Centre**	**(H)**	**18**	***20**
			299	275

1920-21—Won 13, Lost 1.

COACH: George C. Buchheit
CAPTAIN: Basil Hayden

Date	Team	Site	UK	Opp.
Jan. 12	Ky. Wesleyan	(H)	38	13
Jan. 15	Cumberland	(H)	37	21
Jan. 18	Georgetown	(H)	38	23
Jan. 21	Chattanooga	(H)	42	10
Jan. 26	Cincinnati	(A)	26	19
Jan. 29	Auburn	(H)	40	25
Feb. 8	**Centre**	**(A)**	**27**	**29**
Feb. 15	Georgetown	(A)	56	11
Feb. 18	Centre	(H)	20	13
Feb. 22	Vanderbilt	(H)	39	18
	SIAA TOURNAMENT (Atlanta, Ga.)			
Feb. 25	Tulane		50	28
Feb. 26	Mercer		49	24
Feb. 28	Mississippi A & M		28	13
Mar. 1	Georgia (championship)		20	19
			510	266

1921-22—Won 10, Lost 6.

COACH: George C. Buchheit
CAPTAIN: R. E. Lavin

Date	Team	Site	UK	Opp.
Jan. 14	**Georgetown**	**(H)**	**17**	**26**
Jan. 17	Louisville	(A)	38	14
Jan. 18	**Vanderbilt**	**(A)**	**12**	**22**
Jan. 21	Louisville	(H)	29	22
Jan. 26	Miss. A & M	(H)	28	21
Jan. 27	Marshall	(H)	34	12
Feb. 4	Centre	(A)	27	21
Feb. 6	Georgetown	(A)	26	17
Feb. 8	Washington & Lee	(A)	21	20
Feb. 9	**Va. Military Inst.**	**(A)**	**32**	**37**
Feb. 11	**Georgetown U.**	**(A)**	**23**	**28**
Feb. 13	**Virginia**	**(A)**	**30**	**32**
Feb. 16	Clemson	(H)	38	14
Feb. 20	Centre	(H)	40	23
	SIAA TOURNAMENT (Atlanta, Ga.)			
Feb. 24	Georgetown		41	21
Feb. 25	**Mercer**		**22**	**35**
			457	361

1922-23—Won 3, Lost 10.

COACH: George C. Buchheit
CAPTAIN: Fred Fest

Date	Team	Site	UK	Opp.
Jan. 13	Georgetown	(A)	24	13
Jan. 20	**Tennessee**	**(A)**	**26**	**30**
Jan. 22	Chattanooga	(H)	25	18
Jan. 25	**Alabama**	**(H)**	**35**	**45**
Jan. 27	**Centre**	**(H)**	**14**	**21**
Feb. 3	**Georgia**	**(H)**	**19**	**23**
Feb. 5	**Cincinnati**	**(A)**	**24**	**33**
Feb. 7	**Centenary**	**(H)**	**21**	**38**
Feb. 10	**Tennessee**	**(H)**	**23**	**28**
Feb. 14	**Centre**	**(A)**	**10**	**17**
Feb. 15	**Clemson**	**(H)**	**17**	**30**
Feb. 19	**Georgetown**	**(H)**	**21**	**48**
Feb. 23	Sewanee	(H)	30	14
			289	348

1923-24—Won 13, Lost 3.

COACH: G. C. Buchheit
CAPTAIN: A. T. Rice

Date	Team	Site	UK	Opp.
Jan. 1	Vanderbilt	(H)	33	13
Jan. 8	Mexico YMCA	(H)	25	14
Jan. 12	Georgetown	(A)	32	24
Jan. 14	**Miss. A & M**	**(H)**	**16**	**17**
Jan. 15	Sewanee	(H)	50	15
Jan. 18	**Tennessee**	**(A)**	**13**	**20**
Jan. 19	Chattanooga	(A)	24	23
Feb. 4	West Virginia	(H)	24	21
Feb. 9	Centre	(A)	27	18
Feb. 11	Georgetown	(H)	39	35
Feb. 13	Clemson	(H)	38	13
Feb. 14	Virginia	(H)	29	16
Feb. 19	Virginia Tech	(H)	36	14
Feb. 21	Centre	(H)	38	24
Feb. 23	Georgia Tech	(H)	33	27
	SIAA TOURNAMENT (Atlanta, Ga.)			
Feb. 29	**North Carolina**		**20**	**41**
			477	335

ALUMNI GYM ERA (1924-1950)

1924-25—Won 13, Lost 8.

COACH: C. O. Applegran
CAPTAIN: James McFarland

Date	Team	Site	UK	Opp.
Dec. 13	Cincinnati	(H)	28	23
Dec. 18	**Indiana**	**(H)**	**18**	**20**
Dec. 20	**Michigan**	**(H)**	**11**	**21**
Jan. 3	**Cincinnati**	**(A)**	**20**	**24**
Jan. 5	**Illinois**	**(A)**	**26**	**36**
Jan. 6	**Wabash**	**(A)**	**11**	**57**
Jan. 9	Mississippi	(H)	26	23
Jan. 10	Georgetown	(H)	25	17
Jan. 17	Centre	(H)	33	26
Jan. 30	Washington & Lee	(H)	28	22
Feb. 2	West Virginia	(H)	29	19
Feb. 5	**Alabama**	**(A)**	**15**	**24**
Feb. 6	Georgia Tech	(A)	18	16
Feb. 7	**Georgia**	**(A)**	**24**	**28**
Feb. 9	Tennessee	(A)	35	22
Feb. 12	Tulane	(A)	29	22
Feb. 14	Georgetown	(A)	36	21
Feb. 18	Tennessee	(H)	26	21
Feb. 21	Centre	(H)	39	10
	SOUTHERN CONF. TOUR. (Atlanta, Ga.)			
Feb. 27	Mississippi A&M		31	26
Feb. 28	**Georgia**		**31**	**32**
			539	510

1925-26—Won 15, Lost 3.

COACH: Ray Eklund
CAPTAIN: Burgess Carey

Date	Team	Site	UK	Opp.
Dec. 19	**DePauw**	**(H)**	**29**	**38**
Jan. 5	**Indiana**	**(A)**	**23**	**34**
Jan. 9	Berea	(H)	37	23
Jan. 12	Georgetown	(A)	36	21
Jan. 16	Georgia Tech	(H)	25	24
Jan. 22	Centre	(H)	45	25
Jan. 30	Georgetown	(H)	25	20
Feb. 1	Alabama	(H)	27	16
Feb. 4	Centre	(A)	46	19
Feb. 5	Washington & Lee	(H)	44	34
Feb. 8	Auburn	(H)	35	26
Feb. 12	Tennessee	(A)	51	17
Feb. 15	Georgia	(A)	22	18
Feb. 18	Tennessee	(H)	27	21
Feb. 20	Vanderbilt	(H)	30	20
	SOUTHERN CONF. TOUR. (Atlanta, Ga.)			
Feb. 26	Va. Military Inst.		38	25
Feb. 27	Georgia		39	34
Mar. 1	**Mississippi A&M**		**26**	**31**
			605	446

1926-27—Won 3, Lost 13.

COACH: Basil Hayden
CAPTAIN: Paul Jenkins

Date	Team	Site	UK	Opp.
Dec. 18	**Cincinnati**	**(H)**	**10**	**48**
Dec. 21	**Indiana**	**(H)**	**19**	**38**
Dec. 29	**Cincinnati**	**(A)**	**23**	**51**
Dec. 31	**Princeton**	**(H)**	**26**	**30**
Jan. 3	Florida	(H)	43	36
Jan. 10	**Ky. Wesleyan**	**(A)**	**25**	**31**
Jan. 15	**Vanderbilt**	**(H)**	**32**	**48**
Jan. 21	**Tennessee**	**(A)**	**14**	**19**
Jan. 22	**Georgia Tech**	**(A)**	**16**	**48**
Jan. 29	Centre	(H)	27	25
Feb. 1	**Georgetown**	**(A)**	**19**	**26**
Feb. 4	**Washington & Lee**	**(H)**	**34**	**36**
Feb. 7	**West Virginia**	**(H)**	**26**	**44**
Feb. 11	**Mississippi**	**(H)**	**17**	**37**
Feb. 12	Centre	(A)	22	16
Feb. 19	**Tennessee**	**(H)**	**21**	**30**
			374	563

1927-28—Won 12, Lost 6.

COACH: John Mauer
CAPTAIN: Paul Jenkins

Date	Team	Site	UK	Opp.
Dec. 16	Clemson	(H)	33	17
Dec. 20	**Miami (Ohio) U.**	**(H)**	**31**	**36**
Jan. 4	Berea	(H)	37	16
Jan. 9	Centre	(A)	36	25
Jan. 14	Vanderbilt	(H)	43	23
Jan. 16	Virginia	(A)	31	28
Jan. 18	**Naval Academy**	**(A)**	**26**	**32**
Jan. 19	**Maryland**	**(A)**	**7**	**37**
Jan. 28	Tennessee	(H)	48	18
Feb. 3	Washington & Lee	(H)	34	28
Feb. 4	**Indiana**	**(A)**	**29**	**48**
Feb. 8	Vanderbilt	(A)	54	29
Feb. 9	Tennessee	(A)	43	16
Feb. 11	**Georgia Tech**	**(H)**	**31**	**35**
Feb. 18	Centre	(H)	30	20
	SOUTHERN CONF. TOUR. (Atlanta, Ga.)			
Feb. 24	South Carolina		56	40
Feb. 25	Georgia		33	16
Feb. 27	**Mississippi**		**28**	**41**
			630	505

1928-29—Won 12, Lost 5.

COACH: John Mauer
CAPTAIN: Lawrence McGinnis

Date	Team	Site	UK	Opp.
Dec. 15	Eastern Normal	(H)	35	10
Dec. 21	Miami (Ohio) U.	(H)	43***	42
Jan. 4	**North Carolina**	**(H)**	**15**	**25**
Jan. 12	Notre Dame	(A)	19	16
Jan. 16	**Georgia Tech**	**(A)**	**19**	**33**
Jan. 17	Tennessee	(A)	35	29
Jan. 19	Tennessee	(H)	27	22
Jan. 26	**Alabama**	**(H)**	**26**	**27**
Feb. 1	Mississippi A&M	(A)	25	23
Feb. 2	Mississippi A&M	(A)	32	14
Feb. 3	**Tulane**	**(A)**	**22**	**34**
Feb. 8	Washington & Lee	(H)	31	30
Feb. 13	Centre	(H)	47	11
Feb. 22	Mississippi	(H)	35	30
Feb. 23	Mississippi	(H)	32	24
	SOUTHERN CONF. TOUR. (Atlanta, Ga.)			
Mar. 1	Tulane		29	15
Mar. 2	**Georgia**		**24**	**26**
			496	411

*** Denotes 3 overtime periods.

Date	Team	Site	UK	Opp.

1929-30—Won 16, Lost 3.
COACH: John Mauer
CAPTAIN: Paul McBrayer

Date	Team	Site	UK	Opp.
Dec. 14	Georgetown	(H)	46	9
Dec. 20	Miami (Ohio) U.	(H)	35	20
Dec. 31	Berea	(H)	29	26
Jan. 3	Clemson	(H)	31	15
Jan. 10	**Creighton**	**(H)**	**27**	**28**
Jan. 11	Creighton	(H)	25	21
Jan. 18	Tennessee	(H)	23	20
Jan. 24	Mississippi A&M	(H)	43	17
Jan. 25	Mississippi A&M	(H)	20	14
Jan. 31	**Tennessee**	**(A)**	**26**	**29**
Feb. 1	Georgia	(H)	22	21
Feb. 3	Clemson	(A)	34	20
Feb. 8	Georgia Tech	(H)	39	19
Feb. 14	Georgia	(H)	36	23
Feb. 18	Ky. Wesleyan	(H)	32	20
Feb. 22	Washington & Lee	(H)	28	*26

SOUTHERN CONF. TOUR. (Atlanta, Ga.)

Feb. 28	Maryland		26	21
Mar. 1	Sewanee		44	22
Mar. 3	**Duke**		**32**	**37**
			599	408

* Denotes overtime period.

ADOLPH RUPP ERA

1930-31—Won 15, Lost 3.
COACH: Adolph Rupp
CAPTAIN: Carey Spicer

Date	Team	Site	UK	Opp.
Dec. 18	Georgetown	(H)	67	19
Dec. 27	Marshall	(H)	42	26
Dec. 31	Berea	(H)	41	25
Jan. 3	Clemson	(H)	33	21
Jan. 10	Tennessee	(H)	31	23
Jan. 16	Chattanooga	(H)	55	18
Jan. 21	Vanderbilt	(A)	42	37
Jan. 31	Tennessee	(A)	36	*32
Feb. 6	Washington & Lee	(H)	23	18
Feb. 9	Georgia Tech	(H)	38	34
Feb. 13	**Georgia**	**(A)**	**16**	**25**
Feb. 14	**Clemson**	**(A)**	**26**	**29**
Feb. 16	Georgia Tech	(A)	35	16
Feb. 20	Vanderbilt	(H)	43	23

SOUTHERN CONF. TOUR. (Atlanta, Ga.)

Feb. 27	North Carolina State		33	28
Feb. 28	Duke		35	30
Mar. 2	Florida		56	36
Mar. 3	**Maryland (finals)**		**27**	**29**

* Denotes overtime period.   679   469

1931-32—Won 15, Lost 2.
COACH: Adolph Rupp
CAPTAIN: Ellis Johnson

Date	Team	Site	UK	Opp.
Dec. 15	Georgetown	(H)	66	24
Dec. 18	Carnegie Tech	(H)	36	34
Dec. 23	Berea	(H)	52	27
Dec. 30	Marshall	(H)	46	16
Jan. 2	Clemson	(H)	43	24
Jan. 14	Clemson	(A)	30	17
Jan. 15	Sewanee	(A)	30	20
Jan. 16	Tennessee	(A)	29	28
Jan. 21	Chattanooga	(H)	51	17
Jan. 30	Washington & Lee	(H)	48	28
Feb. 6	Duke	(H)	37	30
Feb. 8	Alabama	(H)	50	22
Feb. 10	Vanderbilt	(A)	61	37
Feb. 13	Tennessee	(H)	41	27
Feb. 20	**Vanderbilt**	**(H)**	**31**	**32**

SOUTHERN CONF. TOUR. (Atlanta, Ga.)

Feb. 26	Tulane		50	30
Feb. 27	**North Carolina**		**42**	**43**
			743	456

1932-33—Won 20, Lost 3.
COACH: Adolph Rupp
CATAIN: Forest Sale

Date	Team	Site	UK	Opp.
Dec. 12	Georgetown	(H)	62	21
Dec. 17	Marshall	(N1)	57	23
Dec. 20	Tulane	(H)	53	17
Dec. 21	Tulane	(H)	42	11
Dec. 30	Chicago	(A)	58	26
Jan. 2	**Ohio State**	**(H)**	**30**	**46**
Jan. 6	Creighton	(A)	32	26
Jan. 7	**Creighton**	**(A)**	**22**	**34**
Jan. 10	South Carolina	(H)	44	36
Jan. 16	Tennessee	(A)	42	21
Jan. 16	Clemson	(H)	67	18
Jan. 28	Tennessee	(H)	44	23
Jan. 31	Vanderbilt	(A)	40	29
Feb. 1	Clemson	(A)	42	32
Feb. 2	**South Carolina**	**(A)**	**38**	**44**
Feb. 6	Mexico U.	(H)	81	22
Feb. 11	Georgia Tech	(H)	45	22
Feb. 13	Alabama	(N2)	35	21
Feb. 18	Vanderbilt	(H)	45	28

SEC TOURNAMENT (Atlanta, Ga.)

Feb. 25	Mississippi		49	31
Feb. 26	Florida		48	24
Feb. 27	L.S.U.		51	38
Feb. 28	Mississippi State (championship)		46	27
SEC CHAMPIONS			1073	630

(N1) Ashland, Ky.   (N2) Birmingham

1933-34—Won 16, Lost 1.
COACH: Adolph Rupp
CAPTAIN: John DeMoisey

Date	Team	Site	UK	Opp.
Dec. 5	Alumni	(H)	53	20
Dec. 9	Georgetown	(H)	41	12
Dec. 14	Marshall	(H)	48	26
Dec. 16	Cincinnati	(H)	31	25
Dec. 21	Tulane	(A)	32	22
Dec. 22	Tulane	(A)	42	29
Jan. 12	Sewanee	(A)	55	16
Jan. 13	Tennessee	(A)	44	23
Jan. 20	Chattanooga	(H)	47	20
Jan. 27	Tennessee	(H)	53	26
Feb. 1	Alabama	(N1)	33	28
Feb. 3	Vanderbilt	(A)	48	26
Feb. 8	Alabama	(H)	26	21
Feb. 10	Georgia Tech	(H)	49	25
Feb. 15	Sewanee	(H)	60	15
Feb. 17	Vanderbilt	(H)	47	27

SEC TOURNAMENT (Atlanta, Ga.)

Feb. 24	**Florida**		**32**	**38**
(N1) Birmingham			741	399

1934-35—Won 19, Lost 2.
COACH: Adolph Rupp
CO-CAPTAINS: Dave Lawrence and Jack Tucker

Date	Team	Site	UK	Opp.
Dec. 10	Alumni	(H)	61	10
Dec. 13	Oglethorpe	(H)	81	12
Dec. 20	Tulane	(A)	38	9
Dec. 21	Tulane	(A)	52	12
Jan. 2	Chicago	(H)	42	16
Jan. 8	**New York U.**	**(A)**	**22**	**23**
Jan. 18	Tulane	(H)	63	22
Jan. 19	Tulane	(H)	55	12
Jan. 22	Chattanooga	(H)	66	19
Jan. 26	Tennessee	(H)	48	21
Feb. 1	Alabama	(N1)	33	26
Feb. 2	Vanderbilt	(A)	58	22
Feb. 5	Xavier	(A)	40	27
Feb. 9	Georgia Tech	(H)	57	30
Feb. 11	Alabama	(H)	25	16
Feb. 13	**Michigan State**	**(A)**	**26**	**32**
Feb. 16	Tennessee	(A)	38	36
Feb. 22	Creighton	(H)	63	42
Feb. 23	Creighton	(H)	24	13
Mar. 2	Vanderbilt	(H)	53	19
Mar. 1	Vanderbilt	(H)	46	29
SEC CO-CHAMPIONS			991	448

(N1) Birmingham

1935-36—Won 15, Lost 6.
COACH: Adolph Rupp
CAPTAIN: Milerd Anderson

Date	Team	Site	UK	Opp.
Dec. 6	Georgetown	(H)	42	17
Dec. 17	Berea	(H)	58	30
Dec. 23	Pittsburgh	(H)	35	17
Jan. 8	**New York U.**	**(A)**	**28**	**41**
Jan. 14	Xavier	(A)	36	32
Jan. 17	Tulane	(H)	49	24
Jan. 18	Tulane	(H)	39	21
Jan. 21	Michigan State	(H)	27	19
Jan. 25	Tennessee	(H)	40	31
Feb. 1	**Vanderbilt**	**(A)**	**23**	**32**
Feb. 3	Alabama	(A)	32	30
Feb. 7	Alabama	(H)	40	34
Feb. 10	**Notre Dame**	**(A)**	**20**	**41**
Feb. 11	Butler	(A)	39	28
Feb. 15	**Tennessee**	**(A)**	**28**	**39**
Feb. 18	Xavier	(H)	49	40
Feb. 21	Creighton	(H)	68	38
Feb. 22	**Creighton**	**(H)**	**29**	**31**
Feb. 24	Vanderbilt	(H)	61	41

SEC TOURNAMENT (Knoxville, Tenn.)

Feb. 28	Mississippi State		41	39
Mar. 1	**Tennessee**		**28**	**39**
			812	664

1936-37—Won 17, Lost 5.
COACH: Adolph Rupp
CAPTAIN: Warfield Donohue

Date	Team	Site	UK	Opp.
Dec. 9	Georgetown	(H)	46	21
Dec. 12	Berea	(H)	70	26
Dec. 15	Xavier	(A)	34	28
Dec. 21	Centenary	(H)	37	19
Jan. 2	Michigan State	(H)	28	21
Jan. 5	**Notre Dame**	**(N1)**	**28**	**41**
Jan. 8	Creighton	(H)	59	36
Jan. 14	**Michigan State**	**(A)**	**23**	**24**
Jan. 16	Akron U.	(N2)	32	22
Jan. 23	Tennessee	(H)	43	26
Jan. 30	Vanderbilt	(A)	41	26
Feb. 1	Alabama	(N3)	38	27
Feb. 3	**Tulane**	**(A)**	**28**	**35**
Feb. 4	Tulane	(A)	28	25
Feb. 8	Mexico U.	(H)	60	30
Feb. 10	**Alabama**	**(H)**	**31**	**34**
Feb. 13	**Tennessee**	**(A)**	**24**	**26**
Feb. 20	Vanderbilt	(H)	51	19
Feb. 22	Xavier	(H)	23	15

SEC TOURNAMENT (Knoxville, Tenn.)

Feb. 26	Louisiana State		57	37
Feb. 28	Georgia Tech		40	30
Mar. 1	Tennessee (championship)		39	25
SEC CHAMPIONS			860	593

(N1) Louisville (N2) Cincinnati (N3) Birmingham

1937-38—Won 13, Lost 5.
COACH: Adolph Rupp
CAPTAIN: J. Rice Walker

Date	Team	Site	UK	Opp.
Dec. 5	Berea	(H)	67	33
Dec. 18	Cincinnati	(H)	38	21
Dec. 22	Centenary	(H)	35	25

SUGAR BOWL TOURNAMENT
New Orleans, La.

Dec. 29	Pittsburgh (championship)		40	29
Jan. 8	**Michigan State**	**(A)**	**37**	**42**
Jan. 10	**Detroit**	**(A)**	**26**	**34**
Jan. 15	**Notre Dame**	**(A)**	**37**	**47**
Jan. 22	Tennessee	(H)	52	27
Jan. 29	Vanderbilt	(A)	42	19
Jan. 31	Alabama	(N1)	57	31
Feb. 5	**Xavier**	**(A)**	**32**	**39**
Feb. 7	Michigan State	(H)	44	27
Feb. 12	Alabama	(H)	27	21
Feb. 14	Marquette	(H)	35	33
Feb. 17	Xavier	(H)	45	29
Feb. 21	Vanderbilt	(H)	48	24
Feb. 26	Tennessee	(H)	29	26

SEC TOURNAMENT (Baton Rouge, La.)

Mar. 3	**Tulane**		**34**	**36**
(N1) Birmingham			725	541

1938-39—Won 16, Lost 4.
COACH: Adolph Rupp
CAPTAIN: Bernard Opper

Date	Team	Site	UK	Opp.
Dec. 2	Georgetown	(H)	39	19
Dec. 10	Ky. Wesleyan	(H)	57	18
Dec. 17	Cincinnati	(H)	44	27
Dec. 21	Washington & Lee	(H)	67	47
Jan. 4	**Long Island**	**(A)**	**34**	**52**
Jan. 6	St. Joseph's	(A)	41	30
Jan. 14	**Notre Dame**	**(N1)**	**37**	**42**
Jan. 21	**Tennessee**	**(H)**	**29**	**30**
Jan. 28	**Alabama**	**(N2)**	**38**	**41**
Jan. 30	Vanderbilt	(A)	51	37
Feb. 4	Marquette	(H)	37	31
Feb. 8	Xavier	(A)	41	31
Feb. 11	Alabama	(H)	45	27
Feb. 13	Mississippi State	(H)	39	28
Feb. 18	Tennessee	(A)	36	**34
Feb. 21	Xavier	(H)	43	23
Feb. 25	Vanderbilt	(H)	52	27

SEC TOURNAMENT (Knoxville, Tenn.)

Date	Team	Site	UK	Opp.
Mar. 2	Mississippi		49	30
Mar. 3	Louisiana State		53	34
Mar. 4	Tennessee (championship)		46	38
			878	646

SEC CHAMPIONS
(N1) Louisville (N2) Birmingham
** Denotes 2 overtime periods

1939-40—Won 15, Lost 6.
COACH: Adolph Rupp
CAPTAIN: Layton Rouse

Date	Team	Site	UK	Opp.
Dec. 9	Berea	(H)	74	24
Dec. 16	Cincinnati	(H)	30	39
Dec. 21	Clemson	(A)	55	31
SUGAR BOWL (New Orleans, La.)				
Dec. 27	Ohio State (championship)		36	30
Jan. 1	Kansas State	(H)	53	26
Jan. 6	Xavier	(A)	42	41
Jan. 8	West Virginia	(H)	47	38
Jan. 13	Notre Dame	(A)	47	52
Jan. 20	Tennessee	(H)	35	26
Jan. 27	Alabama	(N1)	32	36
Jan. 29	Vanderbilt	(A)	32	40
Feb. 3	Marquette	(A)	51	45
Feb. 10	Alabama	(H)	46	18
Feb. 12	Xavier	(H)	37	29
Feb. 13	Mississippi State	(H)	45	37
Feb. 17	Tennessee	(A)	23	27
Feb. 19	Georgia Tech	(A)	39	44
Feb. 24	Vanderbilt	(H)	43	38
SEC TOURNAMENT (Knoxville, Tenn.)				
Feb. 29	Vanderbilt		44	31
Mar. 1	Tennessee		30	29
Mar. 2	Georgia (championship)		51	43
			892	724

SEC CHAMPIONS
(N1) Birmingham

1940-41—Won 17, Lost 8.
COACH: Adolph Rupp
CAPTAIN: Lee Huber

Date	Team	Site	UK	Opp.
Dec. 7	Alumni	(H)	62	25
Dec. 12	West Virginia	(H)	46	34
Dec. 13	Maryville	(H)	53	14
Dec. 18	Nebraska	(A)	39	40
Dec. 19	Creighton	(A)	45	54
Dec. 20	Kansas State	(A)	28	25
Dec. 27	Centenary	(H)	70	18
SUGAR BOWL (New Orleans, La.)				
Dec. 30	Indiana		45	48
Jan. 4	Notre Dame	(N1)	47	48
Jan. 9	Xavier		48	43
Jan. 11	West Virginia	(A)	43	56
Jan. 18	Tennessee	(A)	22	32
Jan. 20	Georgia Tech	(A)	47	37
Jan. 25	Xavier	(H)	44	49
Feb. 1	Vanderbilt	(A)	51	50
Feb. 3	Alabama	(A)	38	36
Feb. 8	Alabama	(H)	46	38
Feb. 10	Mississippi	(H)	60	41
Feb. 15	Tennessee	(H)	37	28
Feb. 17	Georgia Tech	(H)	60	41
Feb. 24	Vanderbilt	(H)	58	31
SEC TOURNAMENT (Louisville, Ky.)				
Feb. 27	Mississippi		62	52
Feb. 28	Tulane		59	30
Mar. 1	Alabama		39	37
Mar. 2	Tennessee		33	36
			1182	943

(N1) Louisville

1941-42—Won 19, Lost 6.
COACH: Adolph Rupp
CAPTAIN: Carl Staker

Date	Team	Site	UK	Opp.
Dec. 6	Miami (Ohio) U.	(H)	35	21
Dec. 13	Ohio State	(A)	41	43
Dec. 16	Nebraska	(H)	42	27
Dec. 22	South Carolina	(H)	64	25
Dec. 30	Texas A&M	(H)	49	29
Jan. 2	Washington & Lee	(H)	62	32
Jan. 10	Xavier	(A)	40	39
Jan. 17	Tennessee	(A)	40	46
Jan. 19	Georgia	(A)	51	26
Jan. 20	Georgia Tech	(A)	63	53
Jan. 24	Mexico	(H)	56	26
Jan. 31	Georgia	(H)	55	38
Feb. 2	Alabama	(A)	35	41
Feb. 7	Notre Dame	(A)	43	46
Feb. 9	Alabama	(H)	50	34
Feb. 14	Tennessee	(A)	36	33
Feb. 16	Georgia Tech	(H)	57	51
Feb. 21	Xavier	(H)	44	36
SEC TOURNAMENT Louisville, Ky.				
Feb. 26	Florida		42	36
Feb. 27	Mississippi		59	32
Feb. 28	Auburn		40	31
Mar. 1	Alabama (championship)		36	34

SEC CHAMPIONS

POST SEASON GAME (Louisville, Ky.)

Date	Team	Site	UK	Opp.
Mar. 14	Great Lakes		47	58

NCAA TOURNAMENT (New Orleans, La.)

Date	Team	Site	UK	Opp.
Mar. 20	Illinois		46	44
Mar. 21	Dartmouth		28	47
			1161	928

1942-43—Won 17, Lost 6.
COACH: Adolph Rupp
Co-Captains: Marvin Akers and Melvin Brewer

Date	Team	Site	UK	Opp.
Dec. 12	Cincinnati	(H)	61	39
Dec. 19	Washington	(H)	45	38
Dec. 23	Indiana	(N1)	52	58
Jan. 2	Ohio State	(H)	40	45
Jan. 4	Ft. Knox	(H)	64	30
Jan. 9	Xavier	(A)	43	38
Jan. 16	Tennessee	(A)	30	28
Jan. 18	Georgia	(A)	60	28
Jan. 19	Georgia Tech	(A)	38	36
Jan. 23	Notre Dame	(N1)	60	55
Jan. 26	Vanderbilt	(H)	39	38
Jan. 30	Alabama	(A)	32	41
Feb. 1	Vanderbilt	(A)	54	43
Feb. 6	Alabama	(H)	67	41
Feb. 8	Xavier	(H)	48	36
Feb. 13	Tennessee	(H)	53	29
Feb. 15	Georgia Tech	(H)	58	31
Feb. 20	De Paul	(A)	44	53
SEC TOURNAMENT Louisville, Ky.				
Feb. 25	Tulane		48	31
Feb. 26	Georgia		59	30
Feb. 27	Mississippi State		52	43
Feb. 28	Tennessee		30	33
POST-SEASON GAME (N1)				
Mar. 6	Great Lakes		39	53

(N1) Louisville 1124 887

1943-44—Won 19, Lost 2.
COACH: Adolph Rupp
CAPTAIN:

Date	Team	Site	UK	Opp.
Dec. 1	Ft. Knox	(H)	51	18
Dec. 4	Berea (Naval V-12)	(H)	54	40
Dec. 11	Indiana	(N1)	66	41
Dec. 13	Ohio State	(A)	40	28
Dec. 18	Cincinnati	(H)	58	30
Dec. 20	Illinois	(A)	41	43
Dec. 28	Carnegie Tech	(N2)	61	14
Dec. 30	St. John's	(A)	44	38
Jan. 8	Notre Dame	(N1)	55	54
Jan. 15	Wright Field	(H)	61	28
Jan. 31	Ft. Knox A.R.C.	(H)	76	48
Feb. 5	DePauw	(H)	38	35
Feb. 7	Illinois	(H)	51	40
Feb. 12	Cincinnati	(A)	38	35
Feb. 26	Ohio U.	(H)	51	35
SEC TOURNAMENT (Louisville, Ky.)				
Mar. 2	Georgia		57	29
Mar. 3	Louisiana State		55	28
Mar. 4	Tulane (championship)		62	46

SEC CHAMPIONS

NATIONAL INVITATION TOUR. (New York)

Date	Team	Site	UK	Opp.
Mar. 20	Utah		46	38
Mar. 22	St. John's		45	48
Mar. 26	Oklahoma A&M (consolation)		45	29

(N1) Louisville 1095 745
(N2) Buffalo, N.Y.

1944-45—Won 22, Lost 4.
COACH: Adolph Rupp
CAPTAIN:

Date	Team	Site	UK	Opp.
Dec. 2	Ft. Knox	(H)	56	23
Dec. 4	Berea	(H)	56	32
Dec. 9	Cincinnati	(H)	66	24
Dec. 16	Indiana	(N1)	61	43
Dec. 23	Ohio State	(H)	53	*48
Dec. 26	Wyoming	(N2)	50	46
Dec. 30	Temple	(A)	45	44
Jan. 1	Long Island	(A)	62	*52
Jan. 6	Ohio U.	(H)	59	46
Jan. 8	Arkansas State	(H)	75	6
Jan. 13	Michigan State	(H)	66	35
Jan. 20	Tennessee	(A)	34	35
Jan. 22	Georgia Tech	(A)	64	58
Jan. 27	Notre Dame	(N1)	58	*59
Jan. 29	Georgia	(H)	73	37
Feb. 3	Georgia Tech	(H)	51	32
Feb. 5	Michigan State	(A)	50	66
Feb. 17	Tennessee	(H)	40	34
Feb. 19	Ohio U.	(A)	61	38
Feb. 24	Cincinnati	(A)	65	35
SEC TOURNAMENT (Louisville, Ky.)				
Mar. 1	Florida		57	35
Mar. 2	Louisiana State		68	37
Mar. 3	Alabama		52	41
Mar. 3	Tennessee (championship)		39	35

SEC CHAMPIONS

NCAA TOURNAMENT (New York)

Date	Team	Site	UK	Opp.
Mar. 20	Ohio State		37	45
Mar. 21	Tufts (consolation)		66	56

* Denotes overtime period. 1464 1042
(N1) Louisville
(N2) Buffalo, N. Y.

1945-46—Won 28, Lost 2.
COACH: Adolph Rupp
CAPTAIN: Jack Parkinson

Date	Team	Site	UK	Opp.
Dec. 1	Ft. Knox	(H)	59	36
Dec. 7	Western Ontario	(H)	51	42
Dec. 8	Western Ontario	(H)	71	28
Dec. 15	Cincinnati	(H)	67	31
Dec. 18	Arkansas	(H)	67	42
Dec. 21	Oklahoma	(H)	43	33
Dec. 29	St. John's	(A)	73	59
Jan. 1	Temple	(A)	45	53
Jan. 5	Ohio U.	(H)	57	48
Jan. 7	Fort Benning	(H)	81	25
Jan. 12	Michigan State	(A)	55	44
Jan. 14	Xavier	(A)	62	36
Jan. 19	Tennessee	(A)	50	32
Jan. 21	Georgia Tech	(A)	68	43
Jan. 26	Notre Dame	(N1)	47	56
Jan. 28	Georgia Tech	(H)	54	26
Feb. 2	Michigan State	(H)	59	51
Feb. 4	Vanderbilt	(A)	59	37
Feb. 9	Vanderbilt	(N2)	64	31
Feb. 16	Tennessee	(H)	54	34
Feb. 19	Ohio U.	(A)	60	52
Feb. 23	Xavier	(H)	83	40
SEC TOURNAMENT (Louisville, Ky.)				
Feb. 28	Auburn		69	24
Mar. 1	Florida		69	32
Mar. 2	Alabama		59	30
Mar. 2	Louisiana State (championship)		59	36

SEC CHAMPIONS

POST-SEASON GAME Louisville, Ky.

Date	Team	Site	UK	Opp.
Mar. 9	Temple		54	43

NATIONAL INVITATION TOUR. (New York)

Date	Team	Site	UK	Opp.
Mar. 16	Arizona		77	53
Mar. 18	West Virginia		59	51
Mar. 20	Rhode Island (Championship)		46	45

(N1) Louisville 1821 1198
(N2) Paducah, Ky.

1946-47—Won 34, Lost 3.

COACH: Adolph Rupp
CAPTAIN: Ken Rollins

Date	Team	Site	UK	Opp.
Nov. 28	Indiana Central	(H)	78	36
Nov. 30	Tulane	(H)	64	35
Dec. 2	Ft. Knox	(H)	68	31
Dec. 7	Cincinnati	(A)	80	49
Dec. 9	Idaho	(H)	65	35
Dec. 12	De Paul	(N1)	65	45
Dec. 14	Texas A&M	(H)	83	18
Dec. 16	Miami (Ohio) U.	(H)	62	49
Dec. 21	St. John's	(N2)	70	50
Dec. 23	Baylor	(H)	75	34
Dec. 28	Wabash	(H)	96	24

SUGAR BOWL (New Orleans, La.)

Dec. 30	**Oklahoma A&M**		**31**	**37**
Jan. 4	Ohio U.	(H)	46	36
Jan. 11	Dayton U.	(H)	70	29
Jan. 13	Vanderbilt	(A)	82	30
Jan. 18	Tennessee	(A)	54	39
Jan. 20	Georgia Tech	(A)	70	47
Jan. 21	Georgia	(A)	84	45
Jan. 25	Xavier	(H)	71	34
Jan. 27	Michigan State	(H)	86	36
Feb. 1	Notre Dame	(N1)	60	30
Feb. 3	Alabama	(A)	48	37
Feb. 8	**De Paul**	**(A)**	**47**	**53**
Feb. 10	Georgia	(H)	81	40
Feb. 15	Tennessee	(H)	61	46
Feb. 17	Alabama	(H)	63	33
Feb. 19	Xavier	(A)	58	31
Feb. 21	Vanderbilt	(A)	84	41
Feb. 22	Georgia Tech	(H)	83	46

SEC TOURNAMENT (Louisville, Ky.)

Feb. 27	Vanderbilt		98	29
Feb. 28	Auburn		84	18
Mar. 1	Georgia Tech		75	53
Mar. 1	Tulane (championship)		55	38

SEC CHAMPIONS

POST-SEASON GAME (Louisville)

Mar. 8	Temple	68	29

NATIONAL INVITATION
TOURNAMENT
New York, N. Y.

Mar. 17	Long Island	63	62
Mar. 19	North Carolina State	60	42
Mar. 24	**Utah**	**45**	**49**

(N1) Louisville   2533 1416
(N2) Mad. Sq. Gar., Record Crowd, 18,493

1947-48—Won 36, Lost 3.

COACH: Adolph Rupp
CAPTAIN: Kenneth Rollins

Date	Team	Site	UK	Opp.
Nov. 29	Indiana Central	(H)	80	41
Dec. 1	Ft. Knox	(H)	80	41
Dec. 5	Tulsa U.	(H)	72	18
Dec. 6	Tulsa U.	(H)	71	22
Dec. 10	De Paul	(N1)	74	50
Dec. 13	Cincinnati	(A)	67	31
Dec. 17	Xavier U.	(H)	79	37
Dec. 20	**Temple U.**	**(A)**	**59**	**60**
Dec. 23	St. John's	(A)	52	40
Jan. 2	Creighton	(A)	65	23
Jan. 3	Western Ontario	(H)	98	41
Jan. 5	Miami (Ohio)	(A)	67	53
Jan. 10	Michigan State	(A)	47	45
Jan. 12	Ohio U.	(A)	79	57
Jan. 17	Tennessee	(A)	65	54
Jan. 19	Georgia Tech	(A)	71	56
Jan. 20	Georgia	(A)	88	51
Jan. 24	Cincinnati	(H)	70	43
Jan. 31	De Paul	(A)	68	51
Feb. 2	**Notre Dame**	**(A)**	**55**	**64**
Feb. 5	Alabama	(A)	41	31
Feb. 5	Washington U.	(N2)	69	39
Feb. 9	Vanderbilt	(A)	82	51
Feb. 14	Tennessee	(H)	69	42
Feb. 16	Alabama	(H)	63	33
Feb. 20	Vanderbilt	(H)	79	43
Feb. 21	Georgia Tech	(H)	78	54
Feb. 24	Temple	(N1)	58	38
Feb. 28	Xavier	(A)	59	37

SEC TOURNAMENT (Louisville, Ky.)

Mar. 4	Florida		87	31
Mar. 5	Louisiana State		63	47
Mar. 5	Tennessee		70	47
Mar. 6	Georgia Tech (championship)		54	43

SEC CHAMPIONS

NCAA TOURNAMENT (New York)

Mar. 18	Columbia	76	53
Mar. 20	Holy Cross	60	52
Mar. 23	Baylor (championship)	58	42

NATIONAL CHAMPIONS

OLMYPIC TRIALS (New York)

Mar. 27	Louisville	91	57
Mar. 29	Baylor	77	59
	(Championship—Collegiate Bracket)		
Mar. 31	**Phillips Oilers**		
	(AAU Champs)	**49**	**53**

(N1) Louisville   2690 1730
(N2) Memphis

OLYMPIC TEAM
EXHIBITION GAMES
Kentucky vs. Phillips Oilers

6-30-48 — Tulsa, Okla.		52	60
7- 2-48 — Kansas City, Mo.		70	**69
7- 9-48 — Lexington, Ky.		50	56

†OLYMPIC GAMES (London, England)

July 30	Switzerland	86	21
Aug. 2	Czechoslovakia	53	28
Ang. 3	Argentina	59	57
Aug. 4	Egypt	66	28
Aug. 6	Peru	61	33
Aug. 9	Uruguay	63	28
Aug. 11	Mexico	71	40
Aug. 13	France (championship)	65	21

WORLD CHAMPIONS

** Denotes two overtime periods.
† Kentucky participated as part of U.S. basketball entry.

1948-49—Won 32, Lost 2.

COACH: Adolph Rupp
CAPTAIN:

Date	Team	Site	UK	Opp.
Nov. 29	Indiana Central	(H)	74	38
Dec. 8	De Paul	(N1)	67	36
Dec. 10	Tulsa U.	(H)	81	27
Dec. 13	Arkansas	(H)	76	39
Dec. 16	Holy Cross	(A)	51	48
Dec. 18	St. John's	(A)	57	30
Dec. 22	Tulane	(N1)	51	47

SUGAR BOWL (New Orleans, La.)

Dec. 29	Tulane		78	47
Dec. 30	**St. Louis**		**40**	**42**
Jan. 11	Bowling Green	(N2)	63	61
Jan. 15	Tennessee	(A)	66	51
Jan. 17	Georgia Tech	(A)	56	45
Jan. 22	De Paul	(A)	56	45
Jan. 29	Notre Dame	(N1)	62	38
Jan. 31	Vanderbilt	(A)	72	50
Feb. 2	Alabama	(A)	56	40
Feb. 3	Mississippi	(N3)	75	45
Feb. 5	Tennessee	(N4)	62	52
Feb. 8	Tennessee	(H)	71	56
Feb. 12	Xavier	(H)	96	50
Feb. 14	Alabama	(H)	74	32
Feb. 16	Mississippi	(H)	85	31
Feb. 19	Georgia Tech	(H)	78	32
Feb. 21	Georgia	(H)	95	40
Feb. 24	Xavier	(A)	51	40
Feb. 26	Vanderbilt	(H)	70	37

SEC TOURNAMENT (Louisville, Ky.)

Mar. 3	Florida		73	36
Mar. 4	Auburn		70	39
Mar. 5	Tennessee		83	44
Mar. 5	Tulane (championship)		68	52

SEC CHAMPIONS

NATIONAL INVITATION TOUR. (New York)

Mar. 14	**Loyola of Chicago**	**56**	**67**

NCAA TOURNAMENT
(Eastern Regionals)
New York, N. Y.

Mar. 21	Villanova	85	72
Mar. 22	Illinois	76	47

NCAA FINALS (Seattle, Wash.)

Mar. 26	Oklahoma A&M	46	36
	(championship)		

       2320 1492

NATIONAL CHAMPIONS
(N1) Louisville   (N3) Memphis
(N2) Cleveland   (N4) Owensboro, Ky.

1949-50—Won 25, Lost 5.

COACH: Adolph Rupp
CAPTAIN: Dale Barnstable

Date	Team	Site	UK	Opp.
Dec. 3	Indiana Central	(H)	84	61
Dec. 10	Western Ontario	(H)	90	18
Dec. 15	**St. John's**	**(A)**	**58**	**69**
Dec. 21	De Paul	(N1)	49	47
Dec. 25	Purdue	(A)	60	54

SUGAR BOWL (New Orleans, La.)

Dec. 29	Villanova		57	*56
Dec. 30	Bradley (championship)		71	66
Jan. 2	Arkansas	(A)	57	53
Jan. 4	Mississippi State	(N2)	87	55
Jan. 9	North Carolina U.	(H)	83	44
Jan. 14	**Tennessee**	**(A)**	**53**	**66**
Jan. 16	Georgia Tech	(A)	61	47
Jan. 17	**Georgia**	**(A)**	**60**	**71**
Jan. 21	De Paul	(A)	86	53
Jan. 23	**Notre Dame**	**(A)**	**51**	**64**
Jan. 26	Xavier	(A)	58	47
Jan. 28	Georgia	(H)	88	56
Jan. 30	Vanderbilt	(A)	58	54
Feb. 2	Alabama	(A)	66	64
Feb. 4	Mississippi	(N3)	61	55
Feb. 11	Tennessee	(H)	79	52
Feb. 13	Alabama	(H)	77	57
Feb. 15	Mississippi	(H)	90	50
Feb. 18	Georgia Tech	(H)	97	62
Feb. 23	Xavier	(H)	58	53
Feb. 25	Vanderbilt	(H)	70	66

SEC TOURNAMENT (Louisville, Ky.)

Mar. 2	Mississippi State		56	46
Mar. 3	Georgia		79	63
Mar. 4	Tennessee (championship)		95	58

SEC CHAMPIONS

NATIONAL INVITATION TOUR. (New York)

Mar. 14	**City Col. of N. Y.**	**50**	**89**

       2089 1696

(N1) Louisville
(N2) Owensboro
(N3) Memphis

* Denotes overtime period.

MEMORIAL COLISEUM ERA

1950-51—Won 32, Lost 2.

(Including exhibition games, Kentucky won
39½ games and lost 2.)
COACH: Adolph Rupp
CAPTAIN: Walt Hirsch

Date	Team	Site	UK	Opp.
Dec. 1	West Texas State	(H)	73	43
Dec. 9	†Purdue	(H)	70	52
Dec. 12	Xavier	(A)	67	56
Dec. 14	Florida	(H)	85	37
Dec. 16	Kansas	(H)	68	39
Dec. 23	St. John's	(A)	43	37

SUGAR BOWL (New Orleans, La.)

Dec. 29	**St. Louis**		**42**	***43**
Dec. 30	Syracuse (consolation)		69	59
Jan. 5	Auburn	(H)	79	35
Jan. 8	De Paul	(H)	63	55
Jan. 13	Alabama	(H)	65	48
Jan. 15	Notre Dame	(H)	69	44
Jan. 20	Tennessee	(A)	70	45
Jan. 22	Georgia Tech	(A)	82	61
Jan. 27	Vanderbilt	(A)	74	49
Jan. 29	Tulane	(A)	104	68
Jan. 31	Louisiana State	(A)	81	59
Feb. 2	Mississippi State	(A)	80	60
Feb. 3	Mississippi	(N1)	86	39
Feb. 9	Georgia Tech	(H)	75	42
Feb. 13	Xavier	(H)	78	51
Feb. 17	Tennessee	(A)	86	61
Feb. 19	De Paul	(A)	60	57
Feb. 23	Georgia	(H)	88	41
Feb. 24	Vanderbilt	(H)	89	57

SEC CHAMPIONS

SEC TOURNAMENT (Louisville, Ky.)

Mar. 1	Mississippi State		92	70
Mar. 2	Auburn		84	54
Mar. 3	Georgia Tech		82	56
Mar. 3	**Vanderbilt**		**57**	**61**

POST-SEASON GAME

Mar. 13	Loyola of Chicago	(H)	97	61

NCAA TOURNAMENT

(First Round—Raleigh, N. C.)

Date	Team	Site	UK	Opp.
Mar. 20	Louisville		79	68

(Eastern Regional—New York N.Y.)

Date	Team	Site	UK	Opp.
Mar. 22	St. John's		59	43
Mar. 24	Illinois		76	74

(National Finals—Minneapolis, Minn.)

Date	Team	Site	UK	Opp.
Mar. 27	Kansas St. (championship)		68	58

NATIONAL CHAMPIONS   2540 1783

EXHIBITION GAME

Date	Team	Site	UK	Opp.
Apr. 27	Ky. All-Stars	(H)	92	49

PUERTO RICO EXHIBITION TOUR

Date	Team	Site	UK	Opp.
Aug. 25	San German Athletics		86	38
Aug. 26	Ponce Lions		83	43
Aug. 27	San Turce		93	40
Aug. 29	Univ. of Puerto Rico		91	44
Sept. 2	U. S. Navy		52	23

(Called at half on account of rain)

Date	Team	Site	UK	Opp.
Sept. 3	Puerto Rico All-Stars		75	46

† Memorial Coliseum Dedication Game.
* Denotes overtime period.
(N1) Owensboro, Ky.

1951-52—Won 29, Lost 3.

COACH: Adolph Rupp
CAPTAIN: Robert Watson

Date	Team	Site	UK	Opp.
Dec. 8	Washington & Lee	(H)	96	46
Dec. 10	Xavier	(A)	97	72
Dec. 13	**Minnesota**	**(A)**	**57**	**61**
Dec. 17	St. John's	(H)	81	40
Dec. 20	De Paul	(H)	98	60
Dec. 26	U.C.L.A.	(H)	84	53

SUGAR BOWL (New Orleans, La.)

Date	Team	Site	UK	Opp.
Dec. 28	Brigham Young		84	64
Dec. 29	**St. Louis**		**60**	**61**
Jan. 2	Mississippi†	(N1)	116	58
Jan. 5	Louisiana State	(H)	57	47
Jan. 7	Xavier	(H)	83	50
Jan. 12	Florida	(A)	99	52
Jan. 16	Georgia	(N2)	95	55
Jan. 19	Tennessee	(A)	65	56
Jan. 21	Georgia Tech	(A)	96	51
Jan. 26	Alabama	(A)	71	67
Jan. 28	Vanderbilt	(A)	88	51
Jan. 30	Auburn	(A)	88	48
Feb. 2	Notre Dame	(N3)	71	66
Feb. 4	Tulane	(H)	103	54
Feb. 6	Mississippi	(H)	81	61
Feb. 9	Georgia Tech	(H)	93	42
Feb. 11	Mississippi State	(H)	110	66
Feb. 16	Tennessee	(H)	95	40
Feb. 21	Vanderbilt	(H)	75	45
Feb. 23	De Paul	(A)	63	61

SEC CHAMPIONS

SEC TOURNAMENT (Louisville, Ky.)#

Date	Team	Site	UK	Opp.
Feb. 28	Georgia Tech		80	59
Feb. 29	Tulane		85	61
Mar. 1	Tennessee		81	66
Mar. 1	Louisiana State		44	43
	(championship)			

NCAA TOURNAMENT

(Eastern Regionals)
Raleigh, N. C.

Date	Team	Site	UK	Opp.
Mar. 21	Penn. State		82	54
Mar. 22	**St. John's**		**57**	**64**

2635 1774

† Not counted as SEC game.
(N1) Owensboro, Ky.
(N2) Louisville
(N3) Chicago
Tournament abandoned after 1952.

1952-53—No Schedule.

(Under suspension by NCAA)
Intra-Squad Scrimmage Results
COACH: Adolph Rupp
CO-CAPTAINS: Cliff Hagan and Frank Ramsey

Date				
Dec. 13	Varsity	76	Freshmen	45
Jan. 19	Ramseys	71	Hagans	50
Feb. 4	Hagans	68	Ramseys	55
Feb. 28	Blues	49	Whites	47
		264		197

1953-54—Won 25, Lost 0.

COACH: Adolph Rupp
CO-CAPTAINS: Cliff Hagan and Frank Ramsey

Date	Team	Site	UK	Opp.
Dec. 5	Temple	(H)	86	59
Dec. 12	Xavier	(A)	81	66
Dec. 14	Wake Forest	(H)	101	69
Dec. 18	St. Louis	(A)	71	59

UK INVITATIONAL TOURNAMENT

Date	Team	Site	UK	Opp.
Dec. 21	Duke		85	69
Dec. 22	LaSalle (championship)		73	60
Dec. 28	Minnesota	(H)	74	59
Jan. 4	Xavier	(H)	77	71
Jan. 9	Georgia Tech	(H)	105	53
Jan. 11	De Paul	(H)	81	63
Jan. 16	Tulane	(H)	94	43
Jan. 23	Tennessee	(A)	97	71
Jan. 30	Vanderbilt	(A)	85	63
Feb. 2	Georgia Tech	(N1)	99	48
Feb. 4	Georgia	(H)	106	55
Feb. 6	Georgia	(N2)	100	68
Feb. 8	Florida	(A)	97	55
Feb. 13	Mississippi	(H)	88	62
Feb. 15	Mississippi State	(H)	81	49
Feb. 18	Tennessee	(H)	90	63
Feb. 20	De Paul	(A)	76	61
Feb. 22	Vanderbilt	(H)	100	64
Feb. 27	Auburn	(N3)	109	79
Mar. 1	Alabama	(A)	68	43

SEC PLAYOFF (Nashville, Tenn.)

(Playoff game to determine SEC champion and representative in NCAA Tournament. Kentucky and LSU tied for league title due to a schedule disagreement. Kentucky won but declined NCAA.)

Date	Team	Site	UK	Opp.
Mar. 9	Louisiana State		63	56

2187 1508

SEC CHAMPIONS
(N1) Louisville
(N2) Owensboro, Ky.
(N3) Montgomery

1954-55—Won 23, Lost 3.

COACH: Adolph Rupp
CAPTAIN: Bill Evans

Date	Team	Site	UK	Opp.
Dec. 4	Louisiana State†	(H)	74	58
Dec. 11	Xavier	(A)	73	69
Dec. 18	Temple	(H)	79	61

UNIVERSITY OF KENTUCKY INVITATIONAL TOURNAMENT
Lexington, Ky.

Date	Team	Site	UK	Opp.
Dec. 21	Utah		70	65
Dec. 22	LaSalle (championship)		63	54
Dec. 30	St. Louis	(H)	82	65
Jan. 1	Temple	(H)	101	69
Jan. 8	**Georgia Tech**	**(H)**	**58**	**59**
Jan. 10	De Paul	(H)	92	59
Jan. 15	Tulane	(A)	58	44
Jan. 17	Louisiana State	(A)	64	62
Jan. 22	Tennessee	(A)	84	66
Jan. 29	Vanderbilt	(A)	75	71
Jan. 31	**Georgia Tech**	**(A)**	**59**	**65**
Feb. 3	Florida	(H)	87	63
Feb. 5	Mississippi	(N1)	84	66
Feb. 7	Mississippi State	(A)	61	56
Feb. 9	Georgia	(H)	86	40
Feb. 14	Xavier	(H)	66	55
Feb. 19	De Paul	(H)	76	72
Feb. 21	Vanderbilt	(H)	77	59
Feb. 26	Auburn	(H)	93	59
Feb. 28	Alabama	(H)	66	52
Mar. 1	Tennessee	(H)	104	61

SEC CHAMPIONS

NCAA TOURNAMENT

(Eastern Regionals)
Evanston, Illinois

Date	Team	Site	UK	Opp.
Mar. 11	**Marquette**		**71**	**79**
Mar. 12	Penn State		84	59

1987 1588

† Game not counted in SEC standings.
(N1) Memphis

1955-56—Won 20, Lost 6.

COACH: Adolph Rupp
CAPTAIN: Phil Grawemeyer

Date	Team	Site	UK	Opp.
Dec. 3	Louisiana State†	(A)	62	52
Dec. 10	**Temple**	**(H)**	**61**	**73**
Dec. 12	De Paul	(H)	71	69
Dec. 15	Maryland	(A)	62	61
Dec. 17	Idaho	(H)	91	49

UK INVITATIONAL TOURNAMENT

Date	Team	Site	UK	Opp.
Dec. 20	Minnesota		72	65
Dec. 21	**Dayton**		**74**	**89**
Dec. 28	St. Louis U.	(A)	101	80
Jan. 7	Georgia Tech	(H)	104	51
Jan. 12	Tulane	(H)	85	63
Jan. 14	Louisiana State	(H)	107	65
Jan. 21	Tennessee	(A)	95	68
Jan. 28	**Vanderbilt**	**(A)**	**73**	**81**
Jan. 30	Georgia Tech	(A)	84	62
Feb. 1	Duke	(H)	81	76
Feb. 4	Auburn	(N1)	82	81
Feb. 6	Florida	(A)	81	70
Feb. 11	Mississippi	(H)	88	49
Feb. 13	Mississippi State	(H)	86	65
Feb. 18	**De Paul**	**(A)**	**79**	**81**
Feb. 20	Vanderbilt	(H)	76	55
Feb. 25	**Alabama**	**(N1)**	**77**	**101**
Feb. 27	Georgia	(N2)	143	66
Mar. 3	Tennessee	(H)	101	77

NCAA TOURNAMENT

(Kentucky represented the SEC in NCAA when champion Alabama declined the bid.)
(Eastern Regionals) Iowa City, Iowa

Date	Team	Site	UK	Opp.
Mar. 16	Wayne U.	(A)	84	64
Mar. 17	**Iowa**	**(A)**	**77**	**89**

2197 1802

† Game not counted in SEC standings.
(N1) Montgomery
(N2) Louisville

1956-57—Won 23, Lost 5.

COACH: Adolph Rupp
HONORARY CO-CAPTAINS:
Ed Beck and Gerry Calvert

Date	Team	Site	UK	Opp.
Dec. 1	Washington & Lee	(H)	94	66
Dec. 3	Miami (Fla.)	(H)	114	75
Dec. 8	Temple	(A)	73	58
Dec. 10	**St. Louis**	**(H)**	**70**	**71**
Dec. 15	Maryland	(H)	76	55
Dec. 18	**Duke**	**(A)**	**84**	**85**

UK INVITATIONAL TOURNAMENT

Date	Team	Site	UK	Opp.
Dec. 21	Southern Methodist		73	67
Dec. 22	Illinois (championship)		91	70

SUGAR BOWL (New Orleans, La.)

Date	Team	Site	UK	Opp.
Dec. 28	Virginia Tech		56	55
Dec. 29	Houston (championship)		111	76
Jan. 5	Georgia Tech	(H)	95	72
Jan. 7	Loyola (Chicago)	(H)	81	62
Jan. 12	Louisiana State	(H)	51	46
Jan. 14	**Tulane**	**(A)**	**60**	**68**
Jan. 19	Tennessee	(A)	97	72
Jan. 26	Vanderbilt	(A)	91	83
Jan. 28	Georgia Tech	(A)	76	65
Jan. 30	Georgia	(H)	84	53
Feb. 2	Florida	(H)	88	61
Feb. 8	Mississippi	(N1)	75	69
Feb. 11	**Mississippi State**	**(A)**	**81**	**89**
Feb. 15	Loyola (Chicago)	(A)	115	65
Feb. 18	Vanderbilt	(H)	80	65
Feb. 23	Alabama	(H)	79	60
Feb. 25	Auburn	(H)	103	85
Mar. 2	Tennessee	(H)	93	75

SEC CHAMPIONS

NCAA TOURNAMENT

(Midwest Regional) Lexington, Ky.

Date	Team	Site	UK	Opp.
Mar. 15	Pittsburgh		98	92
Mar. 16	**Michigan State**		**68**	**80**

(N1) Memphis   2357 1953

Date	Team	Site	UK	Opp.

1957-58—Won 23, Lost 6.
COACH: Adolph Rupp
HONORARY CAPT.: Ed Beck

Date	Team	Site	UK	Opp.
Dec. 2	Duke	(H)	78	74
Dec. 4	Ohio State	(A)	61	54
Dec. 7	Temple	(H)	85	***83
Dec. 9	Maryland	(A)	62	71
Dec. 14	St. Louis	(H)	73	60
Dec. 16	Southern Methodist	(A)	64	65

UK INVITATIONAL TOURNAMENT

| Dec. 20 | West Virginia | | 70 | 77 |
| Dec. 21 | Minnesota | | 78 | 58 |

Dec. 23	Utah State	(H)	92	64
Dec. 30	Loyola (Chicago)	(H)	75	42
Jan. 4	Georgia Tech	(H)	76	60
Jan. 6	Vanderbilt	(A)	86	81
Jan. 11	Louisiana State	(H)	97	52
Jan. 13	Tulane	(H)	86	50
Jan. 18	Tennessee	(H)	77	68
Jan. 27	Georgia Tech	(A)	52	71
Jan. 29	Georgia	(N1)	74	55
Jan. 31	Florida	(A)	78	56
Feb. 8	Mississippi	(H)	96	65
Feb. 10	Mississippi State	(H)	72	62
Feb. 15	Loyola (Chicago)	(A)	56	57
Feb. 17	Vanderbilt	(H)	65	61
Feb. 22	Alabama	(N2)	45	*43
Feb. 24	Auburn	(N3)	63	64
Mar. 1	Tennessee	(A)	77	66

SEC CHAMPIONS

NCAA TOURNAMENT
(Mideast Regional) Lexington, Ky.

| Mar. 14 | Miami (Ohio) | | 94 | 70 |
| Mar. 15 | Notre Dame | | 89 | 56 |

(FINALS)
Louisville, Ky.

| Mar. 21 | Temple | | 61 | 60 |
| Mar. 22 | Seattle (championship) | | 84 | 72 |

2166 1817

NATIONAL COLLEGIATE CHAMPIONS
FOR RECORD FOURTH TIME
*** Three overtime periods.
* One overtime period.
(N1) Atlanta (N3) Birmingham
(N2) Montgomery

1958-59—Won 24, Lost 3.
COACH: Adolph Rupp
HONORARY CAPT.: Johnny Cox

Dec. 1	Florida State	(H)	91	68
Dec. 6	Temple	(A)	76	71
Dec. 8	Duke	(A)	78	64
Dec. 11	Southern Methodist	(H)	72	60
Dec. 13	St. Louis	(H)	76	57
Dec. 15	Maryland	(H)	58	*56

UK INVITATIONAL TOURNAMENT

| Dec. 19 | Ohio State | | 95 | 76 |
| Dec. 20 | W. Virginia (championship) | | 97 | 91 |

Dec. 29	Navy	(H)	82	69
Dec. 30	Illinois	(N1)	76	75
Jan. 3	Georgia Tech	(H)	72	62
Jan. 6	Vanderbilt	(A)	66	75
Jan. 10	Louisiana State	(A)	76	61
Jan. 12	Tulane	(A)	85	68
Jan. 17	Tennessee	(H)	79	58
Jan. 26	Georgia Tech	(A)	94	70
Jan. 29	Georgia	(H)	108	55
Jan. 31	Florida	(H)	94	51
Feb. 7	Mississippi	(N2)	97	72
Feb. 9	Mississippi State	(A)	58	66
Feb. 14	Notre Dame	(N3)	71	52
Feb. 18	Vanderbilt	(H)	83	71
Feb. 21	Auburn	(H)	75	56
Feb. 23	Alabama	(H)	39	32
Feb. 28	Tennessee	(A)	69	56

NCAA TOURNAMENT
(Kentucky represented the SEC in NCAA when
champion Miss. State declined the bid.)
(Mideast Regional) Evanston, Ill.

| Mar. 13 | Louisville | | 61 | 76 |
| Mar. 14 | Marquette | | 98 | 69 |

2126 1737

* Denotes overtime period.
(N1) Louisville (N3) Chicago, Ill.
(N2) Jackson, Miss.

1959-60—Won 18, Lost 7.
COACH: Adolph Rupp
CO-CAPTS.: Bill Lickert and Don Mills

Dec. 1	Colorado State	(H)	106	73
Dec. 4	UCLA	(A)	68	66
Dec. 5	So. California	(A)	73	87
Dec. 12	St. Louis	(A)	61	73
Dec. 14	Kansas	(A)	77	*72

UK INVITATIONAL TOURNAMENT

| Dec. 18 | North Carolina | | 76 | 70 |
| Dec. 19 | West Virginia | | 70 | 79 |

Dec. 20	Temple	(N1)	97	92
Dec. 28	Ohio State	(H)	96	93
Jan. 2	Georgia Tech	(H)	54	62
Jan. 5	Vanderbilt	(A)	76	59
Jan. 9	Louisiana State	(H)	77	45
Jan. 11	Tulane	(H)	68	42
Jan. 16	Tennessee	(A)	78	68
Jan. 25	Georgia Tech	(A)	44	65
Jan. 27	Georgia	(N2)	84	60
Jan. 29	Florida	(A)	75	62
Feb. 6	Mississippi	(H)	61	43
Feb. 8	Mississippi State	(H)	90	59
Feb. 13	Notre Dame	(H)	68	65
Feb. 16	Vanderbilt	(H)	68	60
Feb. 20	Auburn	(A)	60	61
Feb. 22	Alabama	(N3)	75	55
Feb. 27	Tennessee	(H)	63	65
Mar. 5	Pittsburgh	(H)	73	66

1838 1642

* Denotes overtime period.
(N1) Louisville (N3) Montgomery, Ala.
(N2) Columbus, Ga.

1960-61—Won 19, Lost 9.
COACH: Adolph Rupp
CAPTAIN: Dick Parsons

Dec. 1	Va. Military Inst.	(H)	72	56
Dec. 3	Florida State	(H)	58	63
Dec. 7	Notre Dame	(N1)	68	62
Dec. 13	North Carolina	(N2)	70	65
Dec. 17	Temple	(A)	58	66

UK INVITATIONAL TOURNAMENT

| Dec. 21 | Illinois | | 83 | 78 |
| Dec. 22 | St. Louis | | 72 | *74 |

Dec. 31	Missouri	(H)	81	69
Jan. 2	Miami (Ohio)	(H)	70	58
Jan. 7	Georgia Tech	(H)	89	79
Jan. 9	Vanderbilt	(A)	62	64
Jan. 13	Louisiana State	(A)	59	73
Jan. 14	Tulane	(A)	70	72
Jan. 21	Tennessee	(H)	83	54
Jan. 30	Georgia Tech	(A)	60	62
Feb. 4	Florida	(H)	89	68
Feb. 6	Georgia	(H)	74	67
Feb. 11	Mississippi	(N3)	74	60
Feb. 13	Mississippi State	(A)	68	62
Feb. 17	UCLA	(H)	77	76
Feb. 21	Vanderbilt	(H)	60	59
Feb. 25	Alabama	(H)	80	53
Feb. 27	Auburn	(H)	77	51
Mar. 4	Tennessee	(A)	68	61

SEC PLAYOFF (Knoxville, Tenn.)
(To determine SEC representative in NCAA
Tournament after champion Miss. State declined bid. Second place Kentucky and Vanderbilt each had 10-4 records.)

| Mar. 9 | Vanderbilt | | 88 | 67 |
| Mar. 11 | Marquette | (N4) | 72 | 88 |

NCAA TOURNAMENT
(Mideast Regional) Louisville, Ky.

| Mar. 17 | Morehead | | 71 | 64 |
| Mar. 18 | Ohio State | | 74 | 87 |

2027 1858

(N1) Louisville, Ky.
(N2) Greensboro, N. C.
(N3) Jackson, Miss.
(N4) Chicago, Ill.
* Denotes one overtime period.

1961-62—Won 23, Lost 3.
COACH: Adolph Rupp
CAPTAIN: Larry Pursiful

Dec. 2	Miami (Ohio)	(H)	93	61
Dec. 4	So. California	(H)	77	79
Dec. 11	St. Louis	(H)	86	77
Dec. 16	Baylor	(H)	94	60
Dec. 18	Temple	(H)	78	55

UK INVITATIONAL TOURNAMENT

Dec. 22	Tennessee		96	69
Dec. 23	Kansas St. (championship)		80	67
Dec. 27	Yale	(H)	79	58
Dec. 30	Notre Dame	(N1)	100	53
Jan. 2	Virginia	(H)	93	73
Jan. 6	Georgia Tech	(H)	89	70
Jan. 8	Vanderbilt	(A)	77	68
Jan. 12	Louisiana State	(H)	84	63
Jan. 15	Tennessee	(A)	95	82
Jan. 29	Georgia Tech	(A)	71	62
Jan. 31	Georgia	(N2)	86	59
Feb. 2	Florida	(A)	81	69
Feb. 10	Mississippi	(H)	83	60
Feb. 12	Mississippi State	(H)	44	49
Feb. 19	Vanderbilt	(H)	87	80
Feb. 24	Alabama	(A)	73	65
Feb. 26	Auburn	(A)	63	60
Mar. 5	Tulane	(H)	97	72

SEC CO-CHAMPIONS

NCAA TOURNAMENT
(Mideast Regional) Iowa City, Iowa

| Mar. 16 | Butler | | 81 | 60 |
| Mar. 17 | Ohio State | | 64 | 74 |

2141 1704

(N1) Freedom Hall, Louisville
(N2) Ga. Tech Coliseum, Atlanta

1962-63—Won 16, Lost 9.
COACH: Adolph Rupp
CAPTAIN: Scotty Baesler

Dec. 1	Virginia Tech	(H)	77	80
Dec. 8	Temple	(A)	56	52
Dec. 12	Florida State	(H)	83	54
Dec. 15	Northwestern	(H)	71	60
Dec. 17	North Carolina	(H)	66	68

UK INVITATIONAL TOURNAMENT

| Dec. 21 | Iowa | | 94 | 69 |
| Dec. 22 | West Va. (Championship) | | 79 | 75 |

Dec. 27	Dartmouth	(H)	95	49
Dec. 29	Notre Dame	(N1)	78	70
Dec. 31	St. Louis	(A)	63	87
Jan. 5	Georgia Tech	(H)	85	**86
Jan. 7	Vanderbilt	(A)	106	82
Jan. 11	Louisiana State	(A)	63	56
Jan. 12	Tulane	(A)	81	72
Jan. 19	Tennessee	(H)	69	*78
Jan. 26	Xavier	(H)	90	76
Jan. 28	Georgia Tech	(A)	62	66
Jan. 31	Georgia	(H)	74	67
Feb. 2	Florida	(H)	94	71
Feb. 9	Mississippi	(N2)	75	69
Feb. 11	Mississippi State	(A)	52	56
Feb. 18	Vanderbilt	(H)	67	69
Feb. 23	Auburn	(H)	78	59
Feb. 25	Alabama	(H)	80	63
Mar. 2	Tennessee	(A)	55	63

1893 1697

(N1) Louisville (N2) Jackson
* Denotes overtime periods

1963-64—Won 21, Lost 6.
COACH: Adolph Rupp
CO-CAPTS.: Cotton Nash and Ted Deeken

Nov. 30	Virginia	(H)	75	64
Dec. 2	Texas Tech	(H)	107	91
Dec. 7	Northwestern	(H)	95	63
Dec. 9	North Carolina	(H)	100	80
Dec. 14	Baylor	(H)	101	65

UK INVITATIONAL TOURNAMENT

| Dec. 20 | Wisconsin | | 108 | 85 |
| Dec. 21 | Wake Forest | | 98 | 75 |

(Championship)

| Dec. 28 | Notre Dame | (N1) | 101 | 81 |

SUGAR BOWL (New Orleans, La.)

| Dec. 30 | Loyola (La.) | | 86 | 64 |
| Dec. 31 | Duke (Championship) | | 81 | 79 |

Jan. 4	Georgia Tech	(A)	67	76
Jan. 6	Vanderbilt	(A)	83	85
Jan. 10	Louisiana State	(H)	103	84
Jan. 11	Tulane	(H)	105	63
Jan. 18	Tennessee	(H)	66	57
Jan. 25	Georgia Tech	(H)	79	62
Feb. 1	Florida	(A)	77	72
Feb. 3	Georgia	(A)	103	83
Feb. 8	Mississippi	(H)	102	59

Date	Team	Site	UK	Opp.
Feb. 10	Mississippi State	(H)	65	59
Feb. 17	Vanderbilt	(H)	104	73
Feb. 22	Auburn	(N2)	99	79
Feb. 24	**Alabama**	**(A)**	**59**	**65**
Feb. 29	Tennessee	(A)	42	38
Mar. 2	St. Louis	(H)	60	67

SEC CHAMPIONS

NCAA TOURNAMENT
(Mideast Regional)
Minneapolis, Minn.

Mar. 13	**Ohio University**		**69**	**85**
Mar. 14	**Loyola (Chicago)**		**91**	**100**

2326 1954

(N1) Louisville
(N2) Montgomery, Ala.

1964-65—Won 15, Lost 10.
COACH: Adolph Rupp
CAPTAIN: Randy Embry

Dec. 4	Iowa	(H)	85	77
Dec. 7	**North Carolina**	**(N1)**	**67**	**82**
Dec. 9	Iowa State	(H)	100	74
Dec. 12	Syracuse	(H)	110	77

UK INVITATIONAL TOURNAMENT

Dec. 18	West Virginia		102	78
Dec. 19	**Illinois**		86	91
Dec. 22	**St. Louis**	**(A)**	**75**	**80**
Dec. 29	**Notre Dame**	**(N2)**	**97**	**111**
Jan. 2	Dartmouth	(H)	107	67
Jan. 5	**Vanderbilt**	**(H)**	**79**	**97**
Jan. 9	Louisiana State	(A)	79	66
Jan. 11	Tulane	(A)	102	72
Jan. 16	**Tennessee**	**(A)**	**58**	**77**
Jan. 18	Auburn	(H)	73	67
Jan. 23	**Florida**	**(A)**	**68**	**84**
Jan. 25	Georgia	(A)	102	82
Jan. 30	Florida	(H)	78	61
Feb. 1	Georgia	(H)	96	64
Feb. 6	Mississippi	(H)	102	65
Feb. 8	Mississippi State	(H)	74	56
Feb. 16	**Vanderbilt**	**(A)**	**90**	**91**
Feb. 20	**Auburn**	**(A)**	**69**	**88**
Feb. 22	**Alabama**	**(A)**	**71**	**75**
Feb. 27	Tennessee	(H)	61	60
Mar. 1	Alabama	(H)	78	72

2109 1914

(N1) Charlotte, N. C.
(N2) Louisville, Ky.

1965-66—Won 32, Lost 2.
COACH: Adolph Rupp
HON. CAPT.: (None)

Oec. 1	Hardin-Simmons	(H)	83	55
Dec. 4	Virginia	(A)	99	73
Dec. 8	Illinois	(A)	86	68
Dec. 11	Northwestern	(H)	86	75

UK INVITATIONAL TOURNAMENT

Dec. 17	Air Force		78	58
Dec. 18	Indiana (Championship)		91	56
Dec. 22	Texas Tech	(A)	89	73
Dec. 29	Notre Dame	(N1)	103	69
Jan. 3	St. Louis	(H)	80	70
Jan. 8	Florida	(A)	78	64
Jan. 10	Ceorgia	(A)	69	**65
Jan. 15	Vanderbilt	(H)	96	83
Jan. 24	Louisiana State	(H)	111	85
Jan. 29	Auburn	(H)	115	78
Jan. 31	Alabama	(H)	82	62
Feb. 2	Vanderbilt	(A)	105	90
Feb. 5	Georgia	(H)	74	50
Feb. 7	Florida	(H)	85	75
Feb. 12	Auburn	(A)	77	64
Feb. 14	Alabama	(A)	90	67
Feb. 19	Mississippi State	(A)	73	69
Feb. 21	Mississippi	(A)	108	65
Feb. 26	Tennessee	(H)	78	64
Mar. 5	**Tennessee**	**(A)**	**62**	**69**
Mar. 7	Tulane	(H)	103	74

SEC Champions

NCAA TOURNAMENT
(Mideast Regional—Iowa City, Iowa)

Mar. 11	Dayton		86	79
Mar. 12	Michigan		84	77

(Finals—College Park, Md.)

Mar. 18	Duke		83	79
Mar. 19	**Texas Western**		**65**	**72**

2519 2028

INTERNATIONAL UNIVERSITIES TOURNAMENT
Tel Aviv, Israel

Aug. 3	Warsaw Univ.		67	58
Aug. 4	Cambridge Univ.		104	45
Aug. 6	Salonika Univ.		91	60
Aug. 10	Instanbul Univ.		82	36
Aug. 11	Warsaw Univ.		87	57

(Championship)

2950 2284

(N1) Louisville
** Double overtime

1966-67—Won 13, Lost 13.
COACH: Adolph Rupp
HON. CAPT.: (None)

Dec. 3	Virginia	(H)	104	84
Dec. 5	**Illinois**	**(H)**	**97**	***98**
Dec. 10	Northwestern	(A)	118	116
Dec. 13	**North Carolina**	**(H)**	**55**	**64**
Dec. 17	**Florida**	**(H)**	**75**	**78**

UK INVITATIONAL TOURNAMENT

Dec. 22	Oregon State		96	66
Dec. 23	Kansas St. (Championship)		83	79
Dec. 28	**Cornell**	**(H)**	**77**	**92**
Dec. 31	**Notre Dame**	**(N1)**	**96**	**85**
Jan. 5	**Vanderbilt**	**(H)**	**89**	***91**
Jan. 14	**Florida**	**(A)**	**72**	**89**
Jan. 16	**Georgia**	**(A)**	**40**	**49**
Jan. 21	Auburn	(H)	60	58
Jan. 23	**Tennessee**	**(H)**	**50**	****52**
Jan. 28	Louisiana State	(H)	102	72
Jan. 30	Mississippi	(H)	96	53
Feb. 4	Louisiana State	(A)	105	84
Feb. 6	Mississippi	(A)	79	70
Feb. 11	**Mississippi State**	**(H)**	**72**	***77**
Feb. 13	**Tennessee**	**(A)**	**57**	**76**
Feb. 18	Mississippi State	(A)	103	74
Feb. 20	Georgia	(H)	101	76
Feb. 25	**Alabama**	**(A)**	**71**	**81**
Feb. 27	**Auburn**	**(A)**	**49**	**60**
Mar. 4	**Vanderbilt**	**(A)**	**94**	**110**
Mar. 6	Alabama	(H)	110	78

2151 2012

(N1) Louisville
* Overtime   ** Double Overtime

1967-68—Won 22, Lost 5.
COACH: Adolph Rupp
CAPTAIN: Thad Jaracz

Dec. 2	Michigan	(A)	96	79
Dec. 4	Florida	(H)	99	76
Dec. 6	Xavier	(H)	111	76
Dec. 9	Pennsylvania	(H)	64	49
Dec. 12	**North Carolina**	**(N1)**	**77**	**84**

UK INVITATIONAL TOURNAMENT

Dec. 22	Dayton		88	85
Dec. 23	South Carolina		76	66

(Championship)

Dec. 30	Notre Dame	(N2)	81	73
Jan. 6	Vanderbilt	(A)	94	78
Jan. 8	Auburn	(A)	84	76
Jan. 13	**Florida**	**(A)**	**78**	**96**
Jan. 15	Georgia	(H)	104	73
Jan. 20	**Auburn**	**(A)**	**73**	**74**
Jan. 22	**Tennessee**	**(A)**	**59**	**87**
Jan. 27	Louisiana State	(A)	121	95
Jan. 29	Mississippi	(A)	85	76
Feb. 3	Louisiana State	(H)	109	96
Feb. 5	Mississippi	(H)	78	62
Feb. 10	Mississippi State	(A)	92	84
Feb. 12	Tennessee	(H)	60	59
Feb. 17	Mississippi State	(H)	107	81
Feb. 19	Georgia	(A)	106	87
Feb. 24	Alabama	(H)	96	83
Feb. 26	Auburn	(H)	89	57
Mar. 2	Vanderbilt	(H)	85	80

SEC Champions

NCAA TOURNAMENT
MIDEAST REGIONAL
Lexington, Ky.

Mar. 15	Marquette		107	89
Mar. 16	**Ohio State**		**81**	**82**

2400 2103

(N1) Greensboro, N.C.   (N2) Louisville

1968-69—Won 23, Lost 5.
COACH: Adolph Rupp
CAPTAIN: Phil Argento

Nov. 30	Xavier	(H)	115	77
Dec. 2	Miami	(H)	86	77
Dec. 7	**North Carolina**	**(H)**	**77**	**87**
Dec. 14	Pennsylvania	(A)	102	78

UK INVITATIONAL TOURNAMENT

Dec. 20	Michigan		112	104
Dec. 21	Army		80	65

(Championship)

Dec. 28	Notre Dame	(N1)	110	90
Dec. 31	**Wisconsin**	**(N2)**	**65**	**69**
Jan. 4	Mississippi	(A)	69	59
Jan. 6	Mississippi State	(A)	91	72
Jan. 11	Florida	(H)	88	67
Jan. 13	Georgia	(H)	88	68
Jan. 18	Tennessee	(H)	69	66
Jan. 25	Louisiana State	(H)	108	96
Jan. 27	Alabama	(A)	83	*70
Feb. 1	Vanderbilt	(H)	103	89
Feb. 3	Auburn	(H)	105	93
Feb. 8	Mississippi	(H)	104	68
Feb. 10	Mississippi State	(H)	91	69
Feb. 15	**Florida**	**(A)**	**81**	**82**
Feb. 17	Georgia	(A)	85	77
Feb. 22	Louisiana State	(H)	103	89
Feb. 26	Alabama	(H)	108	79
Mar. 1	**Vanderbilt**	**(A)**	**99**	**101**
Mar. 3	Auburn	(A)	90	86
Mar. 8	Tennessee	(H)	84	69

SEC Champions

NCAA TOURNAMENT
MIDEAST (Madison, Wisc.)

Mar. 13	**Marquette**	**(N)**	**74**	**81**
Mar. 15	Miami	(N)	72	71

2542 2199

(N1) Louisville; (N2) Chicago

1969-70—Won 26, Lost 2.
COACH: Adolph Rupp
CO-CAPTAINS: Dan Issel and Mike Pratt

Dec. 1	West Virginia	(H)	106	87
Dec. 6	Kansas	(H)	115	85
Dec. 8	North Carolina	(N1)	94	87
Dec. 13	Indiana	(H)	109	92

UK INVITATIONAL TOURNAMENT

Dec. 19	Navy		73	59
Dec. 20	Duke		98	76

(Championship)

Dec. 27	Notre Dame	(N2)	102	100
Dec. 29	Miami (Ohio)	(H)	80	58
Jan. 3	Mississippi	(H)	95	73
Jan. 5	Mississippi State	(H)	111	76
Jan. 10	Florida	(A)	88	69
Jan. 12	Georgia	(A)	72	71
Jan. 17	Tennessee	(H)	68	52
Jan. 24	Louisiana State	(H)	109	96
Jan. 26	Alabama	(H)	86	71
Jan. 31	**Vanderbilt**	**(A)**	**81**	**89**
Feb. 2	Auburn	(A)	84	83
Feb. 7	Mississippi	(A)	120	85
Feb. 9	Mississippi State	(A)	86	57
Feb. 14	Florida	(H)	110	66
Feb. 16	Georgia	(H)	116	86
Feb. 21	Louisiana State	(A)	121	105
Feb. 23	Alabama	(A)	98	89
Feb. 28	Vanderbilt	(H)	90	86
Mar. 2	Auburn	(H)	102	81
Mar. 7	Tennessee	(A)	86	69

SEC Champions

NCAA TOURNAMENT
MIDEAST (Columbus, Ohio)

Mar. 12	Notre Dame	(N3)	109	99
Mar. 14	**Jacksonville**	**(N3)**	**100**	**106**

2709 2253

(N1) Charlotte, N.C.; (N2) Louisville;
(N3) Columbus, Ohio

Date	Team	Site	UK	Opp.

1970-71—Won 22, Lost 6.

COACH: Adolph Rupp
HON. CO-CAPTAINS: Mike Casey and Larry Steele

Date	Team	Site	UK	Opp.
Dec. 1	Northwestern	(A)	115	100
Dec. 5	Michigan	(H)	104	93
Dec. 7	West Virginia	(A)	106	100
Dec. 12	Indiana	(A)	95	93
	UK INVITATIONAL TOURNAMENT			
Dec. 18	De Paul		106	85
Dec. 19	**Purdue**		**83**	**89**
	(Championship)			
Dec. 22	Oregon State	(H)	84	78
Dec. 29	**Notre Dame**	**(N1)**	**92**	**99**
Jan. 2	Mississippi	(A)	103	95
Jan. 4	Miss. State	(A)	79	71
Jan. 9	Florida	(H)	101	75
Jan. 11	Georgia	(H)	79	66
Jan. 16	**Tennessee**	**(A)**	**71**	**75**
Jan. 23	Louisiana State	(A)	82	79
Jan. 25	Alabama	(A)	86	73
Jan. 30	Vanderbilt	(H)	102	92
Feb. 1	Auburn	(H)	114	76
Feb. 6	Mississippi	(H)	121	86
Feb. 8	Miss. State	(H)	102	83
Feb. 13	**Florida**	**(A)**	**65**	**74**
Feb. 15	Georgia	(A)	107	95
Feb. 20	Louisiana State	(H)	110	73
Feb. 22	Alabama	(H)	101	74
Feb. 27	Vanderbilt	(A)	119	90
Mar. 1	Auburn	(A)	102	83
Mar. 6	Tennessee	(H)	84	78
	SEC Champions			
	NCAA TOURNAMENT			
	MIDEAST REGIONAL (Athens, Ga.)			
Mar. 18	**Western Ky.**	**(N2)**	**83**	**107**
Mar. 20	**Marquette**	**(N2)**	**74**	**91**
			2670	2373

(N1) Louisville; (N2) Athens, Ga.

1971-72—Won 21, Lost 7.

COACH: Adolph Rupp
HON. CO-CAPTAINS: Stan Key and Tom Parker

Date	Team	Site	UK	Opp.
Dec. 1	Northwestern	(H)	94	85
Dec. 4	Kansas	(A)	79	69
Dec. 6	Kansas State	(A)	71	64
Dec. 11	**Indiana**	**(N1)**	**89**	****90**
Dec. 13	**Michigan State**	**(H)**	**85**	**91**
	UK INVITATIONAL TOURNAMENT			
Dec. 17	Missouri		83	79
Dec. 18	Princeton		96	82
	(Championship)			
Dec. 28	Notre Dame	(N1)	83	67
Jan. 8	Mississippi	(H)	93	82
Jan. 10	Mississippi State	(H)	104	76
Jan. 15	**Florida**	**(A)**	**70**	**72**
Jan. 17	**Georgia**	**(A)**	**73**	**85**
Jan. 22	Tennessee	(H)	72	70
Jan. 24	Vanderbilt	(H)	106	80
Jan. 29	Louisiana State	(H)	89	71
Jan. 31	Alabama	(H)	77	74
Feb. 5	Vanderbilt	(A)	85	*80
Feb. 7	Auburn	(A)	78	72
Feb. 12	Mississippi	(A)	90	82
Feb. 14	Mississippi State	(A)	63	55
Feb. 19	Florida	(H)	95	68
Feb. 21	Georgia	(H)	87	63
Feb. 26	**Louisiana State**	**(A)**	**71**	**88**
Feb. 28	**Alabama**	**(A)**	**70**	**73**
Mar. 6	Auburn	(H)	102	67
Mar. 9	Tennessee	(A)	67	66
	SEC Co-Champions (Earned NCAA bid by beating Tennessee twice)			
	NCAA TOURNAMENT			
	MIDEAST REGIONAL (Dayton, Ohio)			
Mar. 16	Marquette	(N2)	85	69
Mar. 18	**Florida State**	**(N2)**	**54**	**73**
			2311	2093

(N1) Louisville; (N2) Dayton, Ohio

JOE HALL ERA

1972-73—Won 20, Lost 8.

COACH: Joe B. Hall
HON. CAPTAIN: Jim Andrews

Date	Team	Site	UK	Opp.
Nov. 29	Chilean NAT (Exh)†	(H)	125	62
Dec. 2	Michigan State	(A)	75	66
Dec. 4	**Iowa**	**(H)**	**66**	**79**
Dec. 9	**Indiana**	**(A)**	**58**	**64**
Dec. 11	**North Carolina**	**(N1)**	**70**	**78**
	UK INVITATIONAL TOURNAMENT			
Dec. 15	Nebraska		85	60
Dec. 16	Oregon		95	68
	(Championship)			
Dec. 23	Kansas	(H)	77	71
Dec. 30	Notre Dame	(N1)	65	63
Jan. 6	**Mississippi**	**(A)**	**58**	**61**
Jan. 8	Mississippi State	(A)	90	81
Jan. 13	Florida	(H)	95	65
Jan. 15	Georgia	(H)	89	68
Jan. 20	**Tennessee**	**(A)**	**64**	**65**
Jan. 22	**Vanderbilt**	**(A)**	**75**	**76**
Jan. 27	Louisiana State	(A)	86	71
Jan. 29	Alabama	(A)	95	93
Feb. 3	**Vanderbilt**	**(H)**	**76**	**83**
Feb. 5	Auburn	(H)	88	57
Feb. 10	Mississippi	(H)	88	70
Feb. 12	Mississippi State	(H)	100	*87
Feb. 17	Florida	(A)	94	83
Feb. 19	Georgia	(A)	99	86
Feb. 24	Louisiana State	(H)	94	76
Feb. 26	Alabama	(H)	111	95
Mar. 3	Auburn	(A)	91	79
Mar. 8	Tennessee	(H)	86	81
	SEC Champions			
	NCAA TOURNAMENT			
	MIDEAST REGIONAL (Nashville, Tenn.)			
	Austin Peay	(N2)	106	*100
	Indiana	**(N2)**	**65**	**72**
			2341	2098

(N1) Louisville; (N2) Nashville, Tenn.)
† Not counted in win or pts. total.

1973-74—Won 13, Lost 13

COACH: Joe B. Hall
CAPTAIN: Ronnie Lyons

Date	Team	Site	UK	Opp.
Dec. 1	Miami (O.)	(H)	81	68
Dec. 3	**Kansas**	**(A)**	**63**	**71**
Dec. 8	**Indiana**	**(N1)**	**68**	**77**
Dec. 10	**North Carolina**	**(N2)**	**84**	**101**
Dec. 14	Iowa	(A)	88	80
	UK INVITATIONAL TOURNAMENT			
Dec. 21	Dartmouth		102	77
Dec. 22	Stanford		78	77
	(Championship)			
Dec. 29	**Notre Dame**	**(N1)**	**79**	**94**
Jan. 5	**Louisiana State**	**(A)**	**84**	**95**
Jan. 7	Georgia	(H)	80	74
Jan. 12	Auburn	(H)	79	58
Jan. 14	**Tennessee**	**(A)**	**54**	**67**
Jan. 19	Mississippi	(H)	93	64
Jan. 21	**Alabama**	**(A)**	**77**	**81**
Jan. 26	Florida	(A)	91	82
Jan. 28	**Vanderbilt**	**(H)**	**65**	**82**
Feb. 2	Mississippi State	(A)	82	70
Feb. 4	Louisiana State	(H)	73	70
Feb. 9	Georgia	(A)	86	72
Feb. 11	**Auburn**	**(A)**	**97**	***99**
Feb. 16	Tennessee	(H)	61	58
Feb. 18	**Mississippi**	**(A)**	**60**	**61**
Feb. 23	**Alabama**	**(H)**	**71**	**94**
Feb. 25	**Florida**	**(H)**	**65**	**75**
Mar. 2	**Vanderbilt**	**(A)**	**69**	**71**
Mar. 4	Mississippi State	(H)	108	69

(N1) Louisville; (N2) Greensboro, N.C.

1974 AUSTRALIAN EXHIBITION TOUR
(Not Counted in Won-Lost Record)

Date	Team	UK	Opp.
May 13	Tahitian National Team	116	62
May 17	**Australia**	**87**	**97**
May 18	Newcastle	90	78
May 19	N.S.W. All Stars	123	67
May 21	Illawarra Hawks	115	57
May 22	N.S.W. All Stars	106	50
May 23	A.C.T.	96	69
May 25	Bulleen Heidelberg	88	83
May 26	St. Kilda Business House	80	67
May 27	Nunawading	99	82
May 28	**Melbourne**	**79**	**86**
May 30	Gippsland All Stars	127	74
May 31	Bulleen Heidelberg	72	71
June 1	Laker All Stars	111	83
June 3	So. Australian All Stars	109	96
June 4	So. Australian All Stars	110	81
June 5	So. Australian All Stars	111	84
June 6	Coburg	108	82
June 7	St. Kilda Business House	96	85
		1923	1454

1974-75—Won 26, Lost 5

COACH: Joe B. Hall
CAPTAIN: Jimmy Dan Conner

Date	Team	Site	UK	Opp.
Nov. 25	Ath. in Action†	(H)	103	65
Nov. 30	Northwestern	(H)	97	70
Dec. 2	Miami (O.)	(A)	80	73
Dec. 7	**Indiana**	**(A)**	**74**	**98**
Dec. 9	North Carolina	(N1)	90	78
	UK INVITATIONAL TOURNAMENT			
Dec. 20	Washington State		97	75
Dec. 21	Oklahoma State		90	65
	(Championship)			
Dec. 23	Kansas	(N1)	100	63
Dec. 28	Notre Dame	(N1)	113	96
Jan. 4	L. S. U.	(H)	115	80
Jan. 6	Georgia	(A)	96	77
Jan. 11	**Auburn**	**(A)**	**85**	**90**
Jan. 13	Tennessee	(H)	88	82
Jan. 18	Mississippi	(A)	85	82
Jan. 20	Alabama	(H)	74	69
Jan. 25	Florida	(H)	87	65
Jan. 27	Vanderbilt	(A)	91	90
Feb. 1	Mississippi State	(H)	112	79
Feb. 3	L. S. U.	(A)	77	76
Feb. 8	Georgia	(H)	75	61
Feb. 10	Auburn	(H)	119	76
Feb. 15	**Tennessee**	**(A)**	**98**	**103**
Feb. 17	Mississippi	(H)	108	89
Feb. 22	Alabama	(A)	84	79
Feb. 24	**Florida**	**(A)**	**58**	**66**
Mar. 1	Vanderbilt	(H)	109	84
Mar. 8	Mississippi State	(A)	118	80
	SEC Co-Champions			
	NCAA TOURNAMENT			
	Mideast Regional			
	(Tuscaloosa, Ala., and Dayton, O.)			
Mar. 15	Marquette	(N2)	76	54
Mar. 20	Central Michigan	(N3)	90	73
Mar. 22	Indiana	(N3)	92	90
	Finals (San Diego, CA.)			
Mar. 29	Syracuse	(N4)	95	79
Mar. 31	**UCLA**	**(N4)**	**85**	**92**
			2858	2434

† Exhibition—Not counted in won-lost record. (N1) Louisville; (N2) Tuscaloosa, Ala.; (N3) Dayton, O.; (N4) San Diego, CA.

1975-76—Won 20, Lost 10

COACH: Joe B. Hall
CAPTAIN: Jack Givens

Date	Team	Site	UK	Opp.
Nov. 22	Yugoslavia (EXH.)†	(H)	75	74
Dec. 1	**Northwestern**	**(A)**	**77**	**89**
Dec. 8	**North Carolina**	**(N1)**	**77**	**90**
Dec. 10	Miami	(H)	91	69
Dec. 13	Kansas	(A)	54	48
Dec. 15	**Indiana**	**(N2)**	**68**	***77**
	UK INVITATIONAL TOURNAMENT			
Dec. 19	Georgia Tech		66	64
Dec. 20	Oregon State		82	74
	(Championship)			
Dec. 30	Notre Dame	(N2)	79	77
Jan. 3	**Mississippi State**	**(A)**	**73**	**77**
Jan. 5	**Alabama**	**(A)**	**63**	**76**
Jan. 10	**Tennessee**	**(H)**	**88**	***90**
Jan. 12	Georgia	(H)	92	76
Jan. 17	Vanderbilt	(H)	77	76
Jan. 24	Florida	(A)	89	82
Jan. 26	**Auburn**	**(A)**	**84**	***91**
Jan. 31	Mississippi	(H)	89	81
Feb. 2	Louisiana State	(H)	85	71
Feb. 7	**Tennessee**	**(A)**	**85**	**92**
Feb. 9	**Georgia**	**(A)**	**81**	**86**
Feb. 14	**Vanderbilt**	**(A)**	**65**	**69**
Feb. 21	Florida	(H)	96	89
Feb. 23	Auburn	(H)	93	82
Feb. 28	Mississippi	(A)	94	87
Mar. 1	Louisiana State	(A)	85	70
Mar. 6	Alabama	(H)	90	85
Mar. 8	Mississippi State	(H)	94	*93
	NATIONAL INVITATION TOURNAMENT			
	New York, N.Y.			
Mar. 13	Niagra		67	61
Mar. 16	Kansas State		81	78
Mar. 18	Providence		79	78
Mar. 21	U.N.C. Charlotte		71	67
	(Championship)			
			2415	2345

† Exhibition—Not counted in won-lost record. (N1) Charlotte, N.C.; (N2) Louisville.

1976-77—Won 26, Lost 4

COACH: Joe B. Hall
CAPTAINS: Larry Johnson and Merion Haskins

Date	Team	Site	UK	Opp.
Nov. 22	Marat'n Oil (EXH)†	(N1)	110	93
Nov. 27	Wisconsin	(H)	72	64
Dec. 2	Texas Christian	(H)	103	53
Dec. 6	Indiana	(A)	66	51
Dec. 11	Kansas	(H)	90	63
Dec. 13	South Carolina	(A)	98	67
	UK INVITATIONAL TOURNAMENT			
Dec. 17	Bowling Green		77	59
Dec. 18	**Utah**		**68**	**70**
	(Championship)			

Date	Team	Site	UK	Opp.
Dec. 30	Notre Dame	(N2)	102	78
Jan. 3	Georgia	(H)	64	*59
Jan. 8	Vanderbilt	(A)	64	62
Jan. 12	**Tennessee**	**(H)**	**67**	***71**
Jan. 15	Auburn	(A)	75	68
Jan. 17	Florida	(A)	73	71
Jan. 22	Louisiana State	(H)	87	72
Jan. 24	Mississippi	(H)	100	73
Jan. 29	Alabama	(A)	87	85
Jan. 31	Mississippi State	(A)	92	85
Feb. 5	Vanderbilt	(H)	113	73
Feb. 7	Florida State	(N2)	97	57
Feb. 12	Auburn	(H)	89	82
Feb. 14	Florida	(H)	104	78
Feb. 19	Louisiana State	(A)	90	76
Feb. 21	Mississippi	(A)	81	69
Feb. 26	Alabama	(H)	85	70
Feb. 28	Mississippi State	(H)	77	64
Mar. 5	**Tennessee**	**(A)**	**79**	**81**
Mar. 7	Georgia	(A)	72	54

SEC Co-Champions
NCAA TOURNAMENT
East Regional
(Philadelphia, Pa., and College Park, Md.)

Mar. 12	Princeton	(N3)	72	58
Mar. 17	VMI	(N4)	93	78
Mar. 19	**North Carolina**	**(N4)**	**72**	**79**

2509 2070

† Exhibition—Not counted in won-lost record.
(N1) Memorial Coliseum; (N2) Louisville, Ky.; (N3) Philadelphia, Pa.; (N4) College Park, Md.

1977-78—Won 30, Lost 2

COACH: Joe B. Hall
CAPTAINS: Jack Givens and Rick Robey

Nov. 11	Russia (EXH)‡	(N1)	109	75
Nov. 26	S. Methodist	(H)	110	86
Dec. 5	Indiana	(H)	78	64
Dec. 10	Kansas	(A)	73	66
Dec. 12	South Carolina	(H)	84	65

UK INVITATIONAL TOURNAMENT

Dec. 16	Portland State		114	88
Dec. 17	St. John's		102	72
Dec. 23	Iona	(H)	104	65
Dec. 31	Notre Dame	(N2)	73	68
Jan. 2	Vanderbilt	(H)	72	59
Jan. 7	Florida	(A)	86	67
Jan. 9	Auburn	(A)	101	77
Jan. 14	Louisiana State	(H)	96	76
Jan. 16	Mississippi	(H)	76	56
Jan. 21	Mississippi State	(A)	75	65
Jan. 23	**Alabama**	**(A)**	**62**	**78**
Jan. 30	Georgia	(H)	90	73
Feb. 4	Florida	(H)	88	61
Feb. 6	Auburn	(H)	104	81
Feb. 11	**Louisiana State**	**(A)**	**94**	***95**
Feb. 13	Mississippi	(A)	64	52
Feb. 15	Tennessee	(H)	90	77
Feb. 18	Mississippi State	(H)	58	56
Feb. 20	Alabama	(H)	97	84
Feb. 25	Tennessee	(A)	68	57
Feb. 27	Georgia	(A)	78	67
Mar. 4	Nevada Las Vegas	(H)	92	70
Mar. 6	Vanderbilt	(A)	78	68

SEC CHAMPIONS
NCAA TOURNAMENT
Mideast Regional
(Knoxville, Tenn., and Dayton, Ohio)

Mar. 11	Florida State	(N3)	85	76
Mar. 16	Miami (Ohio)	(N4)	91	69
Mar. 18	Michigan State	(N4)	52	49

FINALS (ST. LOUIS, MO.)

Mar. 25	Arkansas	(N5)	64	59
Mar. 27	Duke	(N5)	94	88

2693 2234

National Collegiate Champions for Fifth Time
‡ Exhibition—Not counted in won-lost record.
(N1) Memorial Coliseum; (N2) Louisville, Ky.; (N3) Knoxville, Tenn.; (N4) Dayton, Ohio, and (N5) St. Louis, Mo.

1978 JAPAN EXHIBITION TOUR
(All Games vs. Japan National Team—Not Counted in Won-Lost Record)

June 13	At Tokyo		104	71
June 15	At Niigata		102	89
June 18	At Nagoya		97	59
June 19	At Osaka		87	82
June 20	At Fukuoka		88	61
June 22	At Nagasaki		122	79
June 24	At Tokyo		105	57

705 498

1978-79—Won 19, Lost 12

COACH: Joe B. Hall
CAPTAINS: Dwane Casey and Truman Claytor

Nov. 26	Poland (EXH)‡	(H)	80	68
Dec. 2	LaSalle	(H)	109	77
Dec. 4	West Texas	(H)	121	67
Dec. 9	Kansas	(A)	67	*66
Dec. 16	**Indiana**	**(A)**	**67**	***68**

UK INVITATIONAL TOURNAMENT

Dec. 22	**Texas A&M**		**69**	**73**
Dec. 23	Syracuse		94	87
Dec. 30	Notre Dame	(N1)	81	76
Jan. 3	**Florida**	**(A)**	**65**	**76**
Jan. 6	**Louisiana State**	**(H)**	**89**	**93**
Jan. 8	Mississippi	(H)	90	64
Jan. 13	**Alabama**	**(A)**	**52**	**55**
Jan. 15	**Mississippi State**	**(A)**	**61**	**63**
Jan. 20	**Tennessee**	**(H)**	**55**	**66**
Jan. 22	Georgia	(H)	73	64
Jan. 25	Auburn	(A)	85	*83
Jan. 27	Florida	(H)	87	81
Jan. 29	Auburn	(H)	66	59
Feb. 3	**Louisiana State**	**(A)**	**61**	**70**
Feb. 5	Mississippi	(A)	87	82
Feb. 7	**Vanderbilt**	**(A)**	**58**	**68**
Feb. 10	Alabama	(H)	80	71
Feb. 12	Mississippi State	(H)	80	65
Feb. 17	**Tennessee**	**(A)**	**84**	**101**
Feb. 19	Georgia	(A)	90	74
Feb. 23	Vanderbilt	(H)	96	70
Feb. 25	South Carolina	(H)	79	74

SEC TOURNAMENT (Birmingham, AL)

Feb. 28	Mississippi		82	77
Mar. 1	Alabama		101	100
Mar. 2	Louisiana State		80	67
Mar. 3	**Tennessee**		**69**	***75**

NATIONAL INVITATION TOURNAMENT
Lexington, Ky.

Mar. 7	**Clemson**		**67**	***68**

2446 2280

‡ Exhibition—Not counted in won-lost record.
(N1) Louisville, Ky.

1979-80—Won 29, Lost 6

COACH: Joe B. Hall
CAPTAIN: Kyle Macy

Nov. 17	**Duke**	**(N1)**	**76**	***82**
Nov. 30	Bradley	(N2)	79	58
Dec. 1	Alaska	(N2)	97	68
Dec. 2	Iona	(N2)	57	50
Dec. 8	Baylor	(H)	80	46
Dec. 10	South Carolina	(H)	126	81
Dec. 12	Kansas	(A)	57	56
Dec. 15	Indiana	(H)	69	58
Dec. 17	Georgia	(N3)	95	69

UK INVITATIONAL TOURNAMENT

Dec. 21	California		78	52
Dec. 22	Purdue		61	60
Dec. 29	Notre Dame	(N4)	86	80
Jan. 2	Auburn	(H)	67	65
Jan. 5	**Tennessee**	**(A)**	**47**	**49**
Jan. 9	Mississippi	(A)	79	73
Jan. 12	**Alabama**	**(H)**	**64**	**78**
Jan. 17	Florida	(A)	76	63
Jan. 19	Vanderbilt	(H)	106	90
Jan. 23	Mississippi State	(A)	89	67
Jan. 26	Georgia	(H)	56	49
Jan. 28	**Louisiana State**	**(H)**	**60**	**65**
Jan. 30	Auburn	(A)	64	62
Feb. 2	Tennessee	(H)	83	75
Feb. 6	Mississippi	(H)	86	72
Feb. 9	Alabama	(A)	72	63
Feb. 13	Florida	(H)	95	70
Feb. 15	Vanderbilt	(A)	91	73
Feb. 17	Nevada Las Vegas	(A)	74	69
Feb. 20	Mississippi State	(H)	71	65
Feb. 24	Louisiana State	(A)	76	*74

SEC CHAMPIONS
SEC TOURNAMENT (Birmingham, AL)

Feb. 28	Auburn		69	61
Feb. 29	Mississippi		69	67
Mar. 1	**Louisiana State**		**78**	**80**

NCAA TOURNAMENT
Mideast Regional
(Bowling Green, Ky., and Lexington, Ky.)

Mar. 8	Florida State	(N5)	97	78
Mar. 13	**Duke**	**(H)**	**54**	**55**

2684 2323

* Denotes overtime period.
(N1) Springfield, Mass.; (N2) Anchorage, Alas.; (N3) Atlanta, Ga.; (N4) Louisville, Ky.; (N5) Bowling Green, Ky.

1980-81—Won 22, Lost 6.

COACH: Joe B. Hall
CAPTAIN: Chuck Verderber

Nov. 29	East Tennessee	(H)	62	57
Dec. 3	Ohio State	(H)	70	64
Dec. 6	Indiana	(A)	68	66
Dec. 13	Kansas	(H)	87	73

UK INVITATIONAL TOURNAMENT

Dec. 19	Alaska		91	56
Dec. 20	Alabama-Birmingham		61	53
Dec. 27	**Notre Dame**	**(N1)**	**61**	**67**
Dec. 30	Maine	(H)	100	54
Jan. 3	Georgia	(H)	76	62
	Auburn	(A)	79	66
Jan. 10	Tennessee	(H)	48	47
Jan. 14	Mississippi	(H)	64	55
Jan. 17	**Alabama**	**(A)**	**55**	**59**
Jan. 19	**Louisiana State**	**(A)**	**67**	**81**
Jan. 21	Florida	(H)	102	48
Jan. 24	Vanderbilt	(A)	78	64
Jan. 28	Mississippi State	(H)	71	64
Jan. 31	Georgia	(A)	71	68
Feb. 4	Auburn	(H)	102	74
Feb. 7	**Tennessee**	**(A)**	**71**	**87**
Feb. 11	Mississippi	(A)	62	55
Feb. 14	Alabama	(H)	77	62
Feb. 18	Florida	(A)	69	56
Feb. 21	Vanderbilt	(H)	80	48
Feb. 25	Mississippi State	(A)	78	74
Mar. 1	Louisiana State	(H)	73	71

SEC TOURNAMENT (Birmingham, AL)

Mar. 5	**Vanderbilt**		**55**	**60**

NCAA TOURNAMENT
Mideast Regional (Tuscaloosa, AL)

Mar. 15	**Alabama-Birmingham**		**62**	**69**

1961 1694

(N1) Louisville, KY

1981-82—Won 22, Lost 8

COACH: Joe B. Hall
CAPTAIN: Chuck Verderber

Nov. 28	Akron	(H)	83	64
Dec. 5	Ohio State	(A)	78	62
Dec. 8	Indiana	(H)	85	69
Dec. 12	Kansas	(A)	77	*74

UK INVITATIONAL TOURNAMENT

Dec. 18	Jacksonville	(H)	107	91
Dec. 19	Seton Hall	(H)	98	74
Dec. 26	**North Carolina**	**(N1)**	**69**	**82**
Dec. 29	Notre Dame	(N2)	34	28
Jan. 2	Georgia	(A)	68	66
Jan. 6	Auburn	(H)	83	71
Jan. 9	**Tennessee**	**(A)**	**66**	**70**
Jan. 13	**Mississippi**	**(A)**	**65**	**67**
Jan. 16	Alabama	(H)	86	69
Jan. 20	Florida	(A)	91	76
Jan. 23	Vanderbilt	(H)	67	58
Jan. 25	Louisiana State	(H)	76	65
Jan. 27	**Mississippi State**	**(A)**	**51**	**56**
Jan. 30	Georgia	(H)	82	73
Feb. 3	**Auburn**	**(A)**	**81**	***83**
Feb. 6	Tennessee	(H)	77	67
Feb. 10	Mississippi	(H)	56	49
Feb. 13	Alabama	(A)	72	62
Feb. 17	Florida	(H)	84	78
Feb. 20	Vanderbilt	(A)	73	69
Feb. 24	Mississippi State	(H)	71	54
Feb. 27	Louisiana State	(A)	78	94

SEC TOURNAMENT (Lexington)

Mar. 4	Auburn		89	66
Mar. 5	Mississippi		62	58
Mar. 6	**Alabama**		**46**	**48**

NCAA TOURNAMENT
Mideast Regional (Nashville)

Mar. 4	**Middle Tennessee (N3)**		**44**	**50**

2199 1993

*Denotes overtime period.
(N1) East Rutherford, N.J.; (N2) Louisville, Ky.; (N3) Nashville, Tenn.

Date	Team	Site	UK	Opp.

1982-83—Won 23, Lost 8
COACH: Joe B. Hall
CAPTAIN: Charles Hurt

Date	Team	Site	UK	Opp.
Nov. 27	Butler	(H)	90	53
Dec. 1	Notre Dame	(A)	58	45
Dec. 4	Vilanova	(H)	93	79
Dec. 7	Detroit	(H)	83	46
Dec. 11	Illinois	(H)	76	57

UK INVITATIONAL TOURNAMENT

Date	Team	Site	UK	Opp.
Dec. 17	Dusquesne		55	42
Dec. 18	Tulane		80	61
Dec. 22	**Indiana**	**(A)**	**59**	**62**
Dec. 29	Kansas	(N1)	83	62
Jan. 3	Mississippi	(H)	72	60
Jan. 5	Louisiana State	(H)	52	50
Jan. 8	**Alabama**	**(A)**	**67**	**74**
Jan. 10	Mississippi State	(A)	59	53
Jan. 15	**Auburn**	**(H)**	**67**	**75**
Jan. 17	Florida	(H)	70	63
Jan. 22	Vanderbilt	(A)	82	77
Jan. 29	**Georgia**	**(A)**	**63**	**70**
Jan. 31	**Tennessee**	**(A)**	**63**	**65**
Feb. 5	Alabama	(H)	76	70
Feb. 8	Mississippi State	(H)	88	67
Feb. 12	Auburn	(A)	71	69
Feb. 14	Florida	(A)	73	61
Feb. 19	Vanderbilt	(H)	82	63
Feb. 26	Georgia	(H)	81	72
Feb. 27	Tennessee	(H)	69	61
Mar. 3	Mississippi	(A)	61	58
Mar. 5	**Louisiana State**	**(A)**	**60**	**74**

SEC TOURNAMENT (Birmingham)

Date	Team	Site	UK	Opp.
Mar. 11	**Alabama**		**64**	**69**

NCAA TOURNAMENT (Tampa and Knoxville)

Date	Team	Site	UK	Opp.
Mar. 19	Ohio	(N2)	57	40
Mar. 24	Indiana	(N3)	64	59
Mar. 26	**Louisville**	**(N3)**	**68**	**80**
			2186	1937

(N1) Louisville; (N2) Tampa; (N3) Knoxville

1983-84—Won 29, Lost 5
COACH: Joe B. Hall
CAPTAIN: Game Captains

Date	Team	Site	UK	Opp.
Nov. 22	Netherlands†	(H)	73	55
Nov. 26	Louisville	(H)	65	44
Dec. 3	Indiana	(H)	59	54
Dec. 10	Kansas	(A)	72	50

UK INVITATIONAL TOURNAMENT

Date	Team	Site	UK	Opp.
Dec. 16	Wyoming	(H)	66	40
Dec. 17	Brigham Young	(H)	93	59
Dec. 20	Cincinnati	(A)	24	11
Dec. 24	Illinois	(A)	56	54
Dec. 28	Purdue	(N1)	86	67
Jan. 2	Mississippi	(A)	68	55
Jan. 7	Louisiana State	(A)	96	80
Jan. 9	Alabama	(H)	68	55
Jan. 11	Mississippi State	(H)	51	42
Jan. 13	**Auburn**	**(A)**	**63**	**82**
Jan. 17	**Florida**	**(A)**	**57**	**69**
Jan. 20	Vanderbilt	(H)	67	46
Jan. 22	Houston	(H)	74	67
Jan. 28	Georgia	(H)	64	40
Jan. 30	Tennessee	(H)	93	74
Feb. 4	**Alabama**	**(A)**	**62**	**69**
Feb. 6	Mississippi State	(A)	77	58
Feb. 11	Auburn	(H)	84	64
Feb. 13	Florida	(H)	67	65
Feb. 19	Vanderbilt	(A)	58	54
Feb. 25	Georgia	(A)	66	64
Feb. 27	**Tennessee**	**(A)**	**58**	**63**
Mar. 1	Mississippi	(H)	76	57
Mar. 3	Louisiana State	(H)	90	68

SEC CHAMPIONS
SEC TOURNAMENT (Nashville)

Date	Team	Site	UK	Opp.
Mar. 8	Georgia		92	79
Mar. 9	Alabama		48	46
Mar. 10	Auburn		51	49

SEC CHAMPIONS
NCAA TOURNAMENT
Mideast Regional (Birmingham and Lexington)

Date	Team	Site	UK	Opp.
Mar. 17	Brigham Young in Birmingham	(N2)	93	68
Mar. 22	Louisville in Lexington	(N3)	72	67
Mar. 24	Illinois in Lexington	(N3)	54	51

FINALS (Seattle)

Date	Team	Site	UK	Opp.
Mar. 31	**Georgetown**		**40**	**53**
			2383	2019

†Exhibition—Not counted in won-lost record.
(N1) Louisville; (N2) Birmingham; (N3) Lexington

Bibliographic Note

The primary sources available for the study of sports in the twentieth century are rich, varied, and abundant. They include manuscript materials, published sources, and oral history. Oral interviews proved to be a particularly valuable source in the preparation of this study. With the help of the University of Kentucky Alumni Association I was able to locate and interview sixty-two current or former players, some living as far away as Florida, California, or the state of Washington. They included at least one member of every Wildcat team from 1920 to the present, with the exception of the 1923 squad. In many cases I talked with more than one team member. For example, I interviewed all five starters on the 1948 team, the "Fabulous Five."

The athletes interviewed and the years they played on the Wildcat varsity were:

John Adams	1962/63-1964/65
Marvin Akers	1940/41-1942/43
Jim Andrews	1970/71-1972/73
Scotty Baesler	1960/61-1962/63
Cliff Barker	1946/47-1948/49
Dicky Beal	1980/81-1983/84
Ralph Beard	1945/46-1948/49
Cecil Bell	1928/29-1930/31
Winston Bennett	1983/84
Gerry Calvert	1954/55-1956/57
Ralph Carlisle	1934/35-1936/37
Dwane Casey	1975/76-1978/79
Truman Claytor	1975/76-1978/79
Ray Edelman	1971/72-1973/74
Elmer (Baldy) Gilb	1926/27-1928/29
Jack Givens	1974/75-1977/78
Phil Grawemeyer	1953/54-1955/56
Alex Groza	1944/45, 1946/47-1948/49
Bob Guyette	1972/73-1974/75
Cliff Hagan	1950/51-1951/52, 1953/54
Joe Hall	1948/49
Basil Hayden	1919/20-1921/22
Derrick Hord	1979/80-1982/83

Lee Huber	1938/39-1940/41
Charles Hurt	1979/80-1982/83
Dan Issel	1967/68-1969/70
Ned Jennings	1958/59-1960/61
Phil Johnson	1955/56-1958/59
Wallace Jones	1945/46-1948/49
William Kleiser	1929/30-1931/32
Ed Lander	1940/41-1942/43
Bo Lanter	1979/80-1981/82
Dave Lawrence	1932/33-1934/35
James Lee	1974/75-1977/78
Jim LeMaster	1965/66-1967/68
Bill Lickert	1958/59-1960/61
Steve Lockmueller	1972/73-1973/74
Paul McBrayer	1927/28-1929/30
James McFarland	1923/24-1925/26
Lawrence McGinnis	1927/28-1929/30
Louis McGinnis	1928/29-1930/31
Kyle Macy	1977/78-1979/80
Don Mills	1957/58-1959/60
Dirk Minniefield	1979/80-1982/83
Terry Mobley	1962/63-1964/65
Cotton Nash	1961/62-1963/64
Bernie Opper	1936/37-1938/39
J. Ed (Buddy) Parker	1944/45-1946/47
Tom Parker	1969/70-1971/72
Dick Parsons	1958/59-1960/61
Linville Puckett	1953/54-1954/55
Sam Ridgeway	1919/20-1920/21
Ken Rollins	1942/43, 1946/47-1947/48
Forest (Aggie) Sale	1930/31-1932/33
James Sharpe	1925/26-1926/27
Carey Spicer	1928/29-1930/31
Bill Spivey	1949/50-1950/51
Guy Strong	1949/50
Lou Tsioropoulos	1950/51-1951/52, 1953/54
Lovell Underwood	1923/24-1925/26
Bob Watson	1949/50-1951/52
LaVon Williams	1976/77-1979/80

In addition to players I also interviewed UK Athletics Board members, athletics directors, coaches, and others connected with the basketball program as well as sportswriters, television sportscasters, and fans. Among the more than fifty interviewees were Mark Bradley, A.B. (Happy) Chandler, Thomas D. Clark, Joe Dean, Pat Etcheberry, D.G. Fitz-Maurice, Leonard Hamilton, Lake Kelly, Harry Lancaster, Mickey Patterson, Russell Rice, and Denny Trease. Baldy Gilb, Cliff Hagan, Joe Hall, and Paul McBrayer have already been listed under the team players.

My research was greatly facilitated by the availability of scrapbooks and photographs from players or their relatives. I found these, like oral interviews, to be virtually untapped sources. Several players or relatives (as in the case of Bill King and Wilbur Schu, who are deceased) lent me their scrapbooks and photos. In addition, I made extensive use of the clippings files maintained on current and former players by the UK Sports Information Office as well as their large collection of individual and team photographs.

For information on former Wildcat coaches and players I used the clipping files maintained in the University Archives. I also examined and made extensive use of the other material in the archives, including copies of the university yearbook, the *Kentuckian* (whose title varies), minutes of the Board of Trustees meetings, and other university records for the years from 1903 to the present. The UK Alumni Office files also contain information and photos which I found useful in the preparation of this study.

The sports pages of several newspapers were read in search of information on individuals, games, and other components of the UK basketball tradition. My undergraduate assistants spent countless hours reading microfilm copies of newspapers at M.I. King Library covering the years from 1903 to the late 1950s, while I concentrated my readings on the more recent decades. We did most of our reading in the *Louisville Courier-Journal* and the *Lexington Herald* and *Lexington Leader*, as well as the campus newspaper, the *Kentucky Kernel* (title varies). Copies of the *Kernel* are on file in the newspaper office. In addition to these papers we read selected issues of the *New York Times, Chicago Tribune, Los Angeles Times, Atlanta Constitution, Atlanta Journal, New Orleans Times-Picayune, Washington Post, Kansas City Star,* and *Miami Herald.*

My discussion of the basketball scandal of 1951 is based in large part on an extensive file on that event made available to me on condition that I not divulge the name of the person who provided it. The file contains, among other things, a typescript copy of Judge Saul Streit's statement on the UK athletic program, a photostatic copy of the indictments of Ralph Beard, Alex Groza, Dale Barnstable, Walt Hirsch, and Jim Line on bribery charges, as well as the perjury indictment of Bill Spivey and the sentencing of Beard, Groza, and Barnstable.

Among other valuable primary sources I used are: *University of Kentucky Basketball Facts* (title varies), a press guide prepared annually since 1944 by the UK Sports Information Office; Adolph F. Rupp, *An Outline of Basketball* (Lexington, 1948) and *Championship Basketball for Player, Coach, Fan* (Englewood Cliffs, New Jersey, 1948); Harry Lancaster as told to Cawood Ledford, *Adolph Rupp as I Knew Him* (Lexington, 1979), a reminiscence by the longtime assistant basketball coach and later athletics director at UK; Dan Chandler and Vernon Hatton, *Rupp, from Both Ends of the Bench* (1972); Jack Givens as told to Bert Nelli, "Goose" (an unpublished autobiography); and *The Official Southeastern Conference Sports Record Book, 1933-1959* (Birmingham, 1959).

The history of the University of Kentucky down to the mid-1960s is traced by James F. Hopkins, *The University of Kentucky: Origins and Early Years* (Lexington, 1951); and Charles G. Talbert, *The University of Kentucky: The Maturing Years* (Lexington, 1965).

Among the books written in recent years about basketball at UK and in the state of Kentucky are three by Russell Rice: *Kentucky Basketball's Big Blue Machine* (Huntsville, Alabama, 1978); *Joe B. Hall: My Own Kentucky Home* (Huntsville, Alabama, 1981); and *The Wildcat Legacy: A Pictorial History of Kentucky Basketball* (Virginia Beach, Virginia, 1982); Tev Laudeman, *The Rupp Years* (Louisville, 1972); Luke Walton, *Basketball's Fabulous Five* (New York, 1950); Oscar Combs, *Kentucky Basketball: A New Beginning* (Lexington, 1979); Dave Kindred, *Basketball: The Dream Game in Kentucky* (Louisville, 1975); and John McGill, *Kentucky Sports* (Lexington, 1978).

I have also used the following more general treatments of basketball in America: Neil D. Isaacs, *All the Moves: A History of College Basketball* (Philadelphia, 1975), the best treatment available on the subject; Larry Fox, *Illustrated History of Basketball* (New York, 1974); James Naismith, *Basketball: Its Origins and Development* (New York, 1941); Al Hershberg, *Basketball's Greatest Teams* (New York, 1966); Sandy Padwe, *Basketball's Hall of Fame* (Englewood Cliffs, N.J., 1970); Jack Berryman and Stephen H. Hardy, "The College Sports Scene," in *Sports in Modern America*, ed. William J. Baker and John M. Carroll (St. Louis, 1981); Bill Russell and Taylor Branch, *Second Wind: The Memoirs of an Opinionated Man* (New York, 1979); John Wooden as told to Jack Tobin, *They Call Me Coach* (New York, 1973); Mike Recht, "Basketball," in *A Century of Sports*, Associated Press Sports Staff (Maplewood, N.J., 1971); Charles Rosen, *Scandals of 51: How the Gamblers Almost Killed College Basketball* (New York, 1978); Pete Axthelm, *The City Game* (New York, 1970); Alexander M. Weyland, *The Cavalcade of Basketball* (New York, 1960); Zander Hollander, ed., *The Modern Encyclopedia of Basketball* (New York, 1969) and *Basketball's Greatest Games* (Englewood Cliffs, N.J., 1970).

Index